The Book of Football

Norman Barrett

Purnell

CONTENTS

INTRODUCTION

by Bobby Charlton

Every morning during my career with Manchester United, I woke feeling elated. I would think what the day held in store for me and count my blessings. I was lucky to be good at the game of football.

Football had been a passion for me since I was a young lad. I still vividly remember my Uncle Tommy buying me my first pair of pigskin football boots and Miss Houston, one of our teachers, making the school team's first proper shorts out of the school blackout curtains. What a thrill football was for me and I was determined to become a professional footballer if I were good enough. My uncles, Stan, George, Jim and Jack Milburn, were all playing at that time and on visits home used to enthral me with stories of all the famous players and games. I couldn't get enough information about the great names— Carter, Doherty, Copping, Matthews, Finney. Later on I was fortunate enough to play against Stan Matthews and Tom Finney and in my first international for England Tom, the great Preston winger, crossed the ball for me to score on my debut. Can you imagine how I felt?

This book is full of the stories of players and managers from different eras, of goalscorers and stoppers, of improvisers and tacticians. It tells of all the men who have made—and are making—soccer history, and of those great matches that will always be talked about and remembered. It will give an insight into the way football has become accepted, not just by players like myself, but by most of the world as the greatest game.

In this country at the moment much is written about what is wrong with our game. But these problems seem small set against the colourful background of football past and present. We are waiting for some new Pelés and Cruyffs to burst on to the scene and by their sheer skill have the public on the edge of their seats and clamouring for more. I am still optimistic that this can happen, as during some soccer schools I ran last summer the skill shown by our youngsters was eye-opening. During my travels abroad, too, I have come across many potential world beaters. They may, one day, take their places among the illustrious company featured in this book. One blessing for me is that I won't have to play against them.

Bobby Charlton

Johnny Haynes

Alex James

Johnny Giles

There are several names that have been used over the years for the brains of the team. Nowadays the tendency is to call him the 'play-maker', because he is the man at the heart of his side's moves, or plays. Another popular name is 'midfield general', for obvious reasons.

Occasionally, the brains of a team will not be a midfield player, but this needs a very special footballer indeed, such as Germany's Franz Beckenbauer, who controlled the game from behind, and Alfredo Di Stefano of Real Madrid fame, who was perhaps more of a deeplying centre-forward.

The special attributes of a midfield general must include the ability to support his team-mates and to set up moves or change the pattern of play. Quickness of thought is as important as speed of action, which is why the term 'schemer' has always been appropriate for this type of footballer.

The Scots built a reputation for producing schemers, often small men with dazzling footwork and inch-perfect passes—Alex James, the daddy of them all, and the waiflike John White, for example. England's schemers have included the master-passer Johnny Haynes and the trickster Len Shackleton, and there can have been few finer midfield generals than Johnny Giles and Peter Doherty, both from across the Irish Sea.

Raich Carter

Wilf Mannion

Len Shackleton

Alex James

The lovable genius

Alex James was the most beloved character in British soccer before the war. He was a footballing genius with a twinkle in his eye and all manner of gifts in his play, which made him perhaps the finest scheming inside-forward of all time. Once a goalscoring forward for Raith and Preston, he modified his game to become the hub of the Arsenal side of the thirties, the driving force that transformed them into the kings of football. He was the one who picked up balls from defence and launched devastating attacks, sending opponents the wrong way before releasing his defence-splitting passes to Bastin or Hulme on either wing or through the middle to Lambert and later Drake. And not only was he a supreme artist himself, but he had the gift to spark the genius in others, to bring out the best in the players around him.

Another quality that particularly distinguished James was described

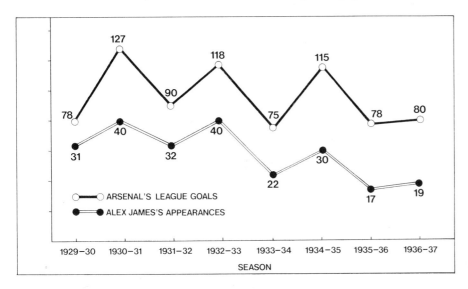

Above: The figures demonstrate just how much Arsenal's goal aggregate depended on James's appearances. Below: The Cup victory of 1936.

Graph data:
ARSENAL'S LEAGUE GOALS: 78, 127, 90, 118, 75, 115, 78, 80
ALEX JAMES'S APPEARANCES: 31, 40, 32, 40, 22, 30, 17, 19
SEASON: 1929–30, 1930–31, 1931–32, 1932–33, 1933–34, 1934–35, 1935–36, 1936–37

THE ACCOLADES

Throughout his career, accolades were heaped on Alex James by the critics, the fans, the men he played with, and the men he played against. Stanley Matthews described him as the greatest footballer he had ever seen, 'a genius of tactics'. Arsenal's manager after Chapman, George Allison, never stopped enthusing about him and used up all the superlatives. Perhaps the most unexpected tribute, however, came from England centre-forward Tommy Lawton, renowned above all for his matchless heading ability. In his book *Football Is My Business*, Lawton had this to say: 'The wee Scottish wizard Alex James could change the whole course of a match with one wiggle of his foot . . . could sell any kind of dummy . . . he taught me, simply by my watching him, one invaluable trick of making a false header.' Lawton went on to describe how he used this trick to score in an international.

Anyone who could teach Tommy Lawton something about heading was indeed a genius.

by one writer (Denzil Batchelor) as 'the gift of absence at the precise moment when the massed attack went in at its strongest.' That was James, all right. One moment he was there, and the next he was gone—striding majestically away with the ball at his feet and a trail of bewildered defenders in his wake.

He also had a certain something that none of the other great ball players seem to have had—not even Pelé or Best, Matthews or Maradona—an indefinable, almost imperceptive gesture when he got the ball that sent a thrill of expectation surging through the crowd, preparing them for a treat to come. Like all the best conjurors, he was getting the audience on his side, setting someone else up for his trickery while they shared the triumph, waiting in awe to see how

---

THE SEARCH FOR A SUCCESSOR

Clubs who tried to emulate Arsenal's success in the 1930s by adopting their style usually came a cropper, for James was the cornerstone of Arsenal's game and there just wasn't another James around. Arsenal themselves tried more than once to find a successor when he retired, eventually paying Wolves £14,000 for Bryn Jones in 1938. But the millstone of this record transfer was too great a burden for the Welsh star, and then the war intervened.

The nearest Arsenal got was another tiny Scot, Jimmy Logie, built in the James mould. A scheming inside-right, he gave them excellent service for ten years after the war. Although he lacked the power to hit those stunning long balls that James used to turn defence into attack, he was a fine dribbler and an immensely popular character. The pass with which he prized open the Liverpool defence for Reg Lewis to put Arsenal ahead in the 1950 Cup final is an often-quoted example of the perfect through ball. Like James, however, Logie was largely ignored by the selectors, winning only one belated cap.

---

it would be accomplished. There he was, that little figure in the baggy pants and flapping sleeves, a Chaplinesque hero, holding the stage, holding his audience spellbound as he weaved his magic around his opponents.

Scottish Beginnings

Like so many other great ball-playing inside forwards, Alex James was a Scot. He was born in 1902 at Mossend, a mining village near Glasgow. As a youth, he worked in the local steelworks, where he formed a friendship with Hughie Gallacher, and the pair of them developed their footballing arts in the streets, often with a ball made of paper and tied with string. These two tiny figures, who were later to play for Scotland and take part in the humbling of England at Wembley in 1928, were soon terrorizing defences in local matches. But they parted, Hughie finding his way to Airdrie and Alex to Raith Rovers (in 1922), and they both spent the first half of the 1920s playing in the Scottish First Division before moving south of the border to win everlasting fame in England.

James was transferred to Second Division Preston in 1925 for £3,275, and made his debut for Scotland—alongside Gallacher—later that year, against Wales at Cardiff. It is perhaps the greatest mystery in football that Alex James played only eight games for Scotland. As far as Scotland are concerned, it is also the greatest crime. Admittedly, James was an outspoken critic of the 'establishment' at times and was his own man, but it is an indictment of the Scottish selectors that Scotland's greatest schemer gained so few caps.

And at first he was a goalscorer, too. In his second international he scored twice for the so-called 'Wembley Wizards', and in that same season (1927-28) was Preston's leading goal-getter with 18. James was much loved at Preston, charming the fans with his trickery, delighting them with his showmanship. He enjoyed his football there, but they never seemed quite able to get back into the First Division.

The Chapman Era

Preston upset James in October 1928, when they kept quiet about an invitation to play for Scotland. James had passed up a cap earlier that year to play for them in an important promotion match, and he was now deeply hurt by their deception. Several big clubs were interested, and it was Arsenal who eventually got him, paying £9,000 for his signature at the end of that season.

It was the beginning of the 'Chapman Era' at Arsenal, the greatest period in their history, when they won world-wide fame and dominated English football. Arsenal's manager Herbert Chapman had already proved himself at Huddersfield, and he was now setting about making Arsenal the greatest club in the land. James was a key figure in his plans, but Alex didn't like the role Chapman had

---

LIMELIGHT

James enjoyed the limelight and was rarely out of the news. A stocky little 5ft 6in (1.68m), with bushy eyebrows and a 'spud' nose that gave him a Puckish appearance, he revelled in his role as a showman. All shorts were long and baggy in his day, but of course on a little man they looked even longer. James took to wearing them extra long as the result of seeing an exaggerated caricature of himself by the newspaper cartoonist Tom Webster, deciding to live up to his popular image.

He also had a reputation as a good-humoured practical joker, but he never allowed his image to affect his game. He was a fierce competitor, and would not tolerate slackness in his team-mates. His seemingly nonchalant manner on the field was due chiefly to the fact that he always had more time than other players—he had the ability to think two moves ahead, and intuitively knew where to pick up a loose ball, even to the extent of anticipating 'miscues' from his colleagues.

Off the field, he was at times rebellious, but his not infrequent clashes with authority usually involved a point of principle.

---

laid out for him. Chapman had developed a new strategy to take advantage of the change in the offside law that came into operation in the mid-twenties. He adopted a stopper centre-half, a 'battering-ram' centre-forward, fast-raiding wingers, and above all a man to convert defence into attack before the opposition could recover. This was where James came in.

But James did not feel that it was a forward's job to chase back to get the ball. He was an individualist,

and like Chapman was used to getting his own way. It took all of Chapman's considerable persuasion to change his mind, for although James was as confident as they come, he was never arrogant enough to assume that he could perform any role allotted him. Nevertheless, Chapman won. He made James believe that he could be the finest goalmaker in the game, and that is just what James became. As a result, his own goalscoring was drastically curtailed: with Raith and Preston he had averaged a goal every three games; with Arsenal, it was about one in ten. But for his team-mates he made goals galore.

In James's first season with them, Arsenal won their first honour, beating Huddersfield 2-0 in the 1930 Cup final. And it was Alex who scored their first goal! It is a goal that has gone down as a Wembley classic, because he caught the opposition out by taking a quick free-kick on a nod from the referee, slipping the ball out to Cliff Bastin on the left and slamming the return into goal. And James had planned it all in the coach on the way to the stadium.

Bastin had arrived at Arsenal as a 17-year-old at about the same time

The magic and wizardry of the little man in the baggy shorts and flapping sleeves is brought to life in this marvellous picture. Sheer bewilderment is etched on the faces of three defenders as he leaves them gaping.

as James, and the older man immediately took him under his wing, forming a superb partnership. Arsenal's forward line in that 1930 final and for the early thirties read: Joe Hulme, David Jack, Jack Lambert, James, and Bastin. Later, Ted Drake was to replace Lambert at centre-forward. It was the perfect combination, and they carried all before them. The cries of 'Lucky Arsenal' became a familiar chant on grounds all over the country, as they would absorb pressure for much of a game and score their goals in explosive breakaways, instigated chiefly by their midfield general, James—the pass inside the back for Bastin to run onto, the long ball through the middle for Jack or the centre-forward to take in their stride, or the spectacular cross-field ball to Hulme, the 'greyhound', on the opposite wing.

In 1931 Arsenal won the League Championship with 127 goals and a record 66 points. In 1932, they narrowly missed both League and Cup, largely because an injury to

James kept him out of the final and the last important League games. Then in 1933 they won the League again, 53 of their 118 goals coming from wingers Bastin and Hulme who fed so voraciously on James's passes. In an unprecedented run of success there was another honour every season—the Championship again in 1934 and 1935 and the Cup in 1936, with James as captain.

But by this time James was being saved for the more important matches—the cumulative effect of the injuries he received throughout his career as the result of the close attention always paid him was making it more difficult for him to recover. He was playing in fewer than half Arsenal's matches, and in 1937 he retired. He joined a pools firm, as a result of which he was barred from taking part in the administrative side of the game, although after the war he returned to Arsenal for a few years as coach. He also wrote match reports for a Sunday newspaper. He was always hugely popular, and a fund of stories—that is, for those who could understand his thick Scottish brogue. When he died in 1953, at the age of 51, such was his fame that he was mourned even by people who had never seen him.

Johnny Haynes

Johnny Haynes was England's first £100-a-week footballer. In the 1950s, he was one of the biggest names in English football, and became captain of England. Yet because he spent the whole of his career with unfashionable Fulham —much of it in Division II—he did not win a single major honour.

Pass Master

Haynes is remembered above all for the pin-point accuracy of his passing, and the well-worn footballing pun 'pass master' has probably been applied to him more than to any other player. He had instant control and was well capable of beating an opponent, but he would disdain the dribble for the telling pass. The most noticeable thing about Haynes was how he invariably seemed to have so much space around him when he received the ball. This was the result of intelligent running off the ball and a fine positional sense, allied to a knack for steering the ball swiftly away from danger. His passes were always designed to do the most damage—the through ball for his centre-forward to run on to, the perfectly weighted pass inside the opposing right-back that sent his wing partner free on the left, or the crossfield ball to his outside-right.

Loyalty to Fulham

Haynes first hit the headlines as a rather small schoolboy in 1950 with a brilliant exhibition at Wembley in England's 8-2 thrashing of Scotland schools. He soon joined Fulham, and made his first-team debut at 18 in December 1952. Eighteen years and some 700 games later, he left to play out the last days of his career in South Africa. In his 594 League matches he scored 148 goals.

A schemer of Haynes's class could have gone anywhere, but he stayed with Fulham through thick and thin. When the maximum wage (£20 a week) was abolished in 1961, the club immediately made him the first £100-a-week footballer in the country. Even so, he could have won greater fame and fortune elsewhere, but he remained loyal to Fulham. Having led them to promotion in 1959, he inspired them throughout the sixties as they played 'Houdini' near the bottom of the table, miraculously avoiding the drop season after season. He was not the only star at the club, but he was the one the team revolved around. It was sad that he should finish his English career in the Third Division, after Fulham finally succumbed to relegation in 1968 and then plummeted straight down again in 1969.

Captain of England

Haynes made his England debut in 1954, and became captain six years later. He won 56 caps (the first 32 as a Second Division player) and scored 18 goals. A car crash in 1962 interrupted his career, at 29, and he never played for England again.

He was a fine captain for both club and country, although he was not universally popular. He did not suffer fools gladly, and would often remonstrate on the field with a colleague he felt could have done better.

Haynes played in two World Cups (1958 and 1962), but failed to do himself justice. Foreign coaches found the England tactics, centred on Haynes, predictable. His deliberate passing game gave their retreating defences time to recover.

Nevertheless, he captained England 22 times, and during his spell at the helm England enjoyed one of the finest runs of success in their history, winning the first six matches of the 1960–61 season with a goal tally of 40 against 8. Haynes himself rated the 9-3 humiliation of Scotland as the best England performance of his time.

For both club and country, Haynes enjoyed at various times a fine midfield partnership with Bobby Robson. But, unlike his colleague, Haynes did not have aspirations to management. Oddly enough, he took over at Fulham when Robson lost the job in 1968, as player-manager. But he was quick to relinquish the post after only 17 days, and he never fancied himself as a manager when his playing days came to an end.

Johnny Haynes (left), captain of England, threatens the Northern Ireland goal at Wembley in 1961. His counterpart, Irish captain Danny Blanchflower, looks on helplessly on the ground, while Terry Neill (right) moves in to challenge. In the background (behind Blanchflower) is Haynes's Fulham club-mate Bobby Robson.

Carter & Shackleton

SUNDERLAND SCHEMERS

Both before and after World War II, Sunderland had one of the most gifted schemers in British football. In the 1930s, it was Raich Carter who won most of the game's honours. After the war, it was Len Shackleton, a controversial figure who won no honours and only a handful of caps, but was nonetheless a marvellous entertainer, the idol of the Roker Park crowd.

Raich Carter

The complete inside-forward, Raich (Horatio) Carter would make or take chances with equal flair. He had a fine footballing brain and an explosive shot. Although normally playing at inside-right, he favoured his left foot and scored most of his goals from 14 or 15 yards out, often pouncing on the loose clearance.

Sunderland-born, Carter was originally signed by Leicester, who misguidedly allowed him to return to his local club before he had represented them at first-class level. He was capped for England in only his second season (1933-34), but it was not until the war that he won a regular international place. In his seven seasons with Sunderland, before the war cut six years out of the heart of his career, he won League and Cup medals and was captain and key man in their success. In their 1935-36 Championship season, he was joint Division I leading scorer, with team-mate Bobby Gurney, with 31 goals.

For England during the war, he was a fine inside partner for winger Stanley Matthews, and at the end of the war joined Derby, where he teamed up with another great inside-forward Peter Doherty. In the first post-war Cup competition, he collected another winner's medal, and in 1946-47 partnered Tom Finney in some memorable matches for England.

But he was past his peak, and in 1948, now in his mid-thirties, he went to Third Division Hull as player-manager, taking them straight up to Division II. He retired from League football in 1952 with 216 goals to his credit in 451 League games and 7 in 13 internationals. He was not finished, however, and went on to win an Irish Cup medal with Cork at the age of 40. His later career as a manager—with Leeds, Mansfield, and Middlesbrough—was sound rather than spectacular, and he eventually drifted out of the game.

Carter

Shackleton

Len Shackleton

One of the great characters of football, Len Shackleton was a highly individual player, always involved in controversy and never afraid to speak his mind. Known as the 'Clown Prince of Soccer'—a nickname he used as the title of his autobiography—he is remembered for his ball juggling and trickery, for the sheer effrontery of his play. And his reputation for bucking authority is typified by the notorious chapter in his book, 'The average director's knowledge of football'. It consists of a blank page!

As a 15-year-old schoolboy international in 1938, Shackleton signed amateur forms with Arsenal, but less than a year later was told by their manager George Allison—kindly but firmly—that he would never make the grade. Rather than go back to his native Bradford with his tail between his legs, the young Shackleton got a job, and he returned to the North only when the war began in earnest.

He made his League debut for Bradford Park Avenue in 1946, hav-ing represented England against Scotland in the last of the victory internationals. After only a few matches, he was transferred to Second Division Newcastle for £13,000, a large fee in those days. His debut for them was sensational—he scored 6 of the record 13 they put past hapless Newport.

But Shackleton didn't settle at Newcastle, and during the following season, after frequent clashes with the management, he went to neighbours Sunderland for £20,050. He stayed at Roker Park for the rest of his career, entertaining an appreciative crowd with all the tricks in the book and a few more besides. A constant critic of the footballing 'establishment' and their treatment of players, he won only five England caps. A leg injury ended his playing career in 1957, and he became a football journalist.

Shackleton's international career was in part limited by the presence of two other great all-round inside-forwards, Carter and Wilf Mann-ion. But it has been said that he was too clever to play for England.

Harmer & White

WHITE HART LANE 'WAIFS'

At the beginning of 1960 Spurs had two waif-like figures in their team, delightful, delicate ball-playing artists who played the game at their own pace and struck up fine midfield partnerships with wing-half Danny Blanchflower. Tommy Harmer, the ball-juggling Cockney, was coming to the end of his days with Spurs, while Scottish international John White was just beginning. For a brief period they played in the same team, although their styles were similar. One match in particular is remembered in which their combination proved effective—a fourth round Cup replay at White Hart Lane, when lowly Crewe were put in their place to the tune of 13-2, the highest Cup score this century.

Tommy Harmer

It was sad that Tommy Harmer never won the honours or got the rewards he deserved in football. He gave immense pleasure to hundreds of thousands, but was in and out of the Spurs team and never won an international cap.

An extraordinary looking figure on the field, Harmer didn't look the part of a footballer. Skinny and short (5ft 6in) with 'matchstick' legs and a large head, he weighed little more than 9 stone. He had the physique of the proverbial weakling who always gets sand kicked in his face. His hollow eyes and sunken cheeks did nothing to dispel the impression that you could blow him off the ball.

Harmer signed for Spurs in 1948, and although he made his League debut in 1951 and won an England 'B' cap in 1952, it was another five years before he won a regular place. He was a master of all the skills, and made the crowd laugh with his sheer cheek, as he weaved in and out of towering defenders, controlling the ball with foot, knee, chest, or whatever. His passing was immaculate, especially the lofted through pass, which he contrived to back-spin so that it didn't run on. He missed out on Spurs' glory years, going to Watford in 1960 when John White was flourishing. He frittered his beautiful skills away in the Third Division, before going to Chelsea in 1962, playing only a handful of games for them, but, at the age of 34, scoring an all-important goal that earned them promotion.

John White

Still mourned at White Hart Lane, home of the Spurs, John White was cut down in his prime by a freak accident. In July 1964, while playing golf, he was killed by a stroke of lightning. Thus Spurs lost one of the finest inside-forwards of the post-war era, a man who had been at the heart of their Cup and League double of 1960-61.

Spurs paid Scottish Second Division side Falkirk a mere £20,000 for him in 1959, although he was already an international, having played a couple of games at centre-forward for Scotland before establishing himself at inside-right. He soon struck up a midfield partnership with Danny Blanchflower that was almost telepathic, and like Blanchflower he had the ability to weight a pass to perfection.

They called him the 'Ghost of White Hart Lane' because of his remarkable capacity for popping up seemingly out of nowhere in the right place to collect a pass.

Tiny Tommy Harmer

He stood just 5ft 7½in (1.71m) and weighed barely 10 stone (64kg), but he had boundless stamina and packed a mighty shot. He drifted into wonderful positions, and his perfect crosses provided countless goals for Bobby Smith, Jimmy Greaves, Cliff Jones, and Les Allen. White was a calming influence on the team when things got tough, and was set to take over from Blanchflower when tragedy struck. Spurs never replaced him, and neither did Scotland, for whom he won 22 caps and was a key figure in their build-up for the 1966 World Cup. He was only 26 when he died.

John White (centre) with midfield partner Danny Blanchflower (left).

Wilf Mannion

Golden Boy

In days when mediocre players are making a fortune from the game, it is sad to look back on Wilf Mannion, the 'Golden Boy' of the North-East, who finished up working on a building site. In a brilliant playing career, interrupted by World War II, Mannion was virtually a one-club man. He was an idol at Ayresome Park, making his debut for Middlesbrough at the age of 17 in 1937. A rift developed with the club in 1948, and he refused to re-sign. But in the end he had to give in, having lost a considerable amount in wages and missed six internationals, for in those days the club always had the whip-hand.

Mannion (right) in action for Middlesbrough against Arsenal.

Complete Inside-Forward

Only 5ft 6in (1.68m), Mannion was a blond bombshell of a player. Playing in either inside-forward berth, he was the link-man of England's great post-war side, the ball-playing midfield genius who could also score goals. He was the complete inside-forward.

A contemporary of his, Alf Ramsey, regarded him as the greatest brain in football, in a class of his own as an inside-forward. Mannion's greatest asset perhaps was his ability to work in a confined space, whether in midfield or near goal. His speed of action matched his speed of thought, and he could turn the course of a game with one stroke of his genius. He was also famed for his classic body-swerve, timed to perfection just as an opponent was committing himself to a tackle.

Golden Days

Mannion made his England debut against Scotland in a wartime international in 1941, and immediately created an impression, popping up in all kinds of positions to confuse the Scottish defence and displaying all his fine ball-playing craftsmanship. He was whipped away in 1943 for active service, but made a sensational come-back after the war, scoring a hat-trick against Ireland in his first full international.

Mannion starred in 13 of England's first 14 post-war internationals in what were golden days for the national side. With that immortal forward line that read 'Matthews - Mortensen - Lawton - Mannion - Finney', they took Portugal apart 10-0 in Lisbon in 1947 and a year later triumphed 4-0 over Italy in Turin.

After his dispute with Middlesbrough, Mannion won back his England place, and in all featured in 26 internationals, scoring 11 goals. In addition to all his skills, he was a great showman and possessed immense courage—never better illustrated than when he was being carried off at Wembley in 1951 against Scotland and tried to climb off the stretcher despite a broken cheek-bone.

The flaxen-haired Mannion was the one bright star in the Middlesbrough firmament, but even his genius could not save them from relegation in 1954. He retired immediately, but Hull City persuaded him to come back a few months later, and although he played only 16 League games in their colours, it was enough for him to score the goal that took his career tally to 100—in 357 League games.

At the end of that season, he was suspended by the League for refusing to substantiate 'illegal payment' allegations he had made in a newspaper article. And although the ban was lifted after two years, Mannion dabbled in non-League management for a time before disappearing from the game altogether.

He won no honours with unfashionable Middlesbrough, but he could look back on a magnificent international career. And one match must stand out in the memory—when he represented Great Britain against the Rest of Europe at Hampden in 1947. He gave a superb exhibition of football that day, scoring twice in Britain's 6-1 triumph and playing havoc with the European defence . . . golden memories indeed.

AHEAD OF HIS TIME

According to his England colleague Billy Wright, one of Mannion's techniques was years ahead of his time. In his book *One Hundred Caps and All That*, Wright tells how Mannion was making flicked passes with the outside of his foot just after the war. This was five years or so before the Europeans began doing it and ten before it first caught on in British football.

Peter Doherty

Widely acclaimed as Northern Ireland's finest inside-forward, Peter Doherty had a tempestuous playing career that spanned World War II and five League clubs. He passionately resented the underprivileged status of the professional footballer, and as a result was often at odds with authority. But despite his fiery temperament off the field, he was the perfect gentleman on it, and never once in trouble with the referee.

Effortless Genius

Whatever he did on the field, Doherty did with seemingly effortless grace. But he always gave a hundred per cent. He displayed a confident Irish charm and a brand of courage that enabled him to ride the severest of tackles. His genius was sometimes halted, but never quenched.

Doherty was a complete inside-forward, a schemer and a goal-scorer. In his chequered League career he notched 197 goals in 403 appearances. Always in the game, in defence as well as attack, he had a razor-sharp footballing brain that alerted him to opportunities and danger alike. He was a master of the long ball, with the ability to switch play in a flash. He possessed a fierce and accurate shot from all angles with either foot, and was an expert penalty-taker. Add to this his immaculate ball control, elusive swerve, and fine heading ability, and it's no wonder they called him 'Peter the Great'.

The Long League Trail

Born in Coleraine in 1914, one of 10 children, Doherty first played for Glentoran as a 17-year-old, but was soon snapped up by Second Division Blackpool for £1,500, in November 1933. He made his international debut in February 1935, against England, and a year later was transferred to Manchester City for £10,000 because Blackpool needed the fee.

In his first season with City, he scored 30 goals to help them win the League—but they were relegated the next season! Doherty's talents were wasted in Division II, and at the end of the war he signed for Derby. There, he struck up a wonderful midfield partnership with Raich Carter—two similar players, yet they dovetailed perfectly.

The 1945-46 season marked the beginning of the post-war era, and although there was no League Championship, the FA Cup was staged on a two-legged basis (up to the sixth round). In winning the Cup, Derby played 11 matches and the inside-forwards scored 22 of their 37 goals, Doherty contributing 10, including one in the final.

But a dispute with the board led to another move half-way through the following season, this time to Huddersfield. Doherty was made captain, and he saved them from relegation. In 1949, he became player-manager of Third Division Doncaster, taking them up to Division II in his first season. He hung up his boots in 1953, and later managed Bristol City. But his greatest managerial success was with his country.

International Career

As a player, Doherty was always critical of the lack of preparation and organization the Northern Ireland side suffered from. He played his last international in 1950, 15 years after his first. His tally of caps was only 16, because Northern Ireland played only the other home countries at that time, and because of the war years.

Doherty took over the national side in the late 1950s, and was their first official team manager. He immediately set about creating an atmosphere of team spirit, and with two cultured players to build his team around—Danny Blanchflower and Jimmy McIlroy—he produced a fine side from exceedingly thin material. They gained confidence from a 3-2 win over England at Wembley in 1957, and then beat Italy to qualify for the 1958 World Cup. As if this was not enough for such a 'Cinderella' side, they proceeded to reach the quarter-finals, before finally succumbing to France. It was a truly remarkable achievement. And it was a tragedy for the game when Doherty eventually drifted out of it.

COURAGE

Doherty won his first honour with Irish club Glentoran, a Cup medal in 1933. The final against Distillery went to two replays, in the first of which Doherty sprained his ankle. After intensive treatment, he was risked for the second replay, but finished the first half hobbling painfully on the wing. Then, in the second half, he pivoted on the ball from the edge of the box and cracked it into the net before losing consciousness. Glentoran went on to win 3-1, and Doherty valued that winners medal even more than the one he won at Wembley 13 years later.

Johnny Giles

Master tactician

The chief cog in the formidable Leeds footballing machine of the 1960s and early 1970s, Johnny Giles had a wonderful feel for the ball. He could hit massive long balls out of defence right to the feet of his colleagues, and was famed for his delicate chips, particularly from free-kicks, which provided many a headed goal for Leeds' big strikers.

Giles was originally an outside-right with Manchester United, having joined them in 1958 straight from youth football in his native Dublin. He made his first-team debut in the 1959-60 season, when he also won his first Irish cap. He won a Cup medal in 1963, but was transferred to Leeds at the beginning of the next season, having fallen out with Matt Busby over tactics.

With Leeds, Giles turned out to be the master tactician. At £35,000, Don Revie got a marvellous bargain. He drafted him into midfield to replace the injured Bobby Collins in 1965, and Leeds never looked back. Giles struck up an outstanding midfield partnership with the dynamic Billy Bremner. Having won promotion in 1964, Leeds went from strength to strength. The newly promoted club just failed to lift the League title at the first attempt—Manchester United headed them on goal average—but they emerged as the side of the sixties, and after more near misses eventually won the Championship in 1969 with a record number of points.

Despite Leeds' all-round strength, they were never the same without their diminutive schemer —Giles stood only 5ft 7 in (1.70m). He was the brains of the team, with the ability to hold the ball and the knack of knowing exactly when to release it. When Giles was missing through injury, Leeds just did not function in the same smooth manner. Giles was often misused by opponents, but was quite able to

Giles (left), Leeds' mastermind, is challenged by Derby's McGovern.

take care of himself—too much so, perhaps, for he earned a reputation for sly fouls.

Giles helped Leeds to further honours, both at home and in Europe, before leaving them when Revie departed in 1975. Giles became player-manager of West Bromwich, immediately guiding them back to the First Division, and at the same time successfully managing the Republic of Ireland side. But despite his success, he found management too inhibiting, and returned to Dublin in 1977, where he became managing-director of Shamrock Rovers. He continued to play for his country, and established a record of 60 caps.

When he hung up his boots at West Bromwich, Giles had played 554 League games, scoring 99 goals. He had a fierce shot and was a master penalty-taker. But he will always be remembered for the countless goals he made for others.

THE GOALSCORERS

Gerd Müller

Steve Bloomer

Jimmy Greaves

How many times have you heard it said that goals are what football is all about? A time-worn cliché, but nevertheless true, and it has usually been the goalscorers who have won the most fame.

Who was the greatest of them all? Well, that's a question that will never be answered, just as most of the great goalscorers find it impossible to explain what it is that makes them just that.

As a footballer, Pelé has few peers, and his marvellous goalscoring record speaks for itself. Dixie Dean's 60 goals in an English League season is a feat that has never even been approached, and his ability to head the ball has been equalled perhaps only by that thoroughbred of centre-forwards Tommy Lawton. Jimmy McGrory and Jimmy Greaves were prolific, while Bobby Charlton was more the scorer of great goals. The Scots will put forward Hughie Gallacher as the finest leader of an attack and Denis Law as the most exciting and explosive finisher.

Pelé

Bobby Charlton

Ted Drake

Dixie Dean

20

Dixie Dean

The 60-goal season

Dixie Dean died in March 1980, but his legend will always live on—he was indisputably the best header of a football there has ever been and he won what is virtually a permanent place in the record books. The indelible record is his 60 League goals in a season, for it stands about as much chance of being beaten as Bob Beamon's famous Olympic long jump or Jim Laker's 19 wickets in a Test.

Dean scored his 60 goals for Everton in the 1927-28 season, two years after the change in the offside law had made goalscoring easier and before third-back tactics had been developed to counteract the new threat. But that should not be allowed to detract from his achieve-

Above: Dean (far left) scores with a typical header against Sunderland on Christmas Day 1926—the first of his four goals in Everton's 5-4 victory. Left: Dean, at 5ft 11in (1.8m), was no giant, but he dwarfs Arsenal's defenders as he heads for goal.

ment, for no one has reached even 50 since, and today's leading First Division scorers rarely surpass 30.

William Ralph Dean—he always disliked the nickname Dixie—had begun his career three years earlier with Tranmere Rovers in Division III. Everton brought the free-scoring 18-year-old centre-forward to Goodison Park in 1925 for £3,000, no mean sum in those days but the best investment the club ever made.

A Taste of Things to Come

Dean was not an automatic choice at the beginning of his first full season and found himself in the reserves—for just one match, in which he scored seven goals! His 32 in 38 First Division games in 1925-26 was a taste of things to come, but in the summer he fractured his skull in a motor-cycle accident and it was feared he would never play again. Dean, however, had a remarkably strong constitution, and was back on the field less than four months later. The relief round the ground when he first headed the ball was a measure of the aspirations the Goodison crowd had for their new young idol. Dean scored 21 goals in his 27 League games that season, and was largely responsible for keeping Everton in the First Division. What's more, he made his debut for England and scored 12 in 5 matches, including two against Scotland in what was England's first win at Hampden Park for 23 years.

All this was leading up to the season of seasons—1927-28. Another great centre-forward was in the news in 1927, George Camsell, who hit a League record of 59 goals to help Middlesbrough win promotion from Division II. But there was little comparison between the divisions, and as it would turn out Middlesbrough finished bottom of Division I while Everton became champions. Yet there was a difference of only 16 points between the clubs (53 to 37) at the end of the season, and Middlesbrough were a mere 7 points behind the team in fourth place—an indication of the tremendous competition in the top division at that time. There were no easy pickings, yet Dean managed to score in 29 of his 39 games and chalked up seven hat-tricks.

The Build-up

The build-up to the record during the season and then the climax comes straight out of the realms of fantasy. The hero was athletic and courageous, a powerful man who stood out in a crowd. His very presence on the field instilled fear in opposing defences. And the whole country, in the depths of economic depression, was dazzled by his skills and great sportsmanship and thrilled to his scoring feats.

He scored in each of the first nine games, culminating in five against Manchester United. Football fans everywhere were now following his progress with avid interest. The first setback came against neigh-

The dramatic goal against Arsenal that gave Dean the record. With only minutes to go, Dean (left) connected with a corner to complete a hat-trick in the last match of the season. It was his 60th goal.

bours and rivals Liverpool, when he failed to score, and he missed Everton's 7-0 drubbing of West Ham because of international duty. But a couple of hat-tricks put him on course again, and, despite the crude tactics some defenders began to adopt to curb this remarkable goal machine, he continued to bang them in remorselessly, reaching 30 after only 18 games. The excitement was mounting nationwide, but none of it affected Dean, whose coolness on the field was one of his trademarks. Everton were riding high in the table, and after a frenzied Christmas programme started the New Year with a lead of four points. Dean's tally was now 35 from 22 games. In two more games he had passed the 20-year-old club goalscoring record of 38, and the next target was the First Division record of 43, set two seasons previously by Ted Harper of Blackburn. It took him four more games to equal this, though, which he finally did with a flourish—a hat-trick at Anfield—and then another four games to pass it. He now had 45 goals, but another two international calls had left him with only seven matches. Everton had slipped badly in the meantime, going nine games without a win.

The Finale

The task facing Dean as Easter approached was daunting—he needed 15 goals in 7 games. Two against Blackburn on Good Friday helped Everton back to the top of the table on goal average. Three more in the next two matches brought up his 50—in 35 matches. Could he do it? Ten more needed and just four matches to go. Only one goal against Newcastle. Not

DEAN'S GOAL RECORD IN 1927-28					

Dean's goals are given after the match result ('X' indicates a missed match due to international duty), and the last column is his running tally.

1	H	Sheffield Wed.	4-0	1	1
2	A	Middlesbrough	2-4	1	2
3	A	Bolton	1-1	1	3
4	H	Birmingham	5-2	2	5
5	H	Bolton	2-2	1	6
6	A	Newcastle	2-2	2	8
7	H	Huddersfield	2-2	2	10
8	A	Tottenham	3-1	2	12
9	H	Manchester Utd	5-2	5	17
10	H	Liverpool	1-1	0	17
11	H	West Ham	7-0	X	
12	A	Portsmouth	3-1	3	20
13	H	Leicester	7-1	3	23
14	A	Derby	3-0	2	25
15	H	Sunderland	0-1	0	25
16	A	Bury	3-2	2	27
17	H	Sheffield Utd	0-0	0	27
18	A	Aston Villa	3-2	3	30
19	H	Burnley	4-1	0	30
20	A	Arsenal	2-3	1	31
21	H	Cardiff	2-1	2	33
22	A	Cardiff	0-2	0	33
23	A	Sheffield Wed.	2-1	2	35
24	A	Blackburn	2-4	2	37
25	H	Middlesbrough	3-1	2	39
26	A	Birmingham	2-2	0	39
27	A	Huddersfield	1-4	1	40
28	H	Tottenham	2-5	0	40
29	A	Liverpool	3-3	3	43
30	A	West Ham	0-0	0	43
31	A	Manchester Utd	0-1	0	43
32	A	Leicester	0-1	0	43
33	H	Portsmouth	0-0	X	
34	H	Derby	2-2	2	45
35	A	Sunderland	2-0	X	
36	H	Blackburn	4-1	2	47
37	H	Bury	1-1	1	48
38	A	Sheffield Utd	3-1	2	50
39	H	Newcastle	3-0	1	51
40	H	Aston Villa	3-2	2	53
41	A	Burnley	5-3	4	57
42	H	Arsenal	3-3	3	60

good enough. The tensions were escalating, and affecting everyone in the team—that is, except Dean. Who thought he could do it? Everyone was willing him to, but 9 goals in 3 games? This could happen, surely, only in schoolboy fiction.

Another home match, and another 60,000 crowd saw Dean edge closer with two goals against Villa. Two games to go, but seven goals still to get—the dream was slipping away. Then came the game at Turf Moor, and Dean hit the Burnley net four times before half-time. But a pulled thigh muscle left him limping for most of the second half, and it was only constant attention from club trainer Harry Cooke, who moved in with Dean, that got him fit for the following Saturday.

So the scene was set. Arsenal were due at Goodison for the last match of the season on the 5th of May and Dean needed a hat-trick. Thanks to Huddersfield's lapses, Everton had already won the Championship, so the only issue was the League goalscoring record. Arsenal had beaten Everton twice

the second period kept a tight rein on Dean. Time slipped by and there was less than five minutes left. Frustrations were building up. Then, a corner on the left wing, and Alec Troup drifted over a hanging centre to the far post. Dean was there, of course, majestically outjumping the Arsenal defence to power his header into the corner of the net. This, a moment in sporting history that has few equals, was greeted with a roar that reverberated around the whole of Merseyside. Dean accepted the congratulations of team-mates and opponents with his usual dignity and modesty. Amidst the rejoicing, which continued for several minutes, Arsenal's equalizer in the dying seconds was barely observed.

Further Triumphs

Dean was just 21, and already he was a giant among men. His goalscoring record would probably stand for all time; in all matches that season he scored 100! He went on to further triumphs, captaining Everton to Cup victory in 1933 and passing Steve Bloomer's record of

352 League goals in 1936. He finished his career with Notts County in the late 1930s, having amassed 379 goals in 437 League games, and a crop of injuries that left his legs covered with the scars of 15 operations. His 349 League goals for Everton is still an English record for one club.

Strangely, Dean played only a handful of games for England after 1928, finishing with a total of 18 goals in 16 matches. But there was no great continuity of selection in those days, and internationals were fewer.

Some 26 years after he left Everton, the club arranged a testimonial for Dean, and 40,000 turned out to honour the former idol. It was a fitting, if belated, tribute to the greatest goalscorer, and one of the finest sportsmen, English football had ever seen.

Dean follows his header into the net to put Everton two up against Manchester City in the 1933 Cup final. The keeper, wearing No. 22 (the players were numbered 1 to 22) is helpless. Inset: Dean receives the Cup from the Duchess of York after Everton's 3-0 victory.

BRITISH RECORD
Spare a thought for Jim Smith of Ayr United, Scottish Second Division champions in 1927-28. While Dixie Dean was grabbing the glory south of the border, Smith was quietly slotting them in from Dumbarton to Dundee—and setting a British record of 66 League goals in 38 games.

that season, 3-2 in the League and 4-3 in the Cup (despite two from Dean).

Arsenal scored within minutes of the kick-off, but from the restart Dean thundered through their defence and hit a scorching shot past the keeper. Two to get. Midway through the first half Dean was brought down in the box, and cracked in the resultant penalty to an eruption of noise and joy from the terraces. He had equalled the record, and now there seemed ample time to beat it. But Arsenal equalized before half-time, and in

George Camsell

The man in Dean's shadow

Because George Camsell scored his record 59 goals in Division II, and the following season Dixie Dean sensationally chalked up 60 in the First Division, his achievement tends to be underestimated. Yet had Camsell played in another age, or perhaps for a more fashionable club than Middlesbrough, he would surely have received wider recognition and perhaps won more caps.

Look how some of the acknowledged 'greats' have fared for their country. Ferenc Puskas scored 83 goals in 84 matches, Pelé 76 in 92, Bobby Charlton 49 in 106, Jimmy Greaves 44 in 57, and Denis Law 30 in 55—all less than one a game. George Camsell scored two a game! He represented England only 9 times, and his appearances were scattered over 8 seasons, but he scored 18 goals. He scored every time he wore an England shirt.

Camsell's 59 goals for Middlesbrough in 1926-27, scored in 37 games, earned them promotion, and their 122 goals is still a Second Division record. It was Camsell's first full season for the club; he had joined them from Third Division Durham City the previous season. Middlesbrough stayed only one season in the First Division, although their demotion could hardly be blamed on Camsell, who found

As Dean was to Goodison Park, Camsell was to Ayresome Park. A shooting star who brightened the lives of the jobless, he lifted their spirits with his non-stop aggression.

First Division defences only marginally more difficult to penetrate. In the second game of the season he outshone Dean, scoring all of his side's goals in their 4-2 victory over Everton. He went on to register 33 that season. Another 33 the following term helped Middlesbrough back up again, and it was due largely to Camsell's consistency that they stayed in the top division and became a force there towards the end of the 1930s. He was their leading scorer for nine seasons.

An ungainly but gritty player, short and stocky, Camsell stayed with Middlesbrough to the end of his career, in which he scored 346 League goals (including 20 for Durham) in 440 games. He was a great hero at Ayresome Park, where his aggression and deadly finishing brought cheer to the terraces in the days of the depression. And he is still on most short lists of the great centre-forwards of all time.

CAMSELL'S INTERNATIONAL RECORD		
9.5.29	France 1 England 4	2
11.5.29	Belgium 1 England 5	4
19.10.29	Ireland 0 England 3	2
20.11.29	Wales 0 England 6	3
6.12.33	England 4 France 1	2
4.12.35	England 3 Germany 0	2
4.4.36	England 1 Scotland 1	1
6.5.36	Austria 2 England 1	1
9.5.36	Belgium 3 England 2	1
	Total goals	18

Jimmy Greaves

Finisher supreme

Jimmy Greaves leaves the Liverpool defence floundering—from the right, Chris Lawler, Ron Yeats (on ground), Tommy Smith, and Ian St John, who seems to be appealing for help from somewhere!

Sad though the decline of Jimmy Greaves was in his later years, it should never be allowed to cloud the memory of the most prolific goalscorer in First Division football since before World War II. Before Greaves came along, no player had led the Division I scorers for more than two seasons (including Dean and Lawton). Greaves did it six times, over a period of 11 years. All of his 357 League goals were scored in Division I, a record unlikely to be beaten. And he scored five goals in a League game on a record four occasions.

Yet it is not so much for his records that Jimmy Greaves is remembered, but for his style, the way he moved with the ball, his dazzling acceleration, his impish character, his ability to lose his marker, and above all his uncanny knack of rifling the ball into the net from all sorts of angles. Not for Greaves the battering-ram tactics of the powerhouse centre-forward, and nor was he especially dangerous in the air. But he had the ability to score by stabbing or flicking the ball with little or no backlift, which made it extremely difficult for defenders to get in their tackles. And despite his slight frame, his mastery of this technique and his perfect timing enabled him to score such goals from the most difficult positions. And there again, he did not just hang around the box waiting to pounce on chances (as was sometimes implied). Certainly he was a master of being in the right place at the right time. But some of his finest goals were started from deep positions, and there was no finer sight in football than Greaves on one of his darting, swerving runs, knifing through the opposing defence and finishing it all off with his deadly left foot.

Boy Prodigy

Greaves was only 17 when he first played for Chelsea in the League. It was in August 1957 at White Hart Lane, and he scored against Spurs. All through his career he was to maintain a remarkable record of scoring in his first match for every team he played for, at whatever level. Only six months earlier, the boy prodigy had hit four on his debut for the England Youth side. He immediately won a regular place with Chelsea and in only his second season topped the First Division scorers for the first time. He passed the hundred mark in November 1960—at the age of 20 years 9 months, the youngest player to do so. He was leading Division I scorer again that season, with 41, still a post-war record, and he hit 13 goals in 8 games for England.

Changes of Scene

At the end of that season Greaves, who felt the need to broaden his footballing horizons, signed for Milan. It was a move that did not work out. His happy-go-lucky personality was stifled by the stern Italian discipline, his salary decimated by the fines; yet he was Milan's top scorer when they let him return to England. They got nearly £20,000 more from Spurs than the £80,000 they had paid

Chelsea a few months earlier.

The move to Spurs was a great challenge—they had just become the first club this century to bring off the League and Cup double. He was an instant success, playing alongside the bustling Bobby Smith. He helped them win the Cup that first season, scoring their

first goal in the final, and the next season broke the club goalscoring record with 37.

International Career

Greaves marked his England debut with his customary goal, in 1959 in Lima, where England were beaten,

Above: Greaves, in Spurs strip, takes on his former Chelsea team-mates. Below: Scoring for England against Scotland at Wembley.

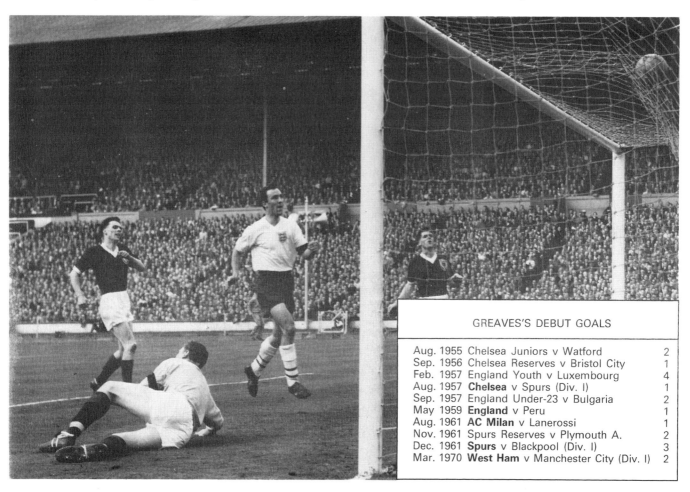

GREAVES'S DEBUT GOALS		
Aug. 1955	Chelsea Juniors v Watford	2
Sep. 1956	Chelsea Reserves v Bristol City	1
Feb. 1957	England Youth v Luxembourg	4
Aug. 1957	**Chelsea** v Spurs (Div. I)	1
Sep. 1957	England Under-23 v Bulgaria	2
May 1959	**England** v Peru	1
Aug. 1961	**AC Milan** v Lanerossi	1
Nov. 1961	Spurs Reserves v Plymouth A.	2
Dec. 1961	**Spurs** v Blackpool (Div. I)	3
Mar. 1970	**West Ham** v Manchester City (Div. I)	2

however, 4-1 by Peru. He established his England place before going to Italy, having scored 11 goals in 5 games, culminating with a hat-trick in the 9-3 destruction of Scotland at Wembley. Despite a disappointing World Cup in Chile, he played in 30 of England's 34 games from 1962 to 1965, and passed Tom Finney's record of 30 goals. In all, he scored 44 goals for England in his 57 games—a tally it took Bobby Charlton 85 internationals to beat.

But an illness in 1965 put him out of football for several months, and he never quite regained his old sparkle. He won back his England place in time for the 1966 World Cup, but poor form in the group matches, then an injury, let Geoff Hurst in, and that was virtually the end of Greaves's international career. He won just three more caps, but did not fit in with the style or philosophy of Alf Ramsey, the England manager.

Anticlimax

Greaves never really got over the disappointment of missing England's triumphant World Cup final. He continued to slot them in for Spurs, though, for three more seasons, winning another Cup medal in 1967 and leading the First Division scorers yet again in 1968-69. But, as he admitted later, he had taken to drink, and his goal touch began to desert him. He moved to West Ham in 1970, and retired a year later, after failing to reach double figures for League goals for the first time in his career.

It was a sad anticlimax. But he had made an indelible impression on the footballing world, not only with his scoring feats and his delightful skills, but also with his sportsmanship and great sense of fun. He might have let himself down in the end, but no one could say that Jimmy Greaves owed anything to the game.

Greaves nips in to score England's winner against the Rest of the World in the FA Centenary match at Wembley in 1963.

JIMMY GREAVES: LEAGUE GOALS				
Club	Season	Games	Goals	*
Chelsea	1957-58	35	22	
	1958-59	42	32	1
	1959-60	40	29	2=
	1960-61	40	41	1
AC Milan	1961-62	(10)	(9)	
Spurs		22	21	
	1962-63	41	37	1
	1963-64	41	35	1
	1964-65	41	29	1=
	1965-66	29	15	
	1966-67	38	25	3
	1967-68	39	23	5
	1968-69	42	27	1
	1969-70	29	8	
West Ham		6	4	
	1970-71	32	9	
		517	357	

*Position in Division I scorers list.

ARTHUR ROWLEY

Only one player has scored more goals in post-war British football than Jimmy Greaves—Arthur Rowley. Playing in the shadow of his more famous elder brother Jack, of Manchester United and England, Arthur scored consistently over 18 seasons. When he retired in 1965, he had amassed 434 goals in 619 League games —an all-time British record. He played for West Bromwich (4 goals), Fulham (27), Leicester (251), and Shrewsbury (152), but only 51 of his goals were scored in the First Division.

A tall and powerful centre-forward, he had a lethal left-foot shot. He led the League's scorers twice, each time in the Second Division with Leicester City, the high point being his 44 in 1956-57.

27

Ted Drake

The 7-goal Gunner

It isn't often that a team scores seven goals away from home in the First Division of the Football League. Arsenal did it on 14 December 1935 at Villa Park—but what was even more remarkable is that all seven were scored by centre-forward Ted Drake. This equalled the record set 47 years earlier by Preston's James Ross, and the feat has still not been repeated in the First Division over 45 years later.

There are other factors, too, that add to the wonder of Drake's achievement that day. First, he was not completely fit, nor had he been in good form. A niggling knee injury had led to his demotion to the reserves, and on this day he had the knee strapped up for the first time. Second, Drake had only eight goal attempts in the whole match—he scored with seven of them and the other one hit the underside of the bar!

The Last Laugh

Drake began the game inauspiciously. Chasing the ball out of play, he slipped on the track surround and tumbled over like a circus clown. That was the last laugh the Villa fans had that day.

Villa were going through a bad patch, and had bought new players in an effort to revitalize the team. The joint attraction of new blood and a visiting side that had won the League title four times in the previous five seasons pulled in the season's biggest crowd, 70,000. Villa began the game well, and were doing most of the attacking. But, typically of sides playing the Arsenal of the thirties, this was no indication of superiority. What was not widely appreciated about the Arsenal strategy was that they tended to control the game even when they were defending. Their build-up from the back was swift and incisive, with Alex James masterminding the breaks, spraying long passes to his forwards. Drake

was the supreme finisher—fast, direct, courageous, and with a cannonball shot.

And so it was that day at Villa Park, when Arsenal broke away after 15 minutes of Villa pressure for Drake's first goal, that the usual cries of 'Lucky Arsenal' went up. By the time he had scored his seventh, the Villa crowd must have realized that there was more than

SCORING TIMETABLE
Aston Villa v Arsenal
14.12.35

15 min: Drake collects a long ball on the left from Pat Beasley, pushes it through the centre-half's legs, and hits a straight drive past the keeper, 0-1.

28 min: Drake runs onto a long ball through the middle from Cliff Bastin, shakes off a dual challenge, and again shoots past the keeper, 0-2.

34 min: Drake picks up a rebound from a defender and rifles the ball in, 0-3.

47 min: Drake races to reach a ball that the centre-half judges is going out, and hooks it cleverly past the keeper, 0-4.

50 min: Drake converts another pass from Cliff Bastin, 0-5.

58 min: Drake collects a bad clearance on the edge of the box and hits the ball first time into the net, 0-6.

65 min: Palethorpe heads a cross past the Arsenal keeper, 1-6.

89 min: Drake heads in another Bastin cross, 1-7.

good fortune involved. And another remarkable thing about Drake's, and Arsenal's, performance was that their great general, James, was not playing.

Drake had his first hat-trick by half-time, his second in under the hour, and, after Villa had obtained their solitary consolation, he registered his record seventh goal in the last minute of the game.

Injuries

He had continuing trouble with injuries that season and, after only one game in two months, turned out in the Cup final with his leg heavily bandaged again. Yet he scored the only goal of the game. The previous season he had finished as the League's leading scorer with 42 goals, an Arsenal record. In all, he scored 123 League goals in 168 games for Arsenal, having joined them from Second Division Southampton (48 goals in 72 games) in 1934. Only Dixie Dean and George Camsell averaged more goals per game. His international career was also restricted, but he scored six goals in his five games for England.

Drake received his final injury in 1945, before the resumption of football after the war. As a manager, he led Chelsea to the League title in 1955. Had not his career been curtailed by injury and war, he would surely have broken more records. It is interesting to look at the results of the matches played in 1939 before war caused the abandonment of League football —results that never appear in any records. Drake missed the first two matches, having been replaced by Reg Lewis. He played in the third game, at home to Sunderland, because Lewis was injured. It turned out to be his last game in first-class football . . . he scored four goals.

THE FIRST SEVEN

The record Drake equalled was set on 6 October 1888 by James Ross of Preston North End, who beat Stoke 7-0. It was the first year of the League, and Preston won the title without losing a game and the Cup without conceding a goal. Ross scored 18 goals in 21 League games, but his club-mate John Goodall was the League's leading scorer with 21.

Joe Payne

Ten-goal hero

Joe Payne was not one of the greatest centre-forwards, but he deserves a place in any goalscoring hall of fame, largely thanks to one afternoon in his life when everything went right.

Although he was signed from his local Derbyshire team by Luton as a centre-forward, Payne had shown so little aptitude for the position in their reserve side that he had been converted into a wing-half. Apparently he had made little more impression in his new role, because by the April of the 1935-36 season he had chalked up only three or four League appearances . . . that is, until fate took a hand.

Three Wishes

It was as if Payne had been granted the proverbial three wishes.

First, both the club centre-forwards were injured.

Second, manager Ned Liddell decided to give Payne another chance in attack because he felt the opposition were not particularly strong.

And third, everything Payne did that Easter Monday was touched with magic. It seemed he could not put a foot wrong.

Luton were in the Third Division at the time, challenging for promotion. Their opponents, Bristol Rovers, were struggling in the bottom half of the table. Despite continuous rain, and sleet later, 13,000 gathered at Kenilworth Road to see what turned out to be the highest-scoring game in the history of the Third Division South.

Yet for over 20 minutes, despite Luton's superiority, Bristol managed to keep the scoresheet clean. Then Payne, gaining in confidence as his side were piling on the pressure, rose to a cross and headed No. 1. This cheered the fans standing in the icy conditions, but little did they realize what was in store. Even when Luton went in at half-

time four up and Payne had notched a hat-trick, there was little to suggest that this was going to be anything more than a heavy thrashing.

Hitting the Jackpot

But in the second half the floodgates opened. Every time Payne got the ball it seemed to finish up in the net. The more he scored, the more his team-mates plied him with passes. It was like feeding a slot machine and hitting the jackpot every time.

Once, Payne found himself on the ground with the ball rolling loose—he stuck out his foot and hooked it into the net!

By the time the final whistle went, the shell-shocked Bristol keeper had picked the ball out of the net a dozen times. His opposite number had hardly touched the ball. Luton's 12-0 victory was an all-time record for the division. And Payne, who was credited with all but one of the second-half goals, had registered 10, the only time in the Football League a player has ever reached double figures. Nat-

urally, it meant instant fame for Payne, but he stayed with Luton. In the remaining four matches he scored all three of their goals; but it was not enough and they missed going up by a couple of points.

The next season, however, Payne proved that he was no flash-in-the-pan by scoring 55 goals and helping Luton to win promotion. At the end of the season he won his only cap, scoring two goals in England's 8-0 victory over Finland in Helsinki.

In 1938 he moved to Chelsea, but injuries sustained in wartime football meant that he never really had a chance to fulfil his potential. He retired in 1948 after spells with West Ham and Millwall. But his magic 10 goals had assured him a permanent place in the annals of British football.

A GLUT OF GOALSCORING

Payne crowned the most amazing outbreak of individual goalscoring in the history of the Football League. Four months earlier, Drake had equalled the League record with 7. Then, on Boxing Day 1935, only two weeks later, Robert Bell scored 9 in Tranmere's 13-4 massacre of Oldham. This was an extraordinary Third Division North result, because only the previous day Oldham had beaten Tranmere 4-1. Bell was aided by an injury to the opposing centre-half and by team-mates who scented the record and poured into the Oldham half to lay on chances for him. He apparently missed some sitters, too, including a penalty.

Then along came Payne with his 10 to settle the argument once and for all.

Footnote: The 55 goals Payne scored in 1936-37 was a Division III South record. In the same season, Ted Harston of Mansfield set a Division III North record—also with 55 goals.

Bloomer & Buchan

STRIKERS OF LONG AGO

Of the goalscoring forwards before and after World War I, two stand out—Steve Bloomer and Charles Buchan. Bloomer was a prolific scorer whose records lasted for decades. Buchan, too, scored goals aplenty, but he was renowned more for his footballing brain, and he was primarily responsible for a tactical revolution that had a long-lasting and profound effect on the history of the game.

Steve Bloomer

In a career that lasted from 1892 to 1914, when he was 40, Steve Bloomer scored 352 goals in League football—297 for Derby County and 55 for Middlesbrough, for whom he played from 1906 to 1910. For England, he scored 28 goals in 23 games, a record that stood for nearly 50 years.

These are the bare statistics. The man himself was a phenomenon. Slightly built and exceedingly pale of face, he did not look like a footballer. Nor did he bother with the niceties of the game. If the ball came to him within sniffing distance of goal, he would shoot. Rarely did he try to bring the ball under control first or think of passing to a better-placed colleague. And when he did pass, it was usually first time. It was said of Bloomer that he 'lived to shoot', always alive to the half-chance, pouncing on accidental deflections. He was a marvellous volleyer in front of goal, and used to slant his ground shots accurately out of the keeper's reach. But above all, it was the suddenness of his shooting that had the keepers foxed, the ability to hit the ball seemingly with the 'wrong' foot. It was a gift perhaps not seen again until the days of Jimmy Greaves.

Bloomer's League record is more remarkable for being compiled with largely unsuccessful clubs, and the nearest he got to honours were two Cup losers' medals with Derby. He was certainly a man for the big occasion, though—a fact borne out by his extraordinary international record. He scored two against Ireland on his debut in 1895, and the following year hit five against Wales, a record since equalled but never passed. And his feat of scoring in each of his first ten internationals is surely a record that will stand for a long, long time.

Charlie Buchan

When Charlie Buchan went from Sunderland to Arsenal in 1925, his transfer caused a stir—the fee was £2,000 plus £100 for every goal he scored in his first season. In the event, he notched 19 League goals and 2 in the Cup. But for every goal Buchan netted, Arsenal manager Herbert Chapman knew he was getting excellent value. A soccer showman, Chapman set out to put Arsenal on the map. Buchan helped him do it, and not just by scoring goals. After Arsenal had conceded seven goals in his first game, it was Buchan who suggested converting the centre-half's role into a purely defensive one, to counteract the effect of the new offside law. Between them, they developed the third-back game, which Arsenal played to such devastating effect in the 1930s and which eventually spread round the world.

Buchan had been on Arsenal's books as an amateur 16 years earlier (his father had been a blacksmith at Woolwich Arsenal). But he turned professional with Southern League Leyton, before joining Sunderland in 1911. He won a Championship medal in 1913, contributing 27 goals. In all, he scored 258 League goals in 482 matches for his two clubs, but he never won an FA Cup medal, reaching the final once for each club. His international career (five games, four goals) was the source of much controversy. Many said that the England side should be built round him; others feared he was far too clever for the rest.

One other significant contribution came from Buchan—he was one of the first players to turn heading into an art. Rather than just 'bang' his head against the ball, as was the style of the day, he would make clever deflections. And he would use his considerable height to rise above the ball and nod it down into goal.

Buchan retired in 1928 and became a football journalist and later a broadcaster, well known for his Saturday night summaries.

Steve Bloomer

Charlie Buchan

Denis Law

The King

George Best (right) watches his flamboyant team-mate Law attempt a 'bicycle kick'.

Denis Law was two great players in one: a midfield general whose stamina, ball control, vision, and passing enabled him to take complete control of a game, and a striker whose deadly finishing, on the ground or in the air, made him the terror of defences throughout Europe.

Yet as a boy, Law was a skinny 'weakling' with thick spectacles, and looked so unlike a footballer that he was not recognized when he turned up at Huddersfield in 1955 as a 15-year-old apprentice. Little more than three years later, he was making his debut for Scotland (and scoring in it). He was to become their highest scorer, be transferred three times for record fees, score a record number of goals in FA Cup matches, be voted European Footballer of the Year, and provide some of the most exciting moments in post-war football.

It became a familiar, yet no less thrilling, sight 'to see the blond striking inside-forward, shirt typically outside his shorts, leaping like a salmon to power headers into the corner of the net or darting through a crowded area in a blur of movement to flash shots into goal with either foot, and then turning to salute his achievement with arm characteristically flung high.

Law never stopped running, he had reflexes as sharp as à cat's, and he would strike like a cobra. Added to this he had tremendous courage, going in with head or foot to take a half-chance, completely oblivious of his own safety.

Although never a prolific scorer in the manner of Dean, Gallacher, or Greaves, Law collected 217 League goals in 452 matches, and would surely have had many more but for injuries that plagued his career—in only 7 out of his 17 seasons did he play more than 30 League games, 38 being his highest. His greatest disappointment was to miss Manchester United's triumph in the European Cup.

Law was the scourge of England. From 1960 he played in eight consecutive games against the 'Auld Enemy' and was on the losing side only twice. In all he won 55 caps (a record until overhauled by Kenny Dalglish) and scored a record 30 goals for Scotland, despite failing to score in his last 11 games for them. He scored four goals against both Northern Ireland and Norway, and notched another hat-trick against Norway.

Always a scrupulously fair player, Law nevertheless had a tempestuous career, forever getting involved in flare-ups and suffering several suspensions. This was due mainly to his inflammable temperament. He often had to put up with severe provocation. And that was his chief problem: he would not put up with it. If a player kicked him, he would kick that player back. And off the field Law would go.

A Long Way to United

Law spent most of his career with Manchester United, but he got there by a devious route, via Italy. Huddersfield could not keep him long, his talents shining far too brightly and obviously for Second Division football. He won his first cap while with Huddersfield, though, when Matt Busby was in charge of the Scottish side, becoming, at 18 years and 236 days, Scotland's youngest international. Busby had been captivated by Law's performance a couple of years earlier in a youth match and had offered £10,000 for him at the time. But Huddersfield's assistant manager was Bill Shankly, who regarded Law as 'the greatest thing on two feet', so Law stayed put. When eventually he did become available, United were well equipped with Bobby Charlton and Dennis Viollet; so Manchester City stepped in and bought him for a record £55,000.

Law had only one full season with City before going to Torino, along with Joe Baker of Hibs. The Italians loved him, but he never settled in Italy. His rebellious nature did not fit in with the strict discipline. Nevertheless, his stay there did him good, and he returned to England a better player for the tight marking he had learnt to overcome.

Matt Busby paid a new British record of £115,000 to bring Law back to Manchester, and made him the highest-paid player in Britain. Busby soon found he had to curb Law's enthusiasm for being in the thick of things all the time and his desire for controlling a match, and although Law objected he played him as a striker. In his first season with United, he scored 23 League goals, and although they just escaped relegation, they won the Cup, Law scoring the first goal in their 3-1 victory over Leicester at Wembley. He also had a marvellous season for Scotland, getting 11 goals in 7 games.

He went on to win two League Championship medals with United in the sixties and in 1964 was voted European Footballer of the Year, the first of the United trio to win that award—Bobby Charlton (1966) and George Best (1968) were the others. What a line-up United had in the mid-sixties, three of the greatest players the world has ever seen all in the same forward-line.

Decline and Comeback

Injuries in the late sixties almost put paid to Law's career. But he doggedly shook them off, and showed as much courage in regaining his fitness and confidence as he had always shown in the penalty box. His goals became fewer, but he was still scoring at the rate of one in just over two games. And he won back his international place in 1972 after a three-year absence, captaining Scotland to a 2-0 win over Peru at Hampden Park.

But the same man who put him back in a Scottish shirt, Tommy Docherty, dropped a bombshell when, now as United's manager, he gave Law a free transfer at the end of the 1972-73 season.

Law would have retired but for Manchester City's offer to sign him, and he had one more season, playing in the League Cup final, although City lost to Wolves. But then, right at the end of his career, he fulfilled a lifelong ambition—he played in the World Cup. He had just one match, the 2-0 win over Zaïre, and he did not score. But it was poetic justice that such a wonderful player should finally grace the world's greatest competition, and it was a fitting end to a sparkling career.

Not particularly tall—about 5ft 9in (1.75m)—Law was usually head and shoulders above the rest when he leapt for the ball. No wonder they called him 'the king'.

DENIS LAW'S GOALS			
Club	Lg	Cup	Euro
Huddersfield 1955-60	16	3	
Manchester City 1960-61 (£55,000)	21	2	
Torino, Italy 1961-62 (£100,000)	10		
Manchester United 1962-73 (£115,000)	171	33	28
Manchester City 1973-74 (free)	9	2	
Scotland (1958-1974)		30 goals	

Law scores for the Rest of the World against England in 1963.

THE LOST SIX GOALS

Question: Who scored seven goals in an FA Cup tie and finished on the losing side?
Answer: Denis Law. He scored six for Manchester City against Luton in a 1961 4th Round tie, but the match had to be abandoned twenty minutes from the end in torrential rain with City's 6-2 scoreline cancelled. Law's goals do not go into the record books, and although he scored one when the match was replayed, Manchester City lost.
Footnote: For the purists, W. H. Minter scored seven goals for St Albans City against Dulwich Hamlet in a qualifying round tie in 1922, and his side lost 8-7!

Hughie Gallacher

A tragic ending

and he signed for First Division club Airdrie. He helped them win the Scottish Cup in 1924, and they finished runners up to Rangers or Celtic in the League on four consecutive occasions. It was the greatest period in the club's history, and no wonder there were demonstrations when the fans discovered approaches were being made for his transfer. They threatened to burn down the stand if their idol was sold. There seemed little danger of that until Newcastle sent a delegation across the border, who, despite being unwelcome, gatecrashed an

Above: Gallacher (right, arms out wide) furiously disputes an offside decision after scoring for Chelsea. Right: Immensely difficult to shake off the ball, he evades a tackle while keeping close control.

Of all the tragic figures in soccer—and there have been a few—Hughie Gallacher, one of the great heroes of Scottish football, is perhaps the saddest. Fame without wealth was the curse of the footballer before the abolition of the maximum wage; too much of both the cross some have had to bear since then. Gallacher, of course, came

The unsmiling Scot in his Newcastle days. Gallacher had originality as well as all the footballing gifts.

into the former category, for his career spanned the period between the wars. Six clubs paid a total of £23,000 for him—some of his transfers were massive for those days—yet, of course, all he got from them was £60 in signing-on fees.

Many experts regarded Gallacher as the finest centre-forward of his time, some as the finest footballer. He had all the gifts—powerful shooting, deceptive body swerve, speed off the mark, footwork and ball control, and, despite his lack of height (he was barely 5ft 6in), remarkable heading ability. Added to this was the positional sense that enabled him to create unexpected chances, the ability (like Dean and Greaves) to poke the ball in with very little backlift, and the toughness to withstand the fiercest, and not always the fairest, challenges.

Born in Bellshill, a Lanarkshire village near Glasgow, Gallacher played schoolboy football with Alex James, a partnership that would later be revived for Scotland. He worked for a time down the mines before signing for Queen of South. But a bout of pneumonia almost ended his soccer career before it had begun. His determination pulled him through, however,

Airdrie board meeting, asked them to name their price, and without hesitation paid the sum jokingly put forward—a record £6,500.

Honours
Gallacher had already been capped by his country, and one of his goals against Wales in 1925, when he dribbled from half-way through the entire Welsh defence, had even the Welsh defenders applauding. He continued to play for Scotland while south of the border and was outstanding when the 'Wembley Wizards' humiliated England in 1928, and he scored five against Ireland in 1929

He captained Newcastle for a

period and led them to the League title in 1926-27. He went to Chelsea in 1930 for a near-record £10,000, but played only twice more for his country. In the late thirties he moved from club to club, still scoring consistently but gradually declining.

Troubles

On the field Gallacher had a reputation for needling opponents—verbally, not physically. He was always in trouble, and was once suspended for two months after an altercation with a referee. But he frequently suffered excessive physical abuse himself—it was the only way they could stop him.

Off the field, too, he was usually in trouble. Although he kept himself scrupulously fit, he had a reputation for 'fast living'—snappy dressing, drinking, and women. Various scandals, including a divorce, plagued him throughout his career. After he retired, he worked in a Gateshead factory and was still turning out in charity matches at the age of 50. But he was a lonely man. His second wife had died, and he took to excessive drinking. He was drunk when he struck his 14-year-old son. The boy was taken out of his care, and Gallacher was to appear before the magistrates to face charges of ill-treatment. The day before the case was due, he threw himself in front of a train.

All of football mourned the passing of Hughie Gallacher. Third in the all-time list of League goal-scorers, the 'wee man' had enormous flair and was a tremendous crowd-puller wherever he played. Was he the greatest centre-forward of them all? Well, inch for inch, there can be no argument.

Jimmy McGrory
Goal-a-game man

The young McGrory (left) in the early 1920s, and in the late 1930s (right) some 400 goals later but still hungry for them.

Jimmy McGrory was a statistician's dream. The only British footballer to average more than a goal a game over his whole career, he kept it up for 15 years. And he amassed 397 of his 410 League goals for one club—Celtic. Three times he led the Scottish League goalscorers. He hit eight goals in one match against Dunfermline in 1928, a Scottish First Division record. In 1936 he notched four against Motherwell in five minutes. In all first-class football, he scored 550 goals.

McGrory was a leader of the old school, an old-fashioned centre-forward whose job it was to score goals. And no one did it better. Not particularly tall, he was fast and powerful, could shoot with either foot, and had that happy knack of being in the right place at the right time. He scored perhaps a third of his goals with his head, often spectacularly diving full length to meet low crosses.

He first appeared for Celtic briefly in 1923, and then went on loan for a season to Clydebank. On his return to Celtic he played on the left wing, but soon established himself in the centre-forward berth. His goals helped Celtic to two League titles and six Cup wins. He had the misfortune to be a contemporary of the peerless Hughie Gallacher, so his international career was limited to just seven matches, in which he scored six goals.

He retired in 1937 to manage Kilmarnock, and he returned to Celtic in 1945 to serve the club as manager for another 20 years.

GALLACHER'S TRAVELS				
Club	Joined	Fee	Games	Goals
Airdrie	(1920)	–	111	91
Newcastle	(1925)	£6,500	160	133
Chelsea	(1930)	£10,000	132	72
Derby	(1935)	£3,000	51	38
Notts Cty	(1936)	£2,000	45	32
Grimsby	(1937)	£1,000	11	3
Gateshead	(1938)	£500	31	18
			541	387
Scotland	(1924-35)		19	22

JIMMY McGRORY: LEAGUE CAREER			
Club		Games	Goals
Celtic	1923	3	1
Clydebank	1923-24	30	13
Celtic	1924-37	375	396
		408	410
Leading Scorer			(games)
1926-27	49 goals		(33)
1927-28	47 goals		(36)
1935-36	50 goals		(32)

Bobby Charlton

Scorer of great goals

Bobby Charlton's career spanned two distinct periods of Manchester United's success, for he was one of the few survivors of the tragic Munich air crash that destroyed the 'Busby Babes', and he was the cornerstone around which the new great team was built. It is often said of Charlton that he was a scorer of great goals rather than a great scorer of goals. Nevertheless, it will be a long time before his scoring record for England is beaten—49 goals in 106 games.

He won every honour in the game—including World Cup and European Cup medals—but above all he won universal respect. For he was more than just a great player. He was a model sportsman both on and off the field, worshipped not only by partisan United or England fans, but by football followers in every part of the world. Whether playing as a striking inside-forward, an outside-left, or a deep-lying centre-forward, he thrilled crowds everywhere for over a decade with his gazelle-like running, dazzling body swerve, and a shot—taken on the run with either foot—that was out of this world. He was the best-loved player of his generation.

. . . a shot out of this world.

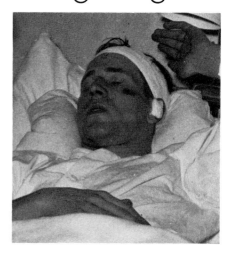

Charlton survived Munich.

A Footballing Family

Charlton was born, in October 1937, in the football-crazy mining village of Ashington, in Northumberland. His mother's four brothers had all been full-backs in the League, and his cousin was the great Newcastle centre-forward Jackie Milburn, idol of the North-East. His elder brother Jack was to become the Leeds and England centre-half, and share in his World Cup triumph.

The young Bobby's talents were evident at an early age, and he was spotted by Manchester United scout Joe Armstrong as a 15-year-old in schoolboy football. United signed him in the face of widespread competition, and he was with them for 20 years. At first, despite his natural ability—or perhaps because of it—he proved difficult to coach. His control, long passing, and shooting ability made him something special, but he had to work on his short game before he could become a fully fledged member of the 'Busby Babes', the sensational young team of all the talents built up by Matt Busby.

Charlton made his League debut in the 1956-57 season against Charlton Athletic, and scored two. He helped United into the Cup final with a typically acrobatic shot

on the turn against Birmingham in the semi-final. He played in enough matches to win a Championship medal, and it was only an injury to United's keeper in the final that robbed him of a Cup winner's medal, too, in his first season.

Munich and After

Charlton's first taste of European competition came in the losing semi-final against Real Madrid in 1957, and he scored in the home leg. With Tommy Taylor at centre-forward and Viollet, Whelan, and Webster also contending for inside-forward places, Charlton was by no means a regular in the side, but he was back the following year for the quarter-final against Red Star. He scored in the home leg, and in the return in Belgrade showed perhaps his first true hint of greatness with two searing goals. But then came the disaster at Munich airport on the way home. Charlton, one of the lucky ones, was found, still strapped to his seat, 60 yards away from the wrecked airliner—cut, bruised, and shocked, but otherwise unhurt.

He recovered to take part, with the few colleagues remaining and a collection of veterans hastily assembled from other clubs, in their brave efforts at the end of the season. Miraculously, they reached Wembley again, but had to be content with another runners-up medal.

ENGLAND RECORD		
Season	Games	Goals
1957-58	3	3
1958-59	9	8
1959-60	6	2
1960-61	9	8
1961-62	12	4
1962-63	6	5
1963-64	10	3
1964-65	3	1
1965-66	16	6
1966-67	4	1
1967-68	9	5
1968-69	8	1
1969-70	11	2
Total	106	49

Charlton playing for England in the 1970 World Cup at the end of his international career.

By this time, Charlton had already made his international debut, against Scotland at Hampden Park, contributing a memorable goal—a spectacular volley on the edge of the box from a Finney cross—to England's 4-0 victory. He went to Sweden for the 1958 World Cup, but to the dismay of Press and public alike he was passed over when England were crying out for some class in the centre.

United switched him to the left wing to give him more room, and he was soon occupying this position for England, too, swerving irresistibly past his man on either side, but never more dangerous than when cutting in for one of his thunderbolt shots. At times he was the best left-winger in the world, but there were games, too, when he seemed to lose his way. There was a tendency sometimes to crowd his inside men in order to get more of the action. Nevertheless, he won his Cup medal at last, in 1963, and another Championship medal in 1965. But there was more to come —very much more.

The Years of Triumph

Although Charlton was a popular hero and at times a genius on the field, he was, in the mid-1960s, somewhat of an enigma. Matt Busby found the answer by playing him as a deep-lying centre-forward, and that's where Alf Ramsey played

Receiving a special award in Mexico.

him in the 1966 World Cup. Balding now, and one of the veterans of the side, he scored a magnificent solo goal against Mexico, and in the semi-final against Portugal played one of his finest internationals, scoring both England's goals. In addition to his World Cup medal that year, he was voted European and England's Footballer of the Year.

Charlton went on to play in the 1970 World Cup and chalk up a record number of appearances (later passed by Bobby Moore) and goals for England. But his greatest and most emotional triumph was to captain the United team in 1968 that won the European Cup at last. The scene was Wembley again, the opponents Benfica, and Bobby scored two goals in their 4-1 victory.

He retired at the end of the 1972-73 season after playing more than 750 games for the club. His 198 goals in 606 League matches were both club records. And, curiously enough, his six goals that season made him their leading scorer for the third time. He joined Preston almost immediately as player-manager, but did not kick a ball again until the following season, when he took his League tally past the 200 mark. He resigned in August 1975 after a dispute with the directors, and it was a sad loss to football.

It is always difficult to know where to put Bobby Charlton in a list of all-time greats, because he often did not make the best use of his undoubted talents. But there can never have been a more popular player with the public as a whole, nor a finer sportsman.

Ferenc Puskas

The Galloping Major

Ferenc Puskas didn't look at all like a footballer—at least, not like one of the all-time 'greats', which he undoubtedly was. With his stocky figure—in his later playing days, 'roly poly' was a term more aptly used to describe it—and chubby face, he looked more like a friendly publican. His appearance was due mainly to his liking for beer and his enormous appetite. Appearances can be deceptive, however, and in Puskas's case they concealed perfect control, startling acceleration, a sparkling football brain and the most devastating left foot in the history of the game. Puskas has often been described as one-footed, but this was not true. It was just that his left foot was so good that he rarely felt the need to use his other peg, and he headed the ball only as a last resort.

Had his career finished at the time of the Hungarian Uprising in 1956 (when, incidentally, there were reports that he had been killed in the fighting), it would have been remarkable enough. A star of arguably the finest international side ever seen, he scored 83 goals in his 84 games for Hungary, and led them to their famous 6-3 victory over England at Wembley in 1953 and their 7-1 humiliation of the same team a year later in Budapest. Then, quite remarkably, he embarked on an entirely new career in a foreign land when he starred for what was probably the greatest club side ever—Real Madrid. And in 1960 he found himself in the European Cup final at Hampden Park, scoring four goals in their memorable 7-3 victory over Eintracht Frankfurt.

Honved and Hungary

Puskas made his debut, in 1943 at the age of 16, for his local side Kispest. Five years later he was the League's leading scorer with 50 goals, although it must be said that there were several weak clubs in the League. Kispest became Honved, the mighty army side who provided most of the national team. Puskas won five Championship medals with Honved and was the League's leading scorer three more times. He shared the goalscoring laurels for both club and country with Kocsis, having made his international debut in 1945 at the age of 18.

The 'Galloping Major', as Puskas became known, played for Hungary for 11 years, much of the time as a superb captain as well as goalscorer and goal-maker. With such great players around him, he was

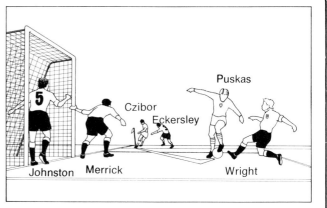

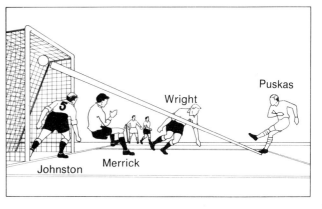

Wright (left) and Puskas exchange pennants before the historic 1953 England-Hungary encounter. The diagrams show how Puskas drags the ball back to leave Wright tackling thin air as he lashes in Hungary's third goal.

COUNTLESS GOALS

There is no complete record of the goals Puskas scored during his career, but he was unimpressed when Pelé scored his 1,000th goal, regarding that milestone as a long way short of his own tally. There is even uncertainty about the number of goals he scored for Hungary—probably 83, although some sources give 85. Whichever

Puskas hammers the nail in England's coffin to complete Hungary's 7-1 triumph in 1954.

is right, it still stands as an all-time international record, ahead of Pelé's 76.

His goal aggregates as leading scorer in the Hungarian and Spanish leagues are as follows:

Hungary:	1947-48 Kispest	50
	1949-50 Honved	31
	1950 Honved	25
	1953 Honved	27
Spain:	1959-60 Real Madrid	26
	1960-61 Real Madrid	27
	1962-63 Real Madrid	26
	1963-64 Real Madrid	20

Czibor, not to return. After a year in Austria, his failure to obtain a playing permit led him to Spain and Real Madrid. Real were the first European champions and the team was a blend of some of the finest footballing talents from around the world. It was dominated by the Argentinian maestro Alfredo Di Stefano.

Other world stars had failed to get on with the temperamental centre-forward, but Puskas struck up a brilliant partnership with him. He played in the 1958-59 European Cup, but not in the final, then scored 12 goals in the 1959-60 campaign in seven games, including his four in the final. He went on to lead the Spanish League scorers four times, hit a hat-trick in the 1962 European Cup final, but had to give best to Eusebio and Benfica, who won 5-3. He won another runners-up medal in 1964. In all, he scored 35 goals in 39 European Cup matches, and won five Championship medals with Real. He also played four times for Spain.

often able to stroll through a match directing operations majestically from the centre of the pitch, making space for others, timing his passes to perfection, and always there with that incomparable left foot to finish off a move. He screened the ball immaculately, could beat a man with a half-turn of his shoulders, and was incredibly difficult to dispossess.

The greatest disappointment for him and for Hungary was the team's defeat in the 1954 World Cup final by Germany. Puskas was criticized for playing in that match, for he had been injured in an earlier group match (in which Hungary beat Germany 8-3!) and was not fully fit. Nevertheless, he scored within six minutes, was thwarted twice in the second half by near-miraculous goalkeeping, and, with Hungary 3-2 down, had what seemed a perfectly good goal disallowed in the dying minutes.

Real and Spain
At the time of the Hungarian Uprising, Puskas was on tour with Honved in South America and decided, together with Kocsis and

Sandor Kocsis of Hungary (left) demonstrates his power in the air against Germany in the 1954 World Cup final.

GOLDEN HEAD

Puskas's goalscoring partner for Honved and Hungary, Sandor Kocsis, was perhaps overshadowed by the great man's personality, but held his own in the matter of statistics. He had two good feet, but it was in the air that he really excelled. Regarded by many as the greatest header of the ball in the history of the game, he became known popularly as 'Golden Head'.

Third in the all-time list of international scorers with 75 goals in 68 matches, Kocsis scored 11 in the 1954 World Cup, a record at that time.

He led Hungary's domestic scoring table three times, in their 26-match season: 1951 (30 goals), 1952 (36), and 1954 (33).

Like Puskas, he settled in Spain after the 1956 uprising, although he had less success with Barcelona than his fellow-countryman. Nevertheless, he won two League, two Cup medals, and a Fairs Cup medal to add to the five Championship medals with Honved and the 1952 Olympic gold he won with Hungary.

Gerd Müller

The Bomber

West German star Gerd Müller is the classic example of the modern striker—stocky, mobile, with immensely powerful thighs, giving him a low centre of gravity. This aids balance and enables him to turn and latch onto loose balls in the penalty box and put them into the back of the net before opponents realize the danger.

Müller's ability to snap up the half-chance played a huge part in the success of West Germany and his club Bayern Munich in the 1970s. When he left Germany in 1979 to play in the United States for Fort Lauderdale, he had scored 628 goals in first-class football. These included 365 in his 14 seasons in the Bundesliga for Bayern, his only club, and 36 for them in

MÜLLER'S 14 WORLD CUP GOALS	
1970	
v Morocco (group)	1
v Bulgaria (group)	3
v Peru (group)	3
v England (quarter-final)	1
v Italy (semi-final)	2
v Uruguay (3rd place game)	0
1974	
v Chile (group)	0
v Australia (group)	1
v E. Germany (group)	0
v Yugoslavia (s-f group)	1
v Sweden (s-f group)	0
v Poland (s-f group)	1
v Netherlands (final)	1

the European Cup. And his record 68 goals for West Germany in only 62 internationals include 14 in the World Cup, more than any other player. None was more important —nor more typical—than his winner in the final of the 1974 World Cup against the Netherlands. Closely marked as usual, he took a low pass from Bonhof on the right bye-line, touched it away from goal, and then swivelled to strike it through his marker's legs into the far corner of the goal from just outside the goal area.

After this triumph, Müller retired from international football to allow himself more time with his family. And goalkeepers and centre-backs around the world, whom Müller never allowed any time, breathed a sigh of relief.

A Bear among Thoroughbreds

Born in the Bavarian village of Zinsen in 1945, Müller left school at 15 when his father died, and worked as a weaver. He joined the

local club Nordlingen, and 46 goals in two seasons attracted the big clubs. Bayern Munich won the race for his signature, and he joined them in 1963. With 35 goals in his first season, he helped them win promotion to the Bundesliga. This effectively silenced the Bayern coach, former Yugoslav international Cajkovski, who had greeted Müller's arrival with the comment: 'Do you want me to put a bear among my racehorses?' The club certainly possessed some thoroughbreds—Franz Beckenbauer and keeper Sepp Maier among them—but it was 'the Bomber', as Müller soon became known, who got the vital goals.

When Bayern pulled off the League and Cup double in 1969, it was Müller who scored both their goals in the 2-1 Cup victory and 30 of their 61 League goals. The following season his 38 goals won him the 'Golden Boot' award, for Europe's leading League scorer, and he won it again in 1971-72 with 40 out of their 101 in 34 matches. The latter season marked the first of a hat-trick of League titles for Bayern, and Müller's further contributions were 36 out of 93 goals in 1973 and 30 out of 95 in 1974.

Yet contrary to widely held opinions, Müller contributed more than just his goals. He played an important part in the build-up of attacks for both club and country, and his very presence in the penalty box took the pressure off his fellow forwards and created space for others moving up from midfield.

Bayern also won a hat-trick of European Cups, from 1974 to 1976. In the 1974 replay against Atlético Madrid, Müller scored two of their four goals, one with a spectacular, uncharacteristically delicate lob over the advancing keeper from the edge of the box. And he clinched the 1975 final against Leeds, typically with a goal from the only chance he had during the whole game.

World Cup winners. Three Müller goals that won World Cup matches: in 1970 against England (left) and 1974 against Poland (right) and Holland (below) in the final.

Vital Goals for Germany

Müller scored so many vital goals for West Germany that one wonders whether they would have won anything without him. He was leading scorer in the 1970 World Cup finals with 10, including two hat-tricks and his memorable extra-time winner against England in the quarter-finals, and he was voted European Footballer of the Year.

He was again a thorn in England's side in the 1972 European Championships. Having scored 6 of West Germany's 10 goals in the 6 qualifying group matches, he scored their third at Wembley which virtually put England out of the tournament. He went on to score both goals in the 2-1 win over host country Belgium in the semifinal and another two in West Germany's fluent 3-0 victory over Russia in the final.

In the 1974 World Cup, held in West Germany, Müller scored four goals, including the only one of the match against Poland which put the Germans into the final. And it was entirely fitting that the greatest striker of modern times should score the winner in the final at Munich, in front of the fans who idolized him.

Tommy Lawton

The thoroughbred

Lawton (left), wearing Notts County colours for the first time, gets up to head home within five minutes of his debut for the Third Division side. England's centre-forward, he joined them from Chelsea in 1947 for a record fee of £20,000.

Tommy Lawton was a joy to watch — and he could score goals. He was everything a centre-forward should be, and more: superb in the air (as befits a pupil of the great Dixie Dean), a cannonball shot with either foot, a sweet volleyer of the ball, robust enough to withstand the strongest of challenges, fast and elusive, and remarkably light on his feet for such a big man.

How the crowds thrilled when Lawton glided between two defenders onto a through ball, collected it smoothly in his stride, and hammered it past the advancing keeper into the corner of the net; or when, prowling round the penalty box like a panther, he would suddenly pounce on a loose ball and lash it into goal; or when he rose to a cross, head and shoulders above the rest, and seemingly hung there in the air before cracking a header goalwards.

His timing in the air was faultless. As he felt the ball touch the skin of his forehead, his powerful neck muscles would come into action, whiplashing his head and directing the ball with remarkable velocity out of the keeper's reach. Lawton himself would say that Dean was the more powerful header of the ball, but it must have been a close-run thing.

Lawton's career spanned 20 years, a world war, six League clubs, and three divisions, as well as a spell as player-manager of a non-League club. He played 23 times for England and scored 22 goals.

Youngest Centre-Forward

At school in Bolton, Lawton was a prolific goalscorer—570 in three seasons—but he never won a schoolboy cap despite scoring a hat-trick in an England trial. He signed amateur forms for Burnley, then in the Second Division, and at $16\frac{1}{2}$ became the youngest centre-forward to play in League football.

He played seven games that first season, 1935-36, and scored five goals to help the club avoid relegation. The following season he signed as a professional as soon as he became 17, and celebrated with a brilliant hat-trick against Spurs. His form attracted most of the top clubs, but it was Everton who won the race for his signature.

Lawton was signed to understudy Dixie Dean, and played several games as inside-right to the great man, whom he was soon to replace. Everton fans had the privilege of watching two of the greatest centre-forwards of all time in one team—one coming to the end of his career, the other just beginning. And what a beginning it was. In his first full season, 1937-38, Lawton headed the League scoring list with 28. He did it again the next season, with 34, won a League Championship medal, and scored six goals in eight games for England.

The War Intervenes

In the first three games of the fated 1939-40 season, Lawton scored all of Everton's five goals. At that rate he might have beaten Dean's record! But that was the end of

The young Lawton, at Everton.

League football for seven years —seven years in which Lawton played some of his finest football, as evidenced by his international record in that time—25 goals in 23 games. Nevertheless, top footballers were luckier than most. They were able to continue their profession while in the services, and Lawton never resented the 'lost' years.

The Third Division

After the war, a dispute with Everton resulted in his transfer to Chelsea. Everton were reluctant to let him go, for he was at his peak, a fact he emphasized with four of England's goals in their historic 10-0 defeat of Portugal in Lisbon. He did not stay with Chelsea long, however, and was involved in perhaps the most sensational transfer in British football, after a pro-

LAWTON: CAREER SUMMARY		
Club (Year signed, fee)	Games	Goals
Burnley (1936)	25	16
Everton (1937, £6,500)	87	65
Chelsea (1945, £11,500)	42	30
Notts County (1947, £20,000)	151	90
Brentford (1952, £12,000)	50	17
Arsenal (1953, £12,000)	35	13
	390	231
England (1938–48)	23	22

tracted dispute with the club. It was not the size of the fee that surprised the footballing world—a record £20,000—but the club that paid it. It was Third Division Notts County.

A part-time job went with the move to County, and Lawton felt he had secured his future. It was, however, virtually the end of his international career, although he was proud to play another four times for England while in the Third Division.

Lawton guided his club to promotion in 1950, and served them well until he moved to Brentford in 1952. By then he had become a provider of goals, playing the deep-lying centre-forward role before the Hungarians 'introduced' it to England. Indeed, his ball control and passing ability were such that he

would always have made a fine inside-forward.

He became player-manager for a few months, but resigned the managership shortly before another curious turn in his career. At the age of 34, he returned to the First Division—with Arsenal, the League champions. They had been going through a bad spell and needed someone of Lawton's experience, not so much to score goals but to provide confidence.

A Final Fling

Lawton enjoyed a pleasant couple of years with Arsenal, showing flashes of his old brilliance and always exhibiting his elegant style. He came out at Highbury for his first game of the 1955-56 season, at the age of nearly 36, and scored a

Lawton enjoyed a final fling in the First Division with Arsenal, treating the Highbury crowd to displays of his heading prowess.

hat-trick against Cardiff. He said farewell with a flourish that season, scoring six goals in eight games.

After a highly successful spell as player-manager of Southern League club Kettering, he unwisely accepted an offer to become manager of his old club Notts County. The club were split over the appointment and Lawton lasted only 14 months. He was in and out of football for some years, and sadly was later to experience financial troubles. It was ironic that a man whose career had been largely determined by the desire to find security in football should be unable to do so.

Pelé

In any argument about the greatest footballer in soccer history, Pelé figures strongly. Many, perhaps most, pundits, say that without doubt he is the No. 1 of all time. Others will say that Di Stefano was a more all-round player with the ability to control a game, others that George Best at his peak had no equal, and still others that Matthews reigned supreme and for longer. Depending on one's allegience, names such as Puskas, Dean, Gallacher, and Beckenbauer will be put forward, and Maradona has been hailed as the 'new Pelé'. The arguments will continue as long as football is played, and it is never possible to make absolute comparisons between footballers of different ages, playing different styles, against different quality opposition. But it is possible to say that Pelé has been the most universally popular footballer, an ambassador for his sport wherever he played, and one of the truly great sportsmen of the century.

If ever the United States become a leading footballing nation, and

A familiar sight—Pelé celebrating a goal. He scored this one against Italy in the 1970 World Cup final, with a soaring leap and a powerful downward header, to put Brazil one up. They went on to win 4-1.

they probably will one day, they can look back and thank one man —Pelé. After a career in which he won every honour in the game, broke record after record, and retired as 'the king of football', Pelé came back, and, with his beautiful skills, wonderful sportsmanship, and above all his great love and enthusiasm for the game, inspired a nation who had more than once rejected the sport, finally to take it to their hearts.

Pelé's feats and records have been analysed, catalogued, and argued about, and many of them are set out on these pages for all to see. But statistics pale before the sight of Pelé in action—his oneness with the ball, his flowing running action, the timing of his shots, his awareness of his team-mates, the way he attacked the ball in the air or unleashed bursts of speed that tore defences apart, his split-second thinking and ability to accomplish the unexpected and the well-nigh impossible, the cheeky way he would sometimes bounce the ball off opponents' shins while dribbling, and his sheer exuberance when he scored—everything he did he did beautifully. He played football in

The Black Pearl

the manner and the spirit in which it should be played, and was the finest possible example for any aspiring youngster to model himself on.

Capped at 16

Born on 23 October 1940 in a small town in Central Brazil and baptized Edson Arantes do Nascimento, Pelé himself does not know how he got his nickname. But from the age of 9, he was known as Pelé to everyone except his family, who call him 'Dico'. Pelé's family were poor, his father a former professional footballer known as Dondinho who had been forced out of the game through injury.

Poverty never stifled Pelé's ambition, and from an early age he not only showed a tremendous talent for the game but also a dedication to it and a fanaticism for it that furnished him with the single-mindedness to perfect his skills. And he was lucky when Brazilian World Cup star of the 1930s, Valdemar de Brito, came to coach the

---

GOALS GALORE

In his 1,254 games, up to the time he retired in 1974, Pelé scored 1,217 goals. His highest score was 8, for Santos against Botafogo (Ribeirão Preto) in an 11-0 win on 21 November 1964. He scored three goals or more on 125 separate occasions, including seven hat-tricks in internationals. His most prolific spell was for Santos in 1961, when he hit 30 in 10 games over a period of only five weeks, as follows: 3, 1, 3, 0, 5, 4, 5, 1, 4, 4. In one spell for Santos, in 1962, he scored in 20 consecutive games. His record of hat-tricks is as follows:

3 goals	89 times
4 goals	29 times
5 goals	6 times
8 goals	1 time

PELÉ YEAR BY YEAR				
Year	All matches		Internationals	
	Games	Goals	Games	Goals
1956	2	2	–	–
1957	73	65	2	2
1958	67	90	7	10
1959	103	126	9	11
1960	82	77	6	4
1961	75	111	–	–
1962	59	71	8	7
1963	59	74	7	7
1964	50	60	3	2
1965	74	105	8	8
1966	50	44	9	5
1967	65	56	–	–
1968	82	59	7	4
1969	78	65	9	7
1970	75	59	15	8
1971	74	31	2	1
1972	74	51	–	–
1973	67	52	–	–
1974	45	19	–	–
Totals	1,254	1,217	92	76

juvenile club Pelé belonged to. De Brito was a top professional coach, but he liked to work with youngsters. So, as a 13-year-old, Pelé began to learn the tricks of his trade and to form good habits. He learnt how to stand sideways before turning to trap a ball, so that he knew where his team-mates were; how to bend a ball to the left or the right; how to screen the ball while dribbling and how to use the arms for balance; how to swerve round an opponent; and how to take off with either or both feet when leaping for

Brazil v England in the 1970 World Cup. Above: Pelé treats Tommy Wright for cramp . . .

the ball. Pelé, who was not the best of students at school, was the perfect soccer pupil.

A year or so later De Brito went back to coaching professionals, but he returned one day to take Pelé to Santos, state champions of São Paulo. A skinny 15-year-old, Pelé had to be built up before he could play for the first eleven. He made his debut before he was 16, and

. . . and exchanges shirts and smiles with England captain Bobby Moore after Brazil's 1-0 victory.

Pelé's famous 'dummy' in the 1970 World Cup semi-final against Uruguay was one of the highlights of a marvellous tournament. With Brazil coasting to a 3-1 victory, Clodoaldo hit a long, low diagonal ball from the left. Pelé raced towards it from the inside-right position, with keeper Mazurkiewicz coming out fast to block his path (below). There didn't seem any way past the keeper —but Pelé found one. He sold the perfect dummy, haring past the keeper on one side while the ball sailed past him on the other (right). Then he put the 'brakes' on, swerved behind the keeper (below centre), and screwed the ball just wide of the goal (below right) as defenders were coming back to cover.

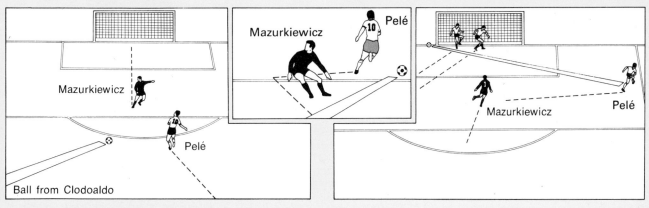

Santos were his only club until he came out of retirement to play in America.

In 1957 Pelé began to play more regularly, alternating with Del Vecchio in the centre-forward berth. Within a few months he also began to score regularly, and on 7 July, at the age of $16\frac{3}{4}$, played his first game for Brazil. It was against Argentina, and he scored Brazil's goal in a 2-1 defeat. It was the first of many games he would play for his country, the first of many goals.

The 1958 World Cup

It was in the World Cup in Sweden the following year that the young Pelé first took the footballing world by storm. Injury kept him out of the side until the last of the group matches, when he played in their 2-0 victory over the USSR. In the quarter-finals they met Wales. Wales were the underdogs, but in the first half their defence, with keeper Jack Kelsey in brilliant form, kept out everything Mazzola, Didi, Garrincha, Zagalo, and Pelé threw at them. Then, after 66 minutes, Pelé scored what he has said was his most unforgettable goal. It wasn't his best by any means —it was in fact somewhat lucky, being deflected past the helpless Kelsey—but it was enough to put Brazil through to the semi-finals and to give the 17-year-old the confidence to turn on his magic for the world to see.

Vava returned to the side against France, and within two minutes of the start accepted a pass from Pelé

Pelé scores for Brazil against Sweden in the 1958 World Cup.

THE 1959 MARATHON

Pelé's most prolific year, for both games and goals, was 1959. In addition to Santos and Brazil, he represented various army teams from August to November. His sole respite was in March, when he played 'only' five matches, but these were all internationals! Here is his month by month record:

Month	Games	Goals
January	8	12
February	8	4
March	5	7
April	9	6
May	8	9
June	15	22
July	6	7
August	8	15
September	9	13
October	9	13
November	11	10
December	7	8
	103	126

The year began with a Santos tour of South America, playing at sea level one day and the next perhaps at 8,000ft. In May they began a tour of Europe, playing 24 games in 50 days in some ten countries. There was no question of resting Pelé and the other big names, because everyone wanted to see them and neither Santos nor the host clubs would risk a loss at the box office. Most of the players were exhausted or sick or in need of treatment for injuries.

Pelé did not enjoy that tour. But the year of 1959 stands as a monument to his remarkable fitness, endurance, and ability to continue to play his beautiful football in the most adverse circumstances.

Pelé shows his perfect heading technique against Portugal in 1966.

and scored. But France, the surprise of the tournament, levelled the scores seven minutes later through the prolific Fontaine. It was the first goal Brazil had conceded, and it shook them. Pelé's reaction startled the rest of his team. He ran to scoop the ball out of the net, dashed back to the centre, placed the ball on the spot, and told his elders to get on with it! It was a completely natural action on his part. Didi put Brazil ahead before half-time; then in the second period, Pelé added three. He was famous.

In the final, Brazil again met unexpected opponents, the host country, Sweden. It turned out to be a classic encounter, despite its one-sidedness, as Brazil unleashed all their brilliance. They shook off an early Liedholm goal with two from Vava before half-time. They gave a marvellous display of football after the interval to win 5-2 and take the Jules Rimet Trophy for the first time. Pelé scored twice, and his first was sheer poetry. Standing in the box, closely marked and with his back to the goal, he took a pass on his thigh, flicked the ball over his head, turned past his marker, and smashed it on the volley into the net.

Czech keeper Ivo Viktor is helpless as Pelé slams the ball past him.

Setbacks

Even a brilliant career such as Pelé's has setbacks, and he experienced them in the most important games of all, the World Cup finals. In Chile in 1962 a pulled groin muscle put him out of action after two matches, and Brazil went on to retain the trophy without him. And four years later, he was savagely hacked down in the match with Portugal and vowed never to play in the World Cup again. Fortunately for Brazil, and for football, that was one promise he didn't keep. But those injuries apart, he continued to have a remarkable career, playing as many as 80 or 100 games a year for Santos, the Army, and Brazil, scoring prolifically all the time. He struck up a deadly partnership with Coutinho for Santos, who won the World Club Championship in 1962 and 1963. In the first leg in 1962, Pelé scored twice and Coutinho once in their 3-2 victory over the European champions, Benfica, and then put on a devastating show in the return in Lisbon, Pelé notching a hat-trick in their 5-2 triumph.

The 1970 World Cup

By June 1970, Pelé was nearly 30. But he was at the peak of his career. The previous year he had scored his thousandth goal, he was as supremely fit as always (and no injuries were going to get in his way this time), and he was the hub of one of the finest sides ever seen. He was partnered by the clever Tostão in the centre of the attack, with Jair-

zinho on the right and Rivelino on the left; Gerson was the moving force and general of the midfield. They were so good that they dominated the tournament despite having a shaky keeper in Felix. They won their six matches, scoring 19 goals against 7. Pelé scored four of them, thrilling the crowds and the world-wide TV audience with everything he did, whether it was leaping high to power his headers at goal, making mazy runs and bouncing the ball off opponent's legs, smashing vicious first-time shots at goal, sliding telepathic passes out to the wings without so much as looking up, or bending delicate chips round opponents.

His goal in the first game, against Czechoslovakia, was spectacular, as he tore into the box to collect a long chip from Gerson on his chest, drop it to his feet, and slam it past the keeper, all the while under pressure. And in the final he opened the score with a magnificent header and laid on two other

Unleashing all his power, Pelé goes for an 'impossible' 60-yard goal against Czechoslovakia in the 1970 World Cup . . . it just missed.

WINNERS MEDALS	
World Cup	1958, 70
World Club Championship	1962, 63
S. American Club Cup	1962, 63
São Paulo League	1958, 60, 61, 62, 64, 65, 67, 68, 69
Brazilian Cup	1962, 63, 64, 68

Pelé and England's Alan Mullery fought a fine duel in Mexico in 1970.

THOUSAND-GOAL MEN

Pelé is not the only 1,000-goal footballer. Comparisons of statistics from different parts of the world or different periods are interesting but not always meaningful. Nevertheless, for the statistically minded, there are two other players who have been credited with scoring over a thousand goals in their career.

The first is another Brazilian, an amateur called Artur Friedenreich who played for several clubs, including São Paulo and Flamengo. His record of 1,329 goals is undocumented but is nevertheless recognized by FIFA. He made his debut for Brazil against Exeter City—and lost two

teeth in a tackle! He helped Brazil win the South American Championship for the first time, in 1919, scoring the only goal of the play-off against Uruguay.

The other 1,000-goal man was an Austrian, Franz 'Bimbo' Binder. In only 756 matches, between 1930 and 1950, he scored 1,006 goals. He won 20 caps playing for Austria and another 9 for Germany, after Austria had been annexed. His chief club was Rapid Vienna, whom he later managed.

Not his greatest goal, but a historic moment for Pelé (right) as he slots in a penalty for Santos to record his 1,000th goal.

goals in the 4-1 defeat of Italy.

Yet he is remembered most for his near misses in 1970, as he seemed bent on scoring the unique goal. There was his lob from behind the half-way line that beat the startled Czech goalkeeper but just missed the goal; a 40-yard return volley from the keeper's kick which brought a brilliant save from Uruguay's Mazurkiewicz; and above all his amazing dummy which left that same player rooted to the spot with the ball and Pelé shooting past on either side of him.

Retirement and Comeback

Pelé bowed out of soccer gradually, playing his last game for Brazil in July 1971 but continuing with Santos for another three years. He resisted all attempts to bring him back to the national side for the 1974 World Cup.

But Pelé's ill-advised business ventures had left him, as they had done before, with serious financial problems. And it was this that made him accept an offer from the New York Cosmos, reputedly of a guaranteed $4.5 million for playing some hundred games over three seasons.

For the record—although NASL (North American Soccer League) records are not statistically accepted—Pelé played 98 games for the Cosmos and scored 60 goals. And in his last season he helped them win the NASL championship. But what is more important is what he did for the game in North America. And for himself, he created another legend. Already a national hero in his own country, he became a hero of a whole continent.

Two England No 9s

'Wor Jackie'

Jackie Milburn, Tommy Lawton's successor in the England No. 9 shirt, was idolized in the North-East and many impartial critics regard him as one of the finest centre-forwards of all time. He was probably the fastest.

Milburn's initials, appropriately enough, were 'JET', but he was known on Tyneside as 'Wor Jackie'. Born in the football-crazy village of Ashington, he virtually lived in his football kit, a fact to which he later attributed his tendency to back pains and his consequent reluctance to head the ball. Nevertheless, he scored a fair proportion of his goals with his head, but it was for his searing runs through the middle and his explosive long-range shooting that he became known.

These attributes were never better demonstrated than on that memorable day at Wembley in 1951 when in five minutes he scored two of the most spectacular goals even that famous stadium has witnessed. The first came soon after half-time, with the score Newcastle 0 Blackpool 0, when he ran onto a pass just inside the Blackpool half and streaked away to slot the ball past the advancing keeper. The second resulted from a back-heel by Ernie Taylor, which found Milburn just outside the box and out to the right. The ball was in the back of the net from Milburn's left foot in a flash. His opposite number Stan Mortensen shook his hand and said, 'That deserves to win any match'.

It was Mortensen, along with other great centre-forwards such as Roy Bentley and Jack Rowley, who kept Milburn's international appearances down to 13, in which he scored 10 goals. For Newcastle, his only League club, he scored 179 goals in 354 League games in the 11 seasons after the war, and helped them to win three triumphant Cup finals in five years.

Jackie Milburn in England action.

The Lion of Vienna

Like Milburn, Lofthouse was a loyal one-club man, playing all his 452 League matches for Bolton Wanderers and amassing 256 goals in the course of them. And, like Milburn, he scored some memorable goals at Wembley. In the 1953 Cup final his 25-yarder after two minutes completed his record of having scored in every round, but that was the famous 'Matthews final' which Blackpool won 4-3. In 1958, the second of his two goals by which Bolton beat Manchester United was the result of a controversial charge on keeper Harry Gregg. It should never have been allowed because both his feet were off the ground when he made contact. But Lofthouse was not a dirty player, simply courageous, unflinching, and always on the look-out for an opportunity. He was what a centre-forward should be— big and strong, powerful in the air, a fine shot with either foot, and difficult to shake off the ball.

It was these qualities that stood him in good stead against Austria in May 1952. Great national pride was at stake for both sides. Vienna was an occupied city; thousands of British servicemen were at the match. The Austrian team were on the crest of a wave, whereas England were in apparent decline.

England scored first through a left-foot volley from Lofthouse, but Austria equalized and the score was 2-2 at half-time. England soaked up mounting pressure and then, eight minutes from time, Lofthouse struck. England's keeper Gil Merrick caught an Austrian corner-kick and threw the ball out to Tom Finney, who caught the Austrian defence on the hop with a shrewd through-pass to Lofthouse. Racing into the Austrian half, Lofthouse made straight for goal. On and on he went until he met the keeper face-on. Down went the players, but Lofthouse had got the last touch and the ball was in the net. He was carried off on a stretcher, but insisted on returning and in the dying moments crashed a shot against the post. Lofthouse played 33 games for England and scored 30 goals (equalling Finney's record), but none was more dramatic than the one that made him 'The Lion of Vienna'.

Lofthouse, both feet clearly off the ground, charges Gregg.

THE TEAM MAKERS

Above: Helmut Schoen

Above: Clough and Taylor
Below: Busby (right) with his 'Babes'

Above: Bill Shankly

Above: Jock Stein
Below: Sir Alf Ramsey

The style of football management varies almost as much as the style of play. At one time a club manager was responsible for the running of the club as well as the team, and this is still so of managers in the lower divisions. But in the higher echelons, the job has become so specialized that a manager will have a whole army of helpers.

Some operate in partnership, such as the highly successful combination of Brian Clough and Peter Taylor, whose ability to bring the best out of players is almost legendary. So many are the qualities required of a top club manager nowadays that it is rare to find them all in one man—he has to be not only a great tactician, but a psychologist, a financial wizard, and a diplomat to boot. He must also have broad shoulders and an iron constitution, for it is the manager who always gets the blame, and anything short of success might mean the loss of his job.

Whereas shrewdness in buying is a major attribute of the club manager, national managers have to rely on the material available, and weld it into a tactical force. Again, though, success is always the yardstick.

Before the days of the tracksuit manager, Herbert Chapman set standards of achievement, with Huddersfield and Arsenal, that have perhaps never been surpassed, and such was his tactical dominance in the game that most soccer histories will have a section headed 'The Chapman Era'.

Herbert Chapman

The great innovator

Herbert Chapman was the most successful and influential manager in the history of the game. A great innovator, he changed the face of football both on and off the field. The period in the 1920s and 1930s during which he 'reignèd' has become known as the 'Chapman Era'. He created two great sides—the Huddersfield of the 1920s and the Arsenal of the 1930s—and introduced tactical methods and all manner of other ideas that had far-reaching effects on the game.

Chapman's own career was undistinguished. He was a reserve team player with Spurs (then a non-League side) in 1907 when he took the player-manager job at Northampton after a colleague had turned it down. He quickly took them to the top of the Southern League. In 1912 he returned to his native Yorkshire and took over ailing Second Division Leeds City, turning them into a successful side during the 1914-18 war. But when, after the war, the club was thrown out of the League for making illegal payments to players, Chapman was temporarily suspended, although he strenuously denied complicity. He made his 'come-back', however, with Huddersfield in 1921, and this marked the beginning of an unprecedented run of success. Under his astute generalship the club won the Cup in 1922 and the League in 1924 and 1925. They went on to win it again in 1926 and became the first club to achieve a hat-trick of League titles, but by then Chapman had left. His far-seeing ambition was to create a great club in London, and when the Arsenal post became vacant he jumped at the chance.

Chapman set out at Highbury to make the game pay and to give the public what it wanted so they would come back for more. He was a born showman and revelled in publicity —but only the kind that would put Arsenal's name on the map. The club always came first. He spent huge sums on transfer fees, but never made a bad buy. His first move was to seduce the great inside-forward Charlie Buchan from Sunderland by agreeing to pay £2,000 down and an extra £100 for each goal Buchan scored in his first season. It was together with Buchan that Chapman devised the 'third back game', a new strategy

Herbert Chapman (left) chats with Alex James at Highbury. Converting the little Scot into a midfield general for Arsenal was Chapman's master-stroke.

that revolutionized football. He bought David Jack for nearly £11,000, almost double the previous transfer record. He bought Alex James for £9,000 and converted him, initially against the player's will, from a goalscorer to the prince of goal-makers. He made ordinary players into internationals; he turned good players into great ones. He knew when to encourage, when to lay down the law, and he had remarkable powers of persuasion.

Chapman piloted Arsenal to Cup triumph in 1930 (they beat his old club Huddersfield in the final) and to League success in 1931 and 1933. He died in 1934, but Arsenal went on. They finished champions again, chalked up their hat-trick in 1935, and won the Cup again in 1936.

In tactical thinking Chapman was years ahead of his contemporaries. Others tried to copy his methods, but without success because they never really understood them. He has been criticized for introducing negativity into the game, for being responsible for the 'safety first' methods that permeated British football in the thirties. For Arsenal it worked, however. Had he lived, he would have found new methods to give the public the entertainment they deserved.

Off the field, too, Chapman was years ahead of his time, and his influence is still felt. He made Highbury the best ground in the country, and had the name of the local underground station changed to Arsenal. He encouraged Tom Whittaker to become the first of the true physiotherapist trainers. He introduced savings schemes for players, regular team meetings (he suggested this for England, too), and high standards of behaviour for players and ground-staff alike. Most of his ideas for improving the game were blocked by the reactionary Football Association and took years to be implemented if they ever were: numbers on shirts, a white ball for bad weather, weather-proof pitches, a 45-minute clock (banned by the FA), special transport for fans, goal judges, and floodlights (suggested in 1932, nearly 20 years before they were finally introduced).

A bust of Herbert Chapman stands in the main entrance hall of Arsenal Stadium as a constant reminder of the man who made the club great. But perhaps the best monument to his memory is the name of the club itself.

51

Sir Matt Busby

The father figure

Sir Matt Busby built three great Manchester United sides after World War II. He survived the Munich air crash in 1958, which destroyed what was potentially the finest club side ever, to make a remarkable personal comeback and mould a new team that, 10 years later, became the first English side to win the European Cup. He was knighted in 1968 for his services to the game, and on retirement became the 'father figure' of British football.

A cultured wing-half for City.

As a player before the war, Busby was a cultured wing-half for Manchester City and Liverpool. He won his solitary cap for Scotland in 1933, but captained them in wartime internationals.

He took over at Manchester United straight after the war, and was soon demonstrating his gift for producing fine footballing sides, for getting talented players together and allowing their natural flair free rein. United, with men such as their captain Johnny Carey and a forward line that read Delaney, Morris, Rowley, Pearson, and Mitten, were First Division runners-up four times before they finally took the title in 1952. But it was their performance in the 1948 Cup that stamped them as a truly great side. They beat six First Division sides to win the Cup, with a goal tally of 22 against 8, and they featured in two of soccer's most memorable matches—a 6-4 third round victory at Villa Park and the 4-2 defeat of Blackpool at Wembley.

As the side began to break up Busby showed the value of the formidable scouting system he had built up under Joe Armstrong and the coaching scheme headed by Jimmy Murphy, which had created a 'layer' of teams. His youth scheme was the finest in the country and the welfare of his fledgelings was always as important to him as their technical progress. He gambled on his youngsters in 1952 when United found themselves near the foot of the table, and they came up trumps—Edwards, Colman, Pegg, Jackie Blanchflower, and others. Gradually, he built up the side that became known as the 'Busby Babes', buying Johnny Berry and Tommy Taylor and later drafting in more young talents, such as Liam Whelan and Dennis Viollet.

They won the Championship in 1956 with a side whose average age was 22, and Busby accepted an invitation to compete in the European Cup against the League's advice. United were the first English club to enter. Reinforced with the young Bobby Charlton, they reached the semi-finals, and they retained the League title. By early 1958, they were riding high again, with a team that promised to dominate English soccer for ten years and break the mighty Real Madrid's hold in Europe. It was after beating Red Star Belgrade to reach the European Cup semi-finals again that Busby's whole world was shattered. His beautiful team, his 'Babes', were cut down in their prime, their bodies scattered with the wreckage of the Elizabethan airliner on the snow of Munich airport. Some survived—Bobby Charlton among them—but eight players died and two others never played again.

Busby himself was seriously injured, and it took all his immense fortitude to recover. It took even more courage to start again and begin rebuilding his beloved United.

But slowly and painfully he did it again for the third time, by blending homegrown talent, such as George Best and Nobby Stiles, with big buys, such as Denis Law and Pat Crerand. They won the Cup and two League titles and in 1968 took the biggest prize of all, the

United's European Cup at last.

European Cup—this with a side containing only three players bought on the transfer market.

When Sir Matt Busby, as he now was, retired in 1969 to become general manager, he had been with the club for 24 years. During that period, the other 90-plus clubs in the League had gone through some seven or eight hundred managers between them! It was almost impossible to replace Busby at United and he had to take over team duties again for a few months before he accepted a place on the Board of Directors in June 1971. He could look back with pride on a quarter of a century of achievement —yet throughout all that time Busby remained the modest, kindly and compassionate man he that had always been.

Bill Shankly

King of the Kop

With his infectious enthusiasm for the game, his ability to instil confidence in his players, and his capacity for shrewd team-building, Bill Shankly created the most consistent and successful club in the history of English football—Liverpool. And at the same time he became a legend himself, known and loved throughout the game for his humanity and wit, and idolized at Anfield. His sudden retirement in 1974, at the height of his success, came as a shock to everyone connected with football. And although Liverpool continued to go from strength to strength, Anfield has never been the same without 'Shanks'.

As a footballer before and after the war, Shankly enjoyed a distinguished career as a half-back for Preston, having started out in the early thirties with Carlisle. A teetotaller and non-smoker, he was known for his fitness. He played five times for Scotland just before the war, and in two Cup finals for Preston, earning a winner's medal in 1938.

As a manager, his early career—Carlisle, Grimsby, Workington, Huddersfield—was largely undistinguished. But then came the offer from Liverpool in 1959. The atmosphere of the big club brought the best out of Shankly, just as his complete dedication to football, his love of the game, and loyalty to Liverpool brought the best out of the club. If ever a man was 'married' to a football club, it was Shankly. Liverpool and football were his life. Such was his belief in the club and the players and so compelling his good-humoured fanaticism, that his fans idolized him as much as any of the team's stars.

Liverpool were in the Second Division when Shankly joined them, but he took them up in 1962. He built a fine side with a mixture of astute buys and homegrown talent—St John, Thompson, Yeats,

Lawrence, Milne, Stevenson, Callaghan, Hunt, Melia. The emphasis was always on teamwork, both on the field and throughout the club. They won the League in 1964, the Cup in 1965, and the League again in 1966 as well as reaching the final of the European Cup-Winners Cup.

Then, as the side began to decline, Shankly built an even better one in the seventies—with men like Clemence, Smith, Hughes, Heighway, Toshack, and of course Kevin Keegan. 'Daylight robbery'

'Shanks'—the fans idolized him as much as any of his stars.

was how Shankly described his £35,000 deal with Fourth Division Scunthorpe, and Keegan proved to be the Shankly masterstroke. Another League title was won in 1973 as well as Liverpool's first European trophy—the UEFA Cup—after years of consistent striving, and in 1974 Liverpool triumphed again at Wembley. Then, on 12 July, came the surprising announcement that Bill Shankly had decided to retire—at 58, he felt he needed a rest. He was working to the last, though, for on the same day he signed Ray Kennedy from Arsenal.

BOB PAISLEY

A loyal servant of the club since 1939, and assistant to Shankly, Bob Paisley was appointed manager a fortnight after Shankly retired. Paisley, a wing-half in the Liverpool championship-winning side of 1947, was 54, and brought to the job a sound knowledge of the game and an unflappable approach. Yet his task was daunting. When you take over a club at the top, there seems to be only one way to go, and that is down. And there are the inevitable comparisons with a distinguished predecessor when the slightest thing goes wrong. But Paisley's record speaks for itself. He took Liverpool to even greater heights. Recruiting men such as Neal, McDermott, Dalglish (to replace the seemingly irreplaceable Keegan when he left in 1977), Souness, Johnson, Hansen, and Alan Kennedy, he blended the most powerful club side in the world—four League titles in five years (never out of the first two), another UEFA Cup win, the European Cup in 1977 and 1978 . . .

Sir Alf Ramsey

The General

Ramsey lifts England after West Germany had equalized in the dying seconds of the 1966 World Cup final to force extra time. His calm 'pep talk' did the trick.

As both player and manager, Alf Ramsey was a thinking man, always cool and unhurried, paying immense attention to the smallest detail. He was knighted for his services to the game after masterminding England's 1966 World Cup triumph, although he eventually lost the job as England team manager in 1974. He always demanded a hundred per cent commitment from his players, and in return gave them unswerving loyalty. His single-mindedness, however, often led to clashes with the Press and with those he regarded as amateur administrators.

The General

In his playing days, Ramsey was known as 'The General', and it was his tactical awareness that helped him overcome a lack of pace. As a full-back for Southampton, Spurs, and England, he was a fine distributor of the ball, and his positional play made up for his slowness on the turn. He was a key member of Spurs' Championship-winning 'push-and-run' side of 1951 and of England's team of the early 1950s, winning 32 caps.

On his retirement in 1955, Ramsey became manager of Third Division Ipswich. And had he not achieved later success with England, he would still be remembered for his remarkable achievements with this small-town club. By careful team-building and without spending large sums of money, he nursed them through to the First Division by 1961. At first, no one outside Suffolk really took 'Ramsey's rustics' seriously. But after an uncertain start, they soon adjusted to the rarefied atmosphere of the 'upper echelon' and swept aside all challenges to win the title in style.

England and the World Cup

Ramsey stuck to his policy of building a side based on work-rate and sheer determination when he became manager of England in 1962. He was England's first 'supremo', taking over all the selection responsibilities, having a team doctor appointed, and bringing to the job the professional approach it had been crying out for for years.

He set about his task of building a World Cup squad with cold efficiency and confidence. As host country, England had no need to qualify, so Ramsey could experiment. He instilled his players with his own confidence and drilled them in his methods. He gradually moulded the tactical system that would win England the World Cup, phasing out his wingers, playing first 4-3-3 and finally 4-4-2, thus dispensing with them altogether. Midfielders Ball and Peters lined up in the Nos. 7 and 11 shirts in the quarter-finals, against Argentina, and that's how the team stayed-—'Ramsey's wingless wonders'.

After his World Cup triumph, however, Ramsey failed to recognize the danger signals. So convinced was he that his methods would continue to be right that he persisted in picking hard men like Stiles in midfield (Hunter and Storey, for example). And even when he could call on a winger of the calibre of Francis Lee, he still favoured the 4-4-2 formation, only occasionally fielding a side with more than two front men.

He was perhaps unfortunate to see England eliminated from the 1970 World Cup finals by West Germany, but humiliation in the European Championships by them in 1972 and then failure to qualify for the 1974 World Cup spelt the end of his England career.

To this day, Ramsey and the Ramsey era remain an enigma. Overall, his 11-year reign can only be regarded as one of England's most successful periods of modern times—the figures speak for themselves. Or do they? Sports writer Hugh McIlvanney summed it up best perhaps when he wrote, about a year before Ramsey was rather clumsily relieved of his post by the FA: 'He is a man who believes in

> ### ENGLAND UNDER RAMSEY
>
> England's first match under Ramsey was in Paris against France in February 1963; their last, in Lisbon against Portugal in April 1974. The full Ramsey record is:
>
> | | |
> |---|---|
> | **Played** | 113 |
> | **Won** | 69 |
> | **Drew** | 27 |
> | **Lost** | 17 |
> | **Goals for** | 224 |
> | **Goals against** | 99 |

destinations rather than journeys. He thinks it is all right to take us to the Promised Land in a cattle truck.' In other words, 'it's only the results that count'. There is a vast body of players, managers, and directors who subscribe to that philosophy today, and to a certain degree they are right. But if they lose sight altogether of the pleasure of the 'journey', they will drive the fans away.

Jock Stein

The man with the Midas touch

The arrival of Jock Stein at Celtic in 1965 ushered in a period of spectacular success for the club unrivalled in British football. As well as brushing aside all domestic challenges, they became the first British side to win the European Cup.

The reasons for Stein's extra-ordinary success as a manager are manifold, although he is basically a simple, straightforward man. First, there is his exceptional knowledge of football and his insatiable appetite for the game. Then there is his ability to bring out the best in his players—to produce all-out effort to compensate for lack of talent or to channel the obvious brilliance of a player such as Jimmy Johnstone into the overall masterplan of the team. Above all, his great love of the game shines through in everything he does, and he believes in an attacking brand of football—the kind of football to entertain.

Plucked out of Obscurity

Stein first joined Celtic as a player in 1951. He was at the time about to give up the game. An undistinguished career as centre-half with Albion Rovers in the 1940s was followed by a spell with Welsh non-League club Llanelly. But when the house he had left behind in Scotland was twice burgled, he decided to call it a day and return to the pits. That is when fate took a hand—Celtic wanted him as a reserve centre-half. He jumped at the chance, and then, because of injury to the regular stopper, found himself drafted straight into the first team. And that was just the beginning of the fairy story.

In 1954 he captained Celtic to the League and Cup double—their first for 40 years. And when, the following year, an ankle injury ended his playing career, he became Celtic's coach—bringing along players of the calibre of Billy McNeill and Pat Crerand.

A Trail of Success

In 1960, Stein left Celtic to take over at Dunfermline, where he breathed instant · life into a club seemingly doomed to relegation. They avoided the drop, and the very next season he guided them to Hampden and Cup victory over Celtic. After a brief but successful spell with Hibs in 1964, there was another call from Celtic, and this time Stein was to be manager.

He joined them a month before they won the Scottish Cup. Then, in his first full season, the man with the Midas touch struck gold again. Celtic won the Championship—their first title since he himself had led them on the field 12 years earlier and only their second since the war. They also won the League Cup, reached the final of the Cup, and were narrowly edged out by Leeds in the semi-finals of the European Cup-Winners Cup.

But this was just a taste of what was in store. In the 1966-67 season, Celtic won the lot—League, Cup, League Cup, and finally the Euro-pean Cup. It was a unique 'grand slam' and a milestone in soccer history. And Stein had accomplished it with a side that cost him next to nothing.

With a constantly changing side, Stein continued to work his magic, and Celtic went on to record after record. It seemed that nothing could stop them—but a serious car accident in July 1975 finally did. It put Stein out of action for several months. But, characteristically, he fought his way back to partial fitness, and took Celtic to another League and Cup double, in 1977, before handing over the reins to Billy McNeill.

In August 1978, Stein made a comeback with Leeds, but before signing a contract and after only 45 days, he answered another urgent call from north of the border. This time it was to take over the Scotland team, in the doldrums after their World Cup debacle. For the man who had done so much to put Scottish soccer on the world map, this was the supreme challenge.

Jock Stein with the Scottish Cup in 1974, the 20th major trophy he had plundered for the club in only nine years as manager.

CELTIC UNDER STEIN

Stein took over at Celtic in 1965, a month before they won the Cup. In July 1975 a near-fatal car crash halted his reign for a season. Celtic's full domestic record under Stein is shown below. In nine seasons of European Cup competition, they won in 1967, were beaten finalists in 1970, and reached the semi-finals twice.

Season	League	Cup	Lg Cup
1965-66	1	2	1
1966-67	1	1	1
1967-68	1	–	1
1968-69	1	1	1
1969-70	1	2	1
1970-71	1	1	2
1971-72	1	1	2
1972-73	1	2	2
1973-74	1	1	2
1974-75	3	1	1
1975-76	Out of action		
1976-77	1	1	2

Bill Nicholson

The big spender

Bill Nicholson's career in football is a story of unswerving loyalty and dedication to one club—Spurs. From the time he joined them as a £2-a-week apprentice in 1936 to his resignation as manager 38 years later, Nicholson gave his life to the club. On the field, he played an important role in Spurs' first-ever Championship side in 1951, and 10 years later guided them to the first League and Cup double of the century. As a player, he was renowned for his fearless tackling; as a manager, for his fearless spending.

A Yorkshireman, born in Scarborough, Nicholson signed as a professional for Spurs in 1938, and played only a handful of first-team games before war put a brake on football. After the war, he enjoyed eight or nine seasons as Spurs' right-half, a thoroughly reliable defender who was one of the key men in Arthur Rowe's 'push-and-run' side that won promotion and then the First Division Championship in consecutive seasons. It was at the end of the latter season, in May 1951, that he won his solitary cap, against Portugal.

When he stopped playing, Nicholson's qualities made him an obvious choice as Spurs' coach, and in 1958 he also became coach to England's World Cup squad. Then, in October of the same year, at 39, he took over the manager's job at Tottenham from the ailing Jimmy Anderson. The very same day, Spurs played Everton in a League match at White Hart Lane and won by the extraordinary score of 10-4. It was an omen of things to come, but it also served initially to throw a smokescreen over the problems facing Nicholson. Spurs, with a suspect defence, were teetering near the bottom of the First Division. From Anderson, Nicholson inherited Bobby Smith, Cliff Jones, Maurice Norman, and a far-from-happy Danny Blanchflower. One of the first things Nicholson did was to restore Blanchflower to the cap-

taincy. He then dipped into the club's coffers and began to earn his reputation as a big—but exceedingly shrewd—spender.

Nicholson did his best shopping in Scotland, where in 1959 he bought midfield dynamo Dave Mackay, keeper Bill Brown, and mercurial schemer John White. He also signed Les Allen from Chelsea in exchange for Brooks.

And so Nicholson had his perfect combination—a world-class midfield in Blanchflower, White, and Mackay, another great creative

player, Cliff Jones, on the wing, with the others blending superbly round them. In that memorable 1960-61 season, Spurs set an all-time record by winning their first 11 League games, and they never looked back. In achieving the 'double', they played some of the finest football seen in the British Isles.

The next season, Nicholson made another masterly sortie into the transfer market to bring Jimmy Greaves back from Italy for nearly £100,000. Spurs retained the Cup, went close in the League, too, and went out of the European Cup in the semi-finals after two classic

encounters with champions Benfica. In 1963 they became the first British side to win a European trophy, the Cup-Winners Cup.

The 'double' side was breaking up, however, the tragic death of John White—struck down by lightning on a golf course in 1964—signalling the end of an era. Nicholson continued to spend, and Spurs won more trophies—the Cup again in 1967, the League Cup in 1971 and 1973, and the UEFA Cup in 1972—but this was small beer for the fans, brought up on the cham-

MAJOR NICHOLSON SIGNINGS			
Date	Signing	From	Fee
Mar. 59	Mackay	Hearts	£30,000
Jun. 59	Brown	Dundee	£16,000
Oct. 59	White	Falkirk	£20,000
Dec. 59	Allen	Chelsea	exchange
Nov. 61	Greaves	Milan	£99,999
Mar. 64	Mullery	Fulham	£72,500
Jun. 64	Jennings	Watford	£27,000
Jul. 64	Knowles	Middles-brough	£45,000
Dec. 64	Gilzean	Dundee	£72,500
Apr. 66	Venables	Chelsea	£80,000
Aug. 66	England	Black-burn	£95,000
Jan. 68	Chivers	South-ampton	£125,000
Feb. 69	Morgan	QPR	£100,000
May 70	Peters	W. Ham	£200,000
May 71	Coates	Burnley	£190,000

pagne football of the 'double' days.

Nicholson's relations with his players had never been close, although with Blanchflower there had been a mutual trust that was the backbone of the club. He worked them hard and criticized rather than coaxed them. And while they respected his knowledge of the game, they were critical of his management. With communication becoming increasingly difficult, Nicholson resigned in September 1974, in his mid-fifties. The club decided to make a clean break rather than keep him on in an advisory capacity, and he joined West Ham's coaching staff.

Supremos of the '70s

Zagalo, Schoen and Menotti

The term 'supremo' has crept into soccer parlance to signify the man in sole charge of a national side. The first supremo in this sense of the England team was Alf Ramsey, who had to fight to win the overlordship denied for so long to his predecessors. He justified the change by guiding England to World Cup victory in 1966.

European team managers have long enjoyed such power. Italy's famous supremo Vittorio Pozzo had sole command of the national side from 1928 to 1948, during which time they won two World Cups and the 1936 Olympic tournament.

It was after Germany's elimination from their 'home' Olympics that Sepp Herberger took over as team manager, and he, too, enjoyed a long run in charge, highlighted by World Cup victory in 1954. He retired 10 years later, after 28 years at the helm.

Zagalo's 'Hat-trick'

Herberger had played for Germany himself in the early 1920s, and Alf Ramsey had tasted World Cup football—albeit a bitter taste, for he was in the England side that lost to the United States in 1950. But Mario Zagalo of Brazil was the first man to enjoy victory as both player and manager. He achieved a unique hat-trick, first as outside-left in the exciting 1958 side, then as a 'withdrawn winger' in 1962, and finally as a last-minute supremo of the magnificent 1970 champions.

As a player, Zagalo was a worker —they called him 'the little ant'—always in action in defence as well as attack. In both 1958 and 1962, he owed his place to the injuries of others, but each time played a key role in the Brazilian team's success. And in 1970, he took over the squad from the sacked Saldanha only two months before the finals. Thanks largely to his former team-mate Pelé, he tasted triumph for the third time.

Home Winners

The mounting pressures of modern football have taken their toll of soccer supremos. A winning run and they're heroes, but as soon as things start to go wrong, the Press and the fans are baying for blood. Brazil's sacking of João Saldanha was symptomatic of the seventies. England gave Sir Alf Ramsey the 'heave-ho' in 1974, Don Revie pre-empted his by resigning in 1977, and Ally McLeod could hardly expect to survive after the Scottish fiasco of 1978.

Two successful supremos of the seventies: Zagalo (left) and Menotti.

Ramsey and Revie went because England had failed to qualify for World Cup finals. The host country, like the holders, does not have to qualify, so building a side is always easier. But the pressures on the home side in the finals can be frightening. Two supremos who withstood these pressures in the seventies and emerged triumphant were Helmut Schoen and Cesar Menotti.

Schoen, a pre-war international, became Herberger's assistant, and took over the West German side when Herberger retired in 1964. Under Schoen, West Germany reached the final in 1966 and won third place in 1970. Yet he still found his policies and style of man-agement under fire. He answered his critics, however, by producing a side to win the 1972 European Championships with attacking, entertaining football. And he silenced them for good with World Cup victory in Munich two years later.

Menotti, in 1978, was under even greater pressure, for Argentina had never won the World Cup. They also had an unenviable reputation in international football to live down. Menotti had turned to coaching when his playing career had been curtailed by injury. He had taken over Argentina's national squad after the 1974 World Cup, and was still only 39 in 1978.

He fought many battles in putting his squad together—preventing the transfer of players abroad, having fixtures rearranged to suit his plans, and getting his players released. And he persisted in his belief in the inherent skill of his players. Argentina won largely because they were the only side in the finals that played attacking football throughout. And Menotti began his defence of the trophy by winning his next big battle, in 1980—a tug-of-war to keep the precocious talents of Diego Maradona in the country.

57

Clough & Taylor
Soccer partnership

The Muhammad Ali of soccer, Brian Clough is rarely out of the headlines for long. Controversial and outspoken, he is not everyone's idea of the perfect manager. But like the former world heavyweight champion, he has backed up his words with achievement. Together with right-hand man Peter Taylor, he has worked some of the more prodigious management miracles of modern football. They each have their strong points—Clough the motivator, Taylor the transfer wizard—and the two have dovetailed perfectly to fashion Championship-winning sides from exceedingly thin material.

They first met in the mid-1950s at Second Division Middlesbrough, where Taylor was a solid goalkeeper and Clough a dashing centre-forward. Clough was a prolific goalscorer, and would surely have collected more than the two caps he won in 1959 had he played for more successful sides. He went to Sunderland in 1961, but a serious knee injury in 1962 virtually ended his career when he was only 27. He finally and reluctantly retired in 1965 with a playing record of 251 goals in 274 League games, and joined Sunderland's coaching staff.

In October 1965, Clough took over at Fourth Division Hartlepool—at 30, he was the youngest manager in the League—and he brought Taylor in as his assistant. It was the beginning of a momentous partnership. Two years later, at Derby, they began the trail that made them the most talked of managers in the game.

Derby were a struggling Second Division side in 1967, but the Taylor-Clough chemistry soon worked its magic, with promotion in 1969 and the First Division Championship in 1972, Derby's first ever League title. But Clough's days at Derby were stormy ones. While Taylor always kept a low profile, Clough was prone to make outrageous statements in the Press

Taylor (left) was a solid goalkeeper with Middlesbrough when he and Clough first met. Clough (right) won two England caps.

and on TV. When the Derby board, embarrassed by his frankness, tried to curb what he regarded as his right to free speech, he resigned, and so did the faithful Taylor.

A month later they were persuaded to join enterprising Third Division club Brighton. But Clough did not stay long, parting company with Taylor to take over the job vacated by the new England supremo Don Revie at Leeds.

After just 44 days at Elland Road, he was sacked. It was an extraordinary decision by the Leeds board, who must have known that Clough would have wanted to change things and would have met with hostility from some of the players —he had once indiscreetly called them 'one of the dirtiest teams in Britain'.

Three months later, Clough was appointed manager of Nottingham Forest, and Peter Taylor joined him once again. The transformation of this Second Division club into the champions of Europe in less than five seasons was nothing short of miraculous. After just scraping through to promotion in 1977, they confounded the pundits the next season by walking away

with the First Division title, the first in their long history. Not only did they thwart a Liverpool hat-trick, but they beat them in the League Cup final, too, and Clough was voted Manager of the Year.

Under Clough and Taylor, Forest went from strength to strength, running up a record 42 League games without defeat. At home, they were the only club to challenge Liverpool's dominance, and in Europe they frustrated another Liverpool hat-trick by knocking them out of the Champion's Cup. They grabbed the headlines again by making Trevor Francis Britain's first million-pound footballer—in time for him to score the winner in the European Cup final. And in 1980 they won it again.

Despite all Clough's indiscretions, his outspoken comments about other personalities in football, his cockiness, and his at times puerile remarks, one thing has always shone through—his enthusiasm and love for the game. It is this, along with his basic honesty, that has enabled him to survive the ups and downs of a tumultuous career and still command respect in the 1980s.

CAPTAINS AND DEFENDERS

Although it is not necessary for a captain to be a defender, many of football's finest defenders have also been inspiring captains, and it is difficult to separate them. Two that stand out immediately are Bobby Moore and Billy Wright, long-time leaders of England and both central defenders.

Some captains do no more than toss for ends at the start of the game, but there is so much more to it than that. Some men are born leaders, capable of lifting the heads of others when things are going badly, and keeping a cool head themselves when the pace is getting hot. Judging when to gee your team-mates up or calm things down is a priceless asset. This is especially so when the tension is greatest, as it is in cup finals, for example. So it is entirely appropriate that it is the captain of the team who is the one who has the honour of receiving the trophy.

Bobby Moore

Johnny Carey

Joe Mercer

George Young

Cullis (left) and Wright

Danny Blanchflower

Rudi Krol

Frank McLintock

59

Billy Wright

Mr Consistency

An inspiring leader of Wolves and England, Billy Wright was the first player from any country to win a hundred international caps. In a career remarkable for the consistent high standard of his performances, he appeared in all but three of England's first 108 games after World War II, first as a hardworking wing-half (59 games) and from 1954 as a centre-half (46). His last 70 appearances, from October 1951, were consecutive, and his last 90 games were as captain.

He captained Wolves during their finest period—Cup victory in 1949 followed by three League titles in the 1950s. Despite his mild manner, he was a forceful leader, and a fine ambassador for football. He was an excellent tactician on the field, and always in the peak of condition. As a wing-half, he was a regular dynamo of a player, with matchless ball control and tackling. His conversion to centre-half was surprising, because he stood only 5ft 8in (1.73m), but his timing and spring-heeled leaping allowed him to outjump the tallest of centre-forwards.

Wolves was Wright's only club, and he gave them magnificent service, playing 490 League and 44 Cup games for them between 1946 and 1959. He had joined the groundstaff as a 14-year-old in 1938, and manager Major Buckley almost sent him home after a few months because he was so small. Originally an inside-left, he soon settled down at right-half, and played for England in four 'Victory' internationals in 1946. After the match at Hampden, which Scotland won 1-0, one football correspondent wrote: 'Wright did three men's work and was the lone England player who looked the part.'

And so it went on throughout Wright's career. A tireless worker, he led by example, getting results from his colleagues by quiet encouragement rather than shouting. When Stan Cullis retired in

THE FIRST 'CENTURION'

Season	Caps	W	D	L
1946-47	8	6	1	1
1947-48	6	5	1	0
1948-49	8	5	1	2
1949-50	10	7	0	3
1950-51	3	2	0	1
1951-52	8	4	4	0
1952-53	8*	4	2	1
1953-54	10	4	2	4
1954-55	7	4	1	2
1955-56	9	6	2	1
1956-57	8	6	2	0
1957-58	11	4	4	3
1958-59	9	3	3	3
Total	105	60	23	21

*One match abandoned.

The first international 'centurion', Billy Wright is chaired off in triumph after his 100th game for England by Ron Clayton and Don Howe.

1947, Wright was appointed captain of Wolves. He first captained England against Northern Ireland in 1948, and led them in three World Cups. It was against Switzerland in the 1954 World Cup that he made his permanent and successful switch to centre-half, when Sid Owen was injured.

Wright was never dropped and never played in any but the first eleven at Wolves. He retired from international duty after he won his 105th cap in May 1959—an 8-1 thrashing of the United States in Los Angeles. And before the start of the next season, he decided to hang up his boots for good.

He became manager of the England youth team, and then in 1962 took over at Arsenal. It was during one of the Highbury club's lowest periods, and although he did much fine work there—bringing along many of the youngsters who were later to restore the club to its former glories—he was perhaps too inexperienced, and he resigned in 1966, to pursue a career in television.

Joe Mercer

'Old Spindly Legs'

Joe Mercer (right) in typical tackling action for Arsenal.

One of the best-loved characters in English football, the genial Joe Mercer established a unique record of League and Cup successes as both player and manager. An attacking wing-half with Everton and England before the war, he assumed a more defensive role with Arsenal in his thirties. In the late 1960s, he built Second Division Manchester City into a fine footballing side. He brought enthusiasm and sparkle to all his activities, greeting triumphs with modesty and setbacks with a smile.

Mercer signed as a professional

In his whole League career, Mercer scored only three goals, and two of these came within a month of each other in 1953, in his last but one season. Mercer himself tells of an extraordinary 'own goal' he once scored—at the second attempt! Playing for Everton in a pre-war match at Stamford Bridge, he played the ball back to his advancing keeper Ted Sagar. But it went past Sagar, who turned and threw himself full length to push the ball onto a post—only for the young Mercer, following up, to knock it into his own net.

for Everton as a 17-year-old in 1932. He made his first-team debut near the end of that season, but had to wait another three before winning a regular place. In those days he was an energetic wing-half. His legs—often likened to a pair of brackets and more suited to the occupation of his namesake, the jockey—were a constant source of amusement to team-mates and opponents alike. But they got him about the field well enough, and he never knew when he was beaten. He was not a strong tackler, having a long, sinewy frame, but his positioning and timing were such that when he went in for the ball he invariably came away with it.

When war broke out, Mercer had a League medal and five England caps. He was at the peak of his fitness and form, and played in 27 of England's wartime and 'victory' internationals, captaining the side from 1943. He hurt his knee against Scotland in 1946, however, and had to have the cartilage removed, so he was not fully fit for the 1946-47 season, the first full season after the war.

Everton sold the 31-year-old Mercer to Arsenal for £7,000. The great side of the thirties was now

broken up and Arsenal were floundering at the bottom of the table. The club and the spindly-legged veteran worked wonders for each other. Tom Whittaker, Arsenal's trainer and the greatest 'healer' in the game, gradually restored his knee. He also got him to recognize his limitations, and turned him into a defensive wing-half. Mercer was given the captaincy, and inspired the team to climb the table to safety. The next season, they won the Championship and in 1950 the Cup, Mercer being voted Footballer of the Year.

He had done his job for Arsenal and no one could have complained had he retired there and then. But 'old spindly legs' wasn't finished yet. He led them in a heroic 10-man performance in the 1952 Cup final, in which Newcastle eventually beat them 1-0, and then to a second League title in 1953. It took a bad leg break the following season finally to put an end to his career.

It was natural for Mercer to go into management, and after a spell with Sheffield United he took over at Aston Villa. But the nervous strain of the job led to a breakdown, and that would have finished most men. But after a year out of the game he returned as manager of Manchester City—forging a brilliant—if unlikely—partnership with the unpredictable Malcolm Allison. Together, they took City first to Division I, then to success in all the major domestic tournaments and also the European Cup-Winners Cup.

He later managed Coventry for a while before becoming a director. As a 'father figure' of English football, he often appeared on television, and his warmth and humanity endeared him to millions of viewers. It was a fitting postscript to his career when in 1977 he was asked to take over as 'caretaker' manager of the England squad, and he enjoyed a successful and popular spell in charge.

Danny Blanchflower

The thinking footballer

Danny Blanchflower was a thinking footballer. This is not to denigrate footballers in general as a race of robots who use their heads only for propelling the ball in the air. But Blanchflower was special. He thought deeply about every aspect of the game. He was a master tactician with the ability to spot weaknesses in the opposition and exploit them or to plug any deficiencies in his own side. He relished his role as captain, and demanded from his manager complete authority to make tactical decisions on the field. As a player, he was a constructive wing-half of great vision, winning the ball by forcing his opponents into errors and distributing it in all manner of subtle ways.

Off the field, his ideas often brought him into conflict with the 'establishment', and he was sometimes accused of being perverse for the sake of it. But whatever he did or said, it was always with the purest of motives, always in the interests of football. And Blanchflower's idea of football was an inventive, attacking game, the brand of football that reached its peak when he led Spurs to League and Cup glory in 1960-61, the first 'double' this century. Blanchflower went on to take Spurs to a second Cup victory in 1962 and the European Cup-Winners Cup in 1963—another milestone, for Spurs were the first British club to win a European trophy.

To Northern Ireland, also, Blanchflower brought his inimitable style of leadership and creativity, and, under the guidance of Peter Doherty, led his small, injury-hit band of 'no-hopers' to the quarter-finals of the 1958 World Cup. In all, he won 56 caps between 1949 and 1962, a record at the time. He was twice voted Footballer of the Year, in 1958 and 1961, an honour he shared with Stanley Matthews and Tom Finney, the only other players to win it more than once.

An Indelible Impression

The Belfast-born Blanchflower studied for a year at St Andrews, Scotland, before starting aircrew training in the RAF towards the end of the war. But on his demob in 1946, he returned to Belfast rather than university, and signed for Glentoran.

He represented the Irish League against the English League in 1947, and it was this game at Goodison, which the English won 4-2, that opened his eyes to the full scope of the game. The patterns woven by the brilliant English

Danny Blanchflower led Spurs to the first 'double' this century.

inside-forward trio of Mannion, Lawton, and Hagan left an indelible impression on the mind of the young Irishman.

Second Division Barnsley signed Blanchflower for £6,000 in 1949.

But he was too much of an individualist for them, questioning their traditional training methods. In March 1951 he went to First Division Aston Villa for £15,000, but his intellectual approach to the game and his passion for trying new ideas met with the same conservative resistance.

The Move to Spurs

At last, his move to Tottenham in 1954 for £30,000 projected him into a footballing environment where he could express himself to the full—although it was not immediately so. Blanchflower succeeded Alf Ramsey as skipper, but was relieved of his responsibility in 1956 when directors criticized him for making tactical changes during a match. Bill Nicholson took over as manager in October 1958, and dropped the 33-year-old Blanchflower, but later that season restored him to the captaincy. Nicholson bought well, and with the tough-tackling Dave Mackay taking care of midfield ball-winning duties, Blanchflower linked up with John White to inspire Spurs to play some of the most cultured and entertaining soccer seen in the country for years, culminating in the great League and Cup double of 1961.

After further triumphs, Blanchflower retired in 1964, at 38 finally unable to hold his place in the team. Already well versed in writing and broadcasting, he took up a career in journalism, writing a highly individual column for a Sunday newspaper—often provocative but always honest. In 1976, he became team manager of Northern Ireland, then in 1978 reluctantly took over at Chelsea for a spell. But he felt so alienated by present-day values and the absence of loyalty and integrity in the game that he resigned after nine months—to continue, often as a lone voice, crying out for the return of some sanity to the game.

Frank McLintock

The 'loser' who wouldn't lie down

It seemed in the 1960s that the gods were against Frank McLintock, that he was destined always to be the 'bridesmaid' and never the 'bride'. Then, dramatically, everything came good at once and he won just about every honour in the game. It was no more than he deserved.

McLintock joined Leicester straight from Glasgow junior football in 1956 at 17, and made his first-team debut in 1959. As an attacking wing-half, he was the driving force in the Leicester side that reached Wembley in 1961 and 1963, only to lose each time. In 1964, he went to Arsenal for £80,000. He added only two more Scottish caps to the three he had won in 1963, and two more losers medals to his collection, these in the League Cup. After their disastrous defeat in the 1969 final by Third Division Swindon, McLintock had to pick up the rest of the side as well as convince himself that he was not one of life's eternal runners-up.

In the 1969-70 season, Arsenal were in the European Fairs Cup thanks to a high position in the previous season's Championship. Early in the season, coach Don Howe decided to use McLintock's drive and determination at the back, and converted him into a central defender. At 5ft 10in (1.78m), he was a little under height for the role, but with his marvellous positional play and immaculate control and distribution, he quickly developed into one of the finest central defenders in the game.

Arsenal reached the final of the Fairs Cup, but lost the first leg 3-1 to Anderlecht. With McLintock's unenviable record in finals and Arsenal's failure to win a trophy for 17 years, it did not bode well for them in the return. But in an emotional night at Highbury, they scored three goals without reply, and McLintock was chaired round the pitch with the Cup.

Frank McLintock in his moment of triumph, having led Arsenal to the League and Cup double 10 years after Spurs did it.

That was only the beginning. Everything McLintock had strived for came to fruition in the 1970-71 season. It needed all his courage, maturity, and powers of leadership, though, to keep Arsenal on course in what was perhaps the most gruelling, cliff-hanging campaign ever waged in first-class football. They spent most of the season struggling in the wake of the unyielding Leeds side, and had to overcome a deficit of seven points at one stage. They did this with a magnificent run of nine consecutive wins near the end of the season, and finally clinched the title with a 1-0 win at Spurs in their last game. This was only five days before the Cup final, which they had reached by overcoming the handicap of an away draw in every round and a two-goal deficit in the semi-final against Stoke.

McLintock led Arsenal out against Liverpool for his fifth Wembley final, and when Liverpool took the lead in extra time it looked like his fifth losing one. But his team just would not lie down. In a breath-taking climax, they scored twice and became only the second side this century to complete the elusive League and Cup double. McLintock went up to receive the Cup exactly 10 years after watching disconsolately as Danny Blanchflower held the second 'leg' of Spurs' double aloft. And to complete his dream season, McLintock, who had won three more Scottish caps and been voted Footballer of the Year, was awarded the MBE.

The following season, Arsenal again reached the final, but lost to Leeds, and McLintock had to be content with the one FA Cup winners medal. In 1973 he joined Queen's Park Rangers, and after retiring in 1977 returned briefly to Leicester as manager. In his 18-year League career, he made 611 appearances in the League and scored 56 goals . . . and won his share of honours after all.

Cullis & Franklin

Constructive stoppers

Stan Cullis

Stan Cullis was a born leader. He skippered Wolves 'A' side at 17, their reserves at 18, their League side at 19, and England at 22. His biggest disappointment was Wolves' failure to win the Cup in 1939. A young team and hot favourites, they went down 4-1 to an inspired Portsmouth. He earned 12 full caps in the last two seasons before the war, taking over the captaincy from the injured Eddie Hapgood for the last of them—a fiery game in Bucharest in which Cullis's calming influence was a major factor in England's 2-0 victory over Romania. He played in 20 wartime internationals, until he was sent on overseas service in 1944.

A powerful tackler and supreme in the air, Cullis was also a fine ball player. He had the ability to hold the ball until he could use it well—making one of his famous long through passes or perhaps taking it through himself with that ungainly, crouching dribbling style of his.

Cullis played only one season after the war, when Wolves narrowly missed the Championship.

Stan Cullis leads Wolves out.

Then, finding himself prone to concussive injuries, he retired at 30. He became assistant manager at Wolves and then manager in 1948. He brought them instant success, with Cup victory in his very first season, three Championships in the 1950s, and a second Cup win in 1960. He built a side that thrived on the quick, long pass and played a brand of direct, robust football, stretching opposing defences with wing-to-wing crosses. In the mid-fifties he matched Wolves against some of the best teams in Europe—Moscow Spartak, Honved, and Moscow Dynamo. Wolves beat them in a celebrated series of 'floodlit friendlies' and were hailed, a little optimistically, as world champions.

Cullis's methods seemed less effective in the sixties, and he was surprisingly dismissed in 1964. He managed Birmingham from 1965 to 1970, but in the end was sadly driven out of office by pressure from the supporters.

> Either side of World War II, England were fortunate enough to have two of the finest centre-halves the world has known. Stan Cullis of Wolves held the position before the war and for much of it. Neil Franklin of Stoke City succeeded him towards the end of the war and retained the position for nearly four years before relinquishing it to join the rebel league in Colombia. In the days of the pure stopper centre-half, whose sole aim was to bottle up the opposing centre-forward, both Cullis and Franklin were refreshingly skilful and constructive players.

Neil Franklin

Neil Franklin

Not a particularly big man, Neil Franklin established himself as far-and-away England's finest centre-half in the immediate post-war years by his technical skill, positional play, and use of the ball.

He joined Stoke just before the war, and in 1944 succeeded Cullis as England's centre-half, playing in 10 unofficial internationals. After the war he won 27 successive caps. Then in 1950 he created a sensation in the soccer world by leaving England (with one of his Stoke team-mates) to play in Colombia.

The attraction was the promise of high wages—the maximum wage in England at the time was only £12 a week. Franklin returned, disillusioned, after only a couple of months, but the FA suspended him—for playing in a country not affiliated to FIFA and perhaps also for letting England down just before the 1950 World Cup. Stoke transferred him to Hull City. He never regained his England place, and, dogged by injury, his career petered out in the late fifties with Crewe Alexandra and Stockport County.

Johnny Carey

The quiet Irishman

Modest and quietly spoken, Johnny Carey was nevertheless an outstanding captain of Manchester United and Ireland in the immediate post-war years. He was also the most versatile of footballers, and during his career played in almost every position for United, including goalkeeper in an emergency, and in seven for the two Irelands. His influence on a team was incalculable. He had a commanding presence, was a natural leader of men, and possessed matchless ability to read the game.

Carey was spotted by chance playing for Dublin side St James's Gate by United scout Louis Rocca, whose visit to Ireland to watch another player had been wasted. United signed him in November 1936 for £200, and he made his debut the following season as inside-left, helping them to go straight back to Division I after their relegation of the previous season. He made his international debut for the Republic of Ireland in

Johnny Carey in pre-war days.

November 1937. He joined the British army in the war, and at the end of hostilities found himself playing for both the Republic and Northern Ireland.

When football resumed in England after the war, Matt Busby was appointed manager of United. He found in Carey the ideal captain, a man with the instinct for transmitting his wishes on the field. It was Busby who converted Carey from a fine inside-forward, first to an even better wing-half, and then to an exceptional full-back.

As a back, Carey was able to call on the footwork and ball skills of an inside-forward and the creative ability of a half-back. A feature of his game was his fine positional play, which allowed him to appear unhurried even though he lacked pace. His distribution was such that it was said he 'spoon-fed' those in front of him.

Carey led the first Busby side, the team whose exploits were to make United one of the great forces in the land. He led them to Cup triumph in 1948, after one of the finest finals of all time, a 4–2 victory over Blackpool. He led them to Championship success in 1952, after finishing runners-up in four of the five previous seasons. And on a personal note—although Carey never encouraged the cult of personality—he was honoured to lead the Rest of Europe against Great Britain in 1947, and in 1949 was voted Footballer of the Year.

In his curious role as a dual international—he had qualifications for both countries and both were pleased enough to obtain his services—he played 29 times for the Republic and 7 times for Northern Ireland. He led the Republic to their shock win over England at Goodison Park in 1949, four years before Hungary were acclaimed as the first 'foreign' side to beat England on her own soil.

Carey retired in 1953, at the age of 34, and went straight into man-

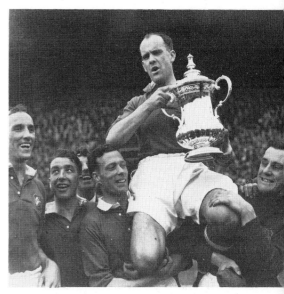

Carey, with the 1948 FA Cup, captained the first great Manchester United side after the war.

agement. He built successful sides at Blackburn, Everton, Orient, and Nottingham Forest and had charge of the Republic of Ireland team for a spell. But he lacked that ruthless streak necessary to survive in certain levels of football management, and eventually departed from the game altogether in 1971.

DIRECTORS' TRIBUTE

So highly did the Manchester club hold Carey in regard that on his retirement the directors invited him to a board meeting to pay him special tribute. The following is an extract from the Minutes of that meeting:

'The Directors . . . unanimously agreed to put on record their great appreciation of his long and loyal service. By his outstanding personality as a true sportsman, the honours he had won as an international and in club matches, he had covered his career with glory and set a shining example to all who follow him.'

Bobby Moore

A cool customer

Bobby Moore won a record 108 caps for England.

England's most capped player, Bobby Moore led them to World Cup glory in 1966. This was the culmination of a remarkable Wembley hat-trick, for in 1964 he captained West Ham to FA Cup victory and in 1965 it was the European Cup-Winners Cup he held aloft. Moore was the perfect captain, remaining completely unruffled whatever the state of the game. His lack of basic speed was rarely evident, because his expert reading of the game and his faultless positional play invariably gave him an edge on opponents. He liked to have a free role at the back, as second stopper, covering his fellow central defender but with no zonal or marking duties himself.

Throughout his career, Moore was criticized for lacking this or that—speed, heading or tackling ability, even passion. He answered all these criticisms on the field of play—by his record of consistency at the highest level. He might have appeared easy to beat, but he rarely gave anyone the chance. He would nip in and 'pinch' the ball rather

---

CULTIVATING A 'GIFT'

Bobby Moore was one of those exceptional players who would collect the ball, often with his back to the way his side were playing, and then hit a pass of stunning accuracy to a team-mate 30 or 40 yards away. Moore cultivated this so-called 'gift' of vision until it became second nature. Whatever the situation, he would ask himself the question: 'If I got the ball now, how would I use it?' Thus he would have the pattern of play in his mind at all times, and he possessed the tactical knowhow to use it to devastating advantage. It was a 'gift' he owed to early coaching by Malcolm Allison.

---

than make a tackle, but his tackling was first class, anyway. He was also sound in the air, without being spectacular. And as for passion—it was his very calmness in the heat of battle that inspired his colleagues. His complete reliability was the springboard for the success of both club and country.

One feature of Moore's play never criticized was his passing. He possessed exceptional vision and knew exactly what he wanted to do with the ball even before he received it. His long passing, in particular, was unrivalled.

Meteoric Rise

Moore was born in 1941, in Barking, East London, and joined West Ham on leaving school. He had excelled at cricket even more than football at school, but developed rapidly at West Ham thanks to Malcolm Allison's coaching and encouragement. He earned a record 18 England Youth caps, and made his League debut in September 1958, three months after turning professional. But it was not until the 1960-61 season that he won a regular place in the side.

His rise after that was meteoric, for the very next season he won the first of his record 108 caps, against Peru in Lima. This was a warm-up game for the 1962 World Cup in Chile, and Moore played in all of England's matches. The following year, at 22, he became the youngest captain of England when he took over from Jimmy Armfield for the game against Czechoslovakia in Bratislava.

A blond six-footer, married to a model and richly rewarded from the game, Moore projected an image of glamour. He was one of the first players to capitalize fully on his name and image commercially. But as the 'golden boy' of British soccer in the 1960s, he experienced mixed receptions when he travelled outside London. The jealous, sometimes hostile, reactions he inadvertently provoked from provincial crowds, however, had absolutely no effect on his play. He continued as always on his majestic way, and never received anything less than the utmost respect from team-mates and opponents alike.

Moore and Managers

Moore's relationship with both Alf Ramsey and West Ham's Ron Greenwood appeared at times somewhat strained.

At West Ham, there were years of 'restrained animosity' between the fiercely independent Moore and his manager. Yet as a youth player he idolized Greenwood, and it was Greenwood's regard for Moore's great talent that attracted him to the manager's job at West Ham in the first place. As far as football was concerned, they got on well. Moore's respect for Greenwood's genius at international level was unqualified. But he was critical of Greenwood's handling of men. And he felt that Greenwood's theories were often completely beyond the scope of the average player.

Although Moore's relationship with England manager Ramsey was perhaps artificial, he was Ramsey's lieutenant on the field, and between them they plotted England's World Cup victory. Moore admired Ramsey's handling of players and his ability to get the best out of them, and Ramsey respected and used Moore's knowledge of players, their capabilities and weaknesses. The one thing they had in common was an icy resolve to take England to the top.

World Cup

Moore's success was achieved despite the fact that he played for the whole of his international career with West Ham, a club with limited prospects. He enjoyed the first-class coaching of first Allison and then Greenwood, but he felt he could better himself, and more than once tried to get away. One clash with Greenwood occurred shortly before the 1966 World Cup. Moore had led West Ham to their FA Cup

and Cup-Winners Cup successes, but defeat in the semi-finals in defence of the European trophy in 1966 left him disillusioned and he began pressing for a move. He would not sign a new contract, and Greenwood would not let him go. Eventually, in order to be eligible to play for England, he compromised and signed a one-month contract.

England can be forever thankful that he did, for Moore was a brilliant leader in 1966. He is remembered most perhaps for the free-kick that gave his West Ham club-mate Geoff Hurst the equalizer in the final, but he scarcely put a foot wrong in the six matches, and was voted Player of the Tournament.

He was even greater in 1970, in Mexico, despite the sensational episode on the way, in which he

An inspiring captain, Moore led England to their World Cup victory in 1966, when his unflappable temperament was invaluable.

was accused of stealing a bracelet in Colombia and released only just in time to compete in the World Cup. For his performance against Brazil, he was acclaimed by Pelé as the greatest defender in the world, and it was no fault of his that England let West Germany back into the game in the quarter-final.

So consistently brilliant were Moore's performances for England that many people remember only his mistakes—one that gifted West Germany a goal at Wembley in 1971, in the European Championships, and another against Poland at Chorzow in 1973, in a World Cup qualifier. Moore was replaced by Hunter later that year and did not play in the return, a draw at Wembley which dashed England's hope of qualifying for the World Cup and virtually ended Ramsey's reign as supremo. But Moore had broken Bobby Charlton's record of England caps, and played his last international in November 1973.

In 1974 he finally departed from West Ham—not to a big club, but to play out the rest of his career with Second Division Fulham. Remarkably, he took them to the Cup final in 1975. But it was not to be a fairytale ending—they lost 2-0 . . . to West Ham!

Moore retired in 1977 after playing his 1,000th game in first-class football. He had made his fortune in football, and he stayed in the game, coaching youngsters and serving his apprenticeship as a manager in non-League football. He surely still had a great deal to offer the game.

THE BOGOTA BRACELET

As part of the 1970 World Cup campaign, England played some warm-up matches in South America. After the Colombia game, Moore and Bobby Charlton visited a jewellery shop in their hotel. Later, Moore was accused of stealing an expensive emerald bracelet, and he was held under formal arrest for several days while the Colombian courts decided whether to proceed with the charge. The Colombian Press denounced the accusation as a national scandal, there having been several recent attempts at framing foreign celebrities for the purpose of extortion. Moore was released four days before the first World Cup match. He proceeded to confirm his unshakable temperament by playing a superb World Cup, which enhanced even his fine reputation.

Young & Woodburn

Iron Curtains

George Young

An imposing figure on the field, George Young stood 6ft 1½in (1.87m) and weighed 14st (89kg). He was a tower of strength for Rangers and Scotland. He joined Rangers in 1941, at 19, as a left-back, but played only right-back and centre-half for them. Whichever position he occupied, he was a master craftsman, commanding in the air or on the ground. He had a fine tactical brain and was highly regarded by opponents for his sportsmanship.

Young played a major role in Rangers' Iron Curtain defence, and his huge punts upfield, though often disparaged as crude, usually found their mark. He could play the

In the immediate post-war years, Scotland could call on the services of some of the finest defenders in their history. Hitherto known rather for their attacking brand of soccer, they began to turn defence into a fine art, and the late 1940s saw the introduction of the so-called 'Iron Curtains'. Outstanding among these defenders were George Young, Sammy Cox, and Willie Woodburn of Rangers and Bobby Evans of Celtic. Young and Cox made a formidable pair of backs for Scotland, probably their best ever, and Woodburn a superb centre-half. Evans was originally a right-half. Young eventually filled the centre-half spot after various replacements for Woodburn had been tried, and Evans later took over from Young.

Scots still argue the respective merits of Young and Woodburn. Which one was Scotland's greatest ever centre-half? Young was a model player and an inspiring captain; Woodburn a brilliant footballer, but with a temper that eventually got him banned. In any event, the general concensus is that they were two of the finest central defenders in the history of the game.

Woodburn (left) watches team-mate Young head clear for Rangers.

ball along the ground to equally devastating effect, and he was masterly in the air.

In the 11 seasons after the war, Young led Rangers to an impressive collection of trophies—six League Championships, four Cups, and two League Cups. He first played for Scotland in wartime internationals, and after the war amassed a record 53 caps. When he was suddenly dropped in 1957, without any explanation or word of thanks from the selectors, he decided to call it a day, and at 35 he retired from football.

Willie Woodburn

Willie Woodburn was 34 when he finished playing, but, unlike Young, he had a suspect temperament and was in the end forcibly retired. He was not a dirty player, but a tendency to 'explode' with anger and violence on the field earned him progressively longer suspensions—two weeks in the 1948-49 season, three in 1952-53, and six early in 1953-54. So when he was sent off at the beginning of the next season for striking an opponent, he was suspended indefinitely. The suspension was

lifted two years later, but it was too late for him to make a comeback.

Woodburn had joined Rangers in 1937, and like Young played a major part in their successes, with five Championship, four Cup, and two League Cup medals. He also won 24 caps.

Tall but lean, he was strong and incisive in the tackle, commanding in the air, and had just about everything a centre-half should have—except, of course, an even temperament. It is said that he is remembered more for his indiscretions than for his outstanding talent.

Rudi Krol

Dutch master

Left-back for Ajax in the early 1970s, Krol played a leading part in their European Cup successes and also in Holland's exciting World Cup win in 1974. Always willing to move up into attack, he would accept goal chances with the confidence of a striker, and typified the 'total football' being played so devastatingly by both club and country. He later became captain and converted to sweeper, rapidly developing into one of the finest in the world. His long raking passes and that same willingness to move upfield put him in the class of Beckenbauer as an attacking sweeper.

Krol joined Ajax in 1967 as a 17-year-old, and made his first-team debut in the 1969-70 season. He was picked for Holland after only a handful of games in the Dutch League, and won his first cap in their 1-0 defeat by England at Amsterdam in November 1969. Ajax brought off the League and Cup double that season, but a broken leg meant Krol missing their first European Cup triumph in 1971. He won European Cup medals in 1972 and 1973, however, and was in the side that beat Independiente of Argentina in the 1972 World Club Championship, the only year Ajax contested it.

As an overlapping full-back, Krol was outstanding in the 1974 World Cup. He showed his ability to attack down either flank, but it was from his own side, the left, that he scored against Argentina in the semi-final group. Pouncing on a half-cleared corner, he lashed a low right-foot drive in from 20 yards.

Krol was the ideal man to take over the captaincy of Ajax when Cruyff left for Barcelona in 1973, and that of Holland when Cruyff retired from international football. Whereas Cruyff's one flaw was his tendency to get involved in arguments with the referee, Krol's behaviour on the field has always been exemplary, and he has been a fine ambassador for Holland off the field, too.

Before the start of the 1978 World Cup final, Krol needed all his diplomacy to deal with the tactics of Argentina, who not only came out minutes late, but then objected to a shield on a Dutch player's hand. It was an obvious piece of gamesmanship, because the player had worn it for the previous five matches, but Krol had to threaten to take his players off before the referee finally got the match going. Despite a booking for a foul after 15 minutes, Krol hardly put a foot wrong during the whole match, and was bitterly disappointed with his second losers' medal.

Krol led Ajax to a domestic revival in the late 1970s, with a League and Cup double in 1979 and another League title in 1980. In May 1979, when he led Holland out at Berne to play Argentina in FIFA's 75th Anniversary match, he set a new Dutch record with his 65th cap. In the 1980 European Championships, he took his international appearances to 74 before leaving Ajax to play in the United States for Vancouver Whitecaps and then for Roma in Italy.

69

THE 'LAST LINE'

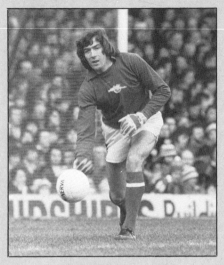

Goalkeepers are a breed apart. As the last line of defence, they have a tremendous responsibility. Other players can make a mistake and get away with it, but a keeper's errors are usually critical.

Few teams have ever achieved greatness without a safe and reliable keeper, Brazil's World Cup winning side of 1970 being a rare exception. Certainly, the success of Liverpool and Nottingham Forest in Europe has been in no small way due to Ray Clemence and Peter Shilton.

The qualities a keeper needs include speed as well as agility; confidence as well as a safe pair of hands. And he needs courage, too —not only to throw himself at the feet of an onrushing forward but also to commit himself every time a cross comes into the box.

And although most of the spectacular moments in football history belong to the goalscorers, saves such as the famous one made by Gordon Banks from Pelé in the 1970 World Cup remain in the memory for just as long.

A gallery of goalkeepers, from the top right, clockwise: Pat Jennings, Frank Swift, Gordon Banks, Ray Clemence (inset), Lev Yachin, Peter Shilton.

Frank Swift

Keeper and clown

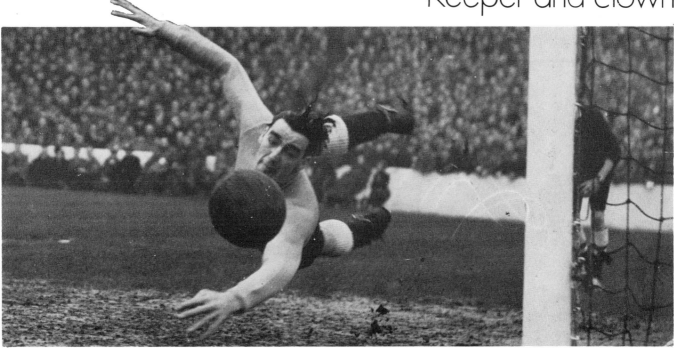

Frank Swift had that rare quality in a keeper—he was a crowd-puller. Fans used to turn up just to see him play, for he was not only a great goalkeeper, he was also a marvellous clown. A giant of a man with huge hands, he always enjoyed his game. He was a familiar picture up and down the country's football grounds in his yellow jersey, and he loved to play to the crowds. But his humour was never taken amiss by either opponents or referees, and his showmanship rarely affected his performance—although he once admitted that his fooling around cost the occasional goal in club football, all 'as part of the entertainment'.

A fine distributor of the ball with hand or foot, Swift was one of the first creative goalkeepers, never wasting a ball. At the top of his form, when he came out to attack the ball he was well nigh unbeatable. He was famous for his one-handed saves, and would break an opponent's heart by contemptuously catching the hardest of drives.

The Blackpool-born Swift joined Manchester City from Lancashire

The well-named Swift flies through the air to thwart a Welsh effort.

Combination club Fleetwood in 1932, and made his first-team debut at Derby on Christmas morning 1933. He remained their first-choice keeper until he retired in 1949. In 1934, only 19, he played in the Cup final at Wembley, and fainted on the way to pick up his winners medal. He won a Championship medal three years later.

Always out to better himself, he was a constant student of goalkeeping techniques. When he let in a

UPS AND DOWNS

Swift suffered ups and downs in his club form in pre-war days, just as Manchester City did. Their Championship-winning side of 1936-37 were leading scorers with 107, and Swift, who played in all their games, conceded 61. The next season, they were again leading scorers in Division I, with 80. Swift was ever-present again, but this time let in 77—and City were relegated!

goal that he felt he should have stopped, he would reconstruct it on paper after the game to discover how he could have saved it.

Swift made his England debut in 1941 and played in 14 wartime internationals. He was England's regular keeper after the war and won 19 full caps. Always a great inspiration to the rest of the team, he was immensely popular with his fellow players, and kept the tension out of the dressing-room with his singing and hilarious mimicry.

Swift was chosen to captain England twice, a rare honour for a goalkeeper and a tribute to his character and powers of leadership. The first of these occasions was England's famous defeat of Italy in Turin in the summer of 1948. It was Swift's brilliance in goal, with some truly remarkable saves, that enabled England to come out on top in what was a pretty even game.

After he retired, Swift became a soccer journalist for a Sunday paper. And it was on one of his match assignments that he died—killed along with much of the Manchester United team in the 1958 Munich air disaster.

71

Courageous Keepers

A TALE OF TWO KEEPERS

Goalkeepers are the most courageous players on the field. They dive sometimes with their heads unprotected into a sea of flailing legs or at the feet of an onrushing forward. Some receive serious injuries as a result of such clashes. These are the stories of two such keepers: one with a tragic outcome, the other, luckily, with less serious consequences.

Bert Trautmann

How do you take the place of England's finest and most popular goalkeeper when he retires after 15 years with his club? How do you win over the fans when you have recently left a prisoner-of-war camp, having fought for England's bitterest enemy? These were the problems facing former German paratrooper Bert Trautmann when he joined Manchester City in 1949 after the retirement of the great Frank Swift. That Trautmann not only filled Swift's shoes successfully but also became a popular hero is a testament to his skills, his courage, and his sportsmanship.

Trautmann needed all his courage when he first appeared for City. He had to suffer the insults and abuse hurled at him by the usual mindless minority of spectators found at most clubs. He didn't let it affect his form, however, and he soon became a favourite with his spectacular cat-like springs, his ability to fingertip goal-bound shots over the bar, and his daring last-second saves. Behind the scenes, too, his kindness and his willingness to give a helping hand endeared the blond giant to everyone who knew him.

He also needed his courage at Wembley in 1956, the second year running that Manchester City had reached the Cup final. After defeat in 1955, they were coasting to a 3-1 victory over Birmingham City when Trautmann came out to make a typically brave plunge at the feet of Peter Murphy. He needed attention, but played on, and then staggered off in great pain after the final whistle to collect his medal. Fortunately he didn't receive any treatment, for the following week a specialist diagnosed a broken neck.

Trautmann, who had also been voted Footballer of the Year that season, recovered from his injury and went on to play a record 508 League games for Manchester City. When he retired after nearly 15 years with the club, one of the finest tributes came from Matt Busby, manager of rivals Manchester United, who spoke of him as one of those players who 'by the very greatness of their gifts belong not so much to one section of football's following as to all of it'.

Two goalkeeping heroes: Bert Trautmann (below left) and the tragic John Thomson (below).

John Thomson

At Ibrox Park, on 5 September 1931, the Celtic goalkeeper dived at the feet of a Rangers forward to deflect the shot past his post. He was injured in the collision, with blood streaming from his head. It was a depressed fracture of the skull. He was stretchered off, but died later that night.

This was a tragedy in any circumstances, but the keeper was John Thomson, only 22 yet one of the most beloved players Scotland has ever had, worshipped by every small boy in the country. 30,000 people jammed the streets on the way to his funeral near his home of Cardenden, and another 20,000 stood in silence at a Glasgow station as his mourners left by train.

What was it that was so special about John Thomson? He was not typically built for a keeper, standing only 5ft 9½in (1.76m), but he was beautifully athletic, a natural sportsman with great speed and agility. His ability to catch a ball cleanly was unsurpassed, and he would often hold a ball when others would have been glad to parry or deflect it. He could change course in mid-air when the flight of the ball or a deflection deceived him. He was, perhaps, the first of a new breed of keepers, in complete command of his penalty area, and his reliability made him an inspiration to his fellow players.

He had firmly established himself in the Scotland team, winning four caps, but was then unlucky enough to break his shoulder bone making a save. Six months later came his fatal accident.

An imposing life-size portrait of John Thomson looks down from the main entrance at Parkhead, and other memorials are to be seen at other Scottish grounds. Schoolboys compete for trophies that perpetuate his name. He was a footballing genius and Scotland have never had another goalkeeper like him.

Lev Yachin

The man in black

The massive frame of Russian goalkeeper Lev Yachin was a familiar sight in international football in the 1950s and 1960s. His country's most popular sportsman, he also won worldwide acclaim and affection, both for his sportsmanship and for his brilliance on the field. In 1963 he became the first Russian to be voted European Footballer of the Year and the first goalkeeper.

Standing just over 6 feet, with long arms, Yachin dominated the penalty area. His sharp reflexes and long reach enabled him to make difficult saves look easy, and his ability to cut out high crosses was a result of his fine positional sense and perfect handling. He had complete confidence in himself and made up his mind in an instant. This was never better demonstrated than in his frequent sorties out of his area to cut out through balls. In training, he always devoted some time to practising as an outfield player so that he could use the ball well when he came out in this way. He was a great believer in the counter-attack, and his distribution was immaculate.

Yachin tried many sports and various positions on the football field before he settled down to be a goalkeeper. In fact, he joined the Moscow Dynamo club as an ice hockey goalminder in 1949, when he was 20. He switched to soccer in 1951, and two years later took over as their regular keeper from Khomich.

He won a gold medal in 1956 when Russia won the Olympic title, and played in three World Cups: in 1958 and 1962, when Russia reached the quarter-finals only to lose to the host country each time, and in 1966, when they reached the semi-finals. He also travelled as a reserve to Mexico for the 1970 World Cup. He was in the Russian side that won the first ever European Football Championship (then the Nations' Cup) in 1960 and were runners-up in 1964.

Almost invariably attired in a black jersey, Yachin won 78 international caps and five League and two Cup medals with Dynamo. He represented FIFA against England in 1963 and Brazil in 1968. When he retired at 41 he captained a Dynamo side against a Rest of the World team led by Bobby Charlton for a final testimonial. Over 100,000 people flocked to the Lenin Stadium to pay tribute to Yachin, who kept a clean sheet for the 50 minutes that he played. The next day he took over as general manager of Dynamo.

For once not in black, Yachin saves for FIFA at Wembley, with England's Jimmy Greaves hovering.

'TIGER' KHOMICH

Alexei Khomich was the spectacular Dynamo keeper of the sensational Moscow side that flashed all too briefly onto the soccer scene in 1945 with a short tour of Britain, before Russian football disappeared from international view again for several years.

His sparkling catlike displays between the posts caught the public imagination, and the British Press christened him 'Tiger'. He won two League medals with Dynamo before Lev Yachin took over, but he never had the opportunity of playing for his country.

'Tiger' leaps to save for Moscow Dynamo against Chelsea.

Gordon Banks

The save of the century

World Cups are known for making and breaking reputations. Gordon Banks went to the 1970 World Cup as the world's leading goalkeeper. He had confirmed himself in the No. 1 position with his displays in England's 1966 World Cup triumph, and maintained his position at the top during the ensuing years, gaining the respect and the admiration of the world's greatest strikers. In 1970, in the cauldron of Guadalajara against one of the finest attacks of all time, Banks not only lived up to his reputation, he enhanced it.

His famous save from Pelé in the match against Brazil is remembered as much as any goal or incident in the tournament. It encapsulated in one brief snatch of time all his skills—his perfect positioning, his remarkable speed across goal as Jairzinho cut back a superb cross, and his catlike reflexes as he dived to deflect Pelé's downward power-header. Pelé described it as the greatest save he had ever seen.

Banks stood 6ft 1in (1.85m) and weighed 13st 6lb (85kg). A master of the angles, he presented a formidable obstacle to any oncoming forward. Often, in desperate situations, he would deliberately leave a slight gap to entice an opponent into going for it—and then spring to block the ball as if by magic.

Banks of England

When Banks wrote his autobiography in 1980, the title was a foregone conclusion—*Banks of England*. His marvellous consistency over the years for his country had earned him the title, alluding to the proverbial impregnability of the Bank of England. He won his first international cap at Wembley against Scotland in April 1963, Alf Ramsey's second match in charge of the England team. He took over from Ron Springett, who had let in five against France in the previous game. Springett added a few more caps to bring his collection up to 33, a record for an England keeper which, with Banks taking over, did not last very long. Banks played his last game for England, also against Scotland, nine years later. He had

made the position his own, and amassed 73 caps. Who knows how many more he would have won had his career not been cut short by a car crash.

During Banks's distinguished international career, other goalkeepers were given the occasional opportunity to gain experience. But Banks's reign spanned one of the most successful decades in English international soccer, and his record speaks for itself—only 57 goals conceded in the 73 games. Meantime, his team-mates were scoring 152 goals, as England won 49 matches, drew 15, and lost only 9. His standing was just as high abroad as it was at home, and he was universally recognized as the world's No. 1.

Banks's importance to the

The famous save from Pelé in the 1970 World Cup: Banks is at the near post (below left) as Jairzinho crosses. He is still only half-way across goal as Pelé's powerful header is about to hit the ground (arrowed above), but manages incredibly to reach it and flick it over the bar with the palm of his outstretched right hand (below).

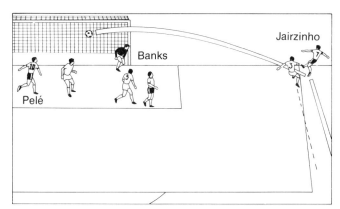

England team was never better demonstrated than when he was taken ill before the 1970 World Cup quarter-final with West Germany. It is probably fair to say that with Banks in goal England would never have lost their 2-0 lead, although it would be unfair to blame his deputy, Peter Bonetti, for being less than perfect.

Not that Banks was always quite the perfect goalkeeper—there were flaws in his game, albeit minor ones. His distribution was occasionally awry. And there was a tendency to get over-excited if he felt he was being unjustly treated or if the other side were being allowed to take liberties. But as a rule his temperament was sound. His colleagues always had complete confidence in him, and off the field, too, he was an immensely popular figure, easy-going and possessing a ready wit.

Late Starter

Banks made a relatively late start to first-class football. Born in Sheffield, he had no footballing ambitions, and drifted into minor-league soccer after he left school. He was spotted by a scout and signed amateur forms for Chesterfield. Later, as a part-time professional at £2 a match, he made the reserve side and also played for the youth team, which remarkably reached the 1956 FA Youth Cup final. And although they lost 4-3 —to a Manchester United side that included Bobby Charlton—this taste of the big-match atmosphere convinced Banks that his career lay in soccer.

But he still had his national service to complete, and was drafted to West Germany, where he met and married his German wife Ursula. So it was another two years before he returned and made his first-team debut, at 22. He played one season (23 League games) for Third Division Chesterfield before being snapped up by Leicester for £7,000. The rest of his career was spent in the First Division, with Leicester (293 League games) and Stoke (194), neither of them fashionable clubs and neither of whom had ever won a major trophy.

With Leicester, Banks had two big disappointments—the losing Cup finals of 1961 and 1963. In 1964 he won a League Cup winners medal and in 1965 a runners-up medal—these at a time when the final was a two-legged affair and did not have the glamour of a Wembley occasion.

In 1967, the season after England's World Cup triumph, Leicester stunned Banks by transfer-listing him. They felt that their 17-year-old reserve keeper Peter Shilton deserved a chance, but the implication was that Banks was 'over the hill'. This left a bitter taste in his mouth, for he had given Leicester fine service despite always having to struggle to get paid half as much as most of his England colleagues earned.

Stoke paid £52,000 for Banks. They were lucky to get him, for West Ham, who had first option, had already begun negotiations for another keeper, and the Liverpool board thwarted Bill Shankly's

With his Fernandel grin, Gordon Banks proudly holds his 1971-72 Footballer of the Year award.

STICKY FINGERS

Banks went through the same ritual before every match. He would first tone up his muscles with a series of stretching exercises and movements. This had the added effect of relaxing him. Then he would talk to himself, 'psyching' himself up mentally for the game. Finally, he did something that another great goalkeeper, Jack Kelsey of Wales and Arsenal, used to do. He would spit the coating of his chewing-gun onto his hands and rub them together, to get a tacky feel. Was this the secret of why the ball always seemed to 'stick' when he caught it?

attempts to buy him because they felt the fee was too high!

At Stoke, there was little chance of League honours. But they were twice within a whisker of reaching Wembley, in 1971 and 1972, each time being knocked out by Arsenal in semi-final replays. But they did reach Wembley in 1972, in the League Cup, thanks largely to Banks's brilliant penalty save from Geoff Hurst in the semi-final with West Ham. They went on to beat Chelsea in the final, and although

hardly comparable with an England World Cup medal six years earlier, it gave Banks great pleasure to be associated with the winning of the first major title in Stoke's 109-year history. He was also voted Footballer of the Year—an honour to go with the OBE he was awarded in 1970.

A few months later, on 22 October 1972, Banks was involved in a head-on collision with a van. Pieces of glass from his windscreen entered his right eye and he lost the sight in it. Admittedly, he was nearly 35, but there is no reason why he could not have continued to play for England right up to the 1974 World Cup. There had been no decline in his form.

After the accident, Banks tried to 're-educate' himself to play with one eye, but he reluctantly came to the conclusion that his first-class career was over. He made a comeback in the United States, however, and enjoyed playing for another two years, even being voted the NASL Goalkeeper of the Year. He later returned to England, eventually to stay in football as a coach.

Peter Shilton

The man who followed Banks

Shilton dominates the England goalmouth against Scotland in 1973.

When Gordon Banks's international career was ended by a car crash in 1972, England were fortunate to have, not one, but two fine replacements—Peter Shilton and Ray Clemence. Shilton had a good run as No. 1, with Clemence making the occasional appearance, and then in 1974 the roles were reversed, with Clemence in the driving

Peter Shilton established himself in the 1970s as the natural successor to Gordon Banks in the England goal. But a loss of form let in Ray Clemence, and Shilton had to fight to win back his place, and eventually finished up sharing it. He made a habit of following in Banks's footsteps, first at Leicester and then at Stoke. It looked like he too would struggle for domestic honours, and he even suffered the ignominy of relegation twice. But then came his move to Nottingham Forest, where he soon picked up most of the honours at home and in Europe.

At 6ft (1.83m) and 12st 10lb (81kg), Shilton is a commanding figure between the posts. He has an unflappable temperament and a burning ambition. He is quick to spot danger and come off his line, and his mastery of the angles and ability to spread himself makes him a formidable opponent in one-to-one situations. His courage in diving to smother the ball at an opponent's feet and his knack of snaking out a hand to grab the ball when seemingly beaten can be quite disconcerting. He also excels at catching crosses, and he displays an ability to hold shots that most keepers would be glad merely to block.

Snapping at Banks's Heels

Shilton was born in Leicester in 1949, and as a schoolboy used to take part in City's twice-weekly coaching classes. He joined the groundstaff at 15 and, as Banks's understudy, made his League debut in May 1966, not yet 17.

From the very start, he was a model professional, dedicated to the game and to improving his play. He was fortunate in having the world's best goalkeeper to study, and although Banks never claimed any credit for Shilton's progress, there is no doubt that Shilton benefited from his advice and example.

So good was Shilton at 17 that several clubs were after him. Leicester realized they could not keep him in the reserves any longer, and chose to sell the 29-year-old Banks instead. Shilton lived up to Leicester's expectations, but unfortunately the reverse did not hold. He became disillusioned with the club when they were relegated in 1969, even though the same season they reached the final of the Cup, losing only 1-0 to Manchester City. How much their Cup run was due to Shilton's efforts may be gauged from the fact that they progressed from the fourth round to the final

by means of 1-0 victories.

Shilton made his England debut in 1970 after the World Cup, having been in England's squad but not in the final 22. He was in dispute with his club for 18 months, though, before settling down when Leicester gained promotion in 1971. And he made the England goalkeeping spot his own early in 1973—at least for a while.

Then his career took another turn. In 1974, he lost his England place to Clemence when Don Revie took charge of England, and he signed for Stoke.

Clough's Masterstroke

It looked as if Shilton had escaped out of the frying-pan into the fire when Stoke were relegated in 1977. But then Nottingham Forest stepped in, in the persons of Brian Clough and Peter Taylor, paying Stoke £250,000 for him, a huge fee for a keeper and much criticized at the time. It turned out to be a masterstroke. Shilton thrived on the encouragement he received at Forest, and he played as great a part in their astonishing successes as anyone else—a League title followed by two European Cups. Forest were the only side to challenge the supremacy of Liverpool, and Shilton challenged their goalkeeper Clemence for his England place again.

Ray Clemence

A record of success

seat. There were other world-class keepers, too, such as Phil Parkes and Joe Corrigan, but they rarely got a look-in. Eventually, in 1980, it became increasingly difficult to choose between Shilton and Clemence, and England manager Ron Greenwood resorted to playing them alternately. Off the field the two remained good friends.

Playing for such a successful side as Liverpool, Ray Clemence's biggest problem at times is maintaining his concentration behind their superb defence. In his first 10 seasons as their regular keeper, Clemence amassed a prolific collection of medals—two European Cups, two UEFA Cups, five League Championships, two FA Cups —and during that time appeared in 415 out of 420 League games. In the 1970-71 season, he missed only one match of their League campaign in which they equalled their First Division record set two years earlier of conceding only 24 goals. And then in the 1978-79 season, Clemence played in all 42, with the extraordinary record of letting in only 16 goals.

Not quite as big as his England rival Peter Shilton, Clemence stands 5ft 11½in (1.82m) and weighs 12st 9lb (80kg). He has no apparent weaknesses. His ability to read the game and speed off the mark enable him virtually to act as a sweeper behind his back four, and he frequently makes sorties outside his penalty area to cut out danger. He has lightning reflexes and spring-heeled agility. He dominates his defence and his distribution, especially by hand, is unerring and intelligent.

Clemence was born in Skegness, Lincolnshire, in 1948 and joined Scunthorpe in 1964. He won a regular place in their first team in the 1966-67 season, and his displays for the struggling Third Division side drew scouts from far and wide. Bill Shankly wasted no time, and in the close season brought him to Liverpool for under £20,000.

As understudy to the reliable Tommy Lawrence, the 18-year-old Clemence settled down in the reserves to learn about the game. In his first two seasons, he made only one appearance in the first team, in a League Cup tie, yet he won an England Under-23 cap, against Wales in October 1968. Then, in February 1970, after Liverpool's disastrous 1-0 defeat at Watford in the sixth round of the Cup, there was a shake-up and Clemence found himself in the first team. He has never looked back.

In the 1972-73 season, with Gordon Banks out of the game, the England spot was open. Clemence played in the two World Cup qualifiers against Wales (making his debut at Cardiff in November 1972), but by then the year-younger Shilton had already won five caps. Shilton then established himself as the No. 1, and by the time Clemence won his place back, against East Germany in May 1974, had collected 20 caps. But Don Revie had replaced Alf Ramsey as England manager, and he now made Clemence first choice. Under Revie, Clemence overtook Shilton, and he kept his place when Ron Greenwood took over in 1977.

Ray Clemence continued to turn out brilliant performances in England's goal, and by the time Greenwood decided to alternate him with Shilton, in 1980, had won his 50th cap, some 20 ahead of his friend and fellow contender for the No. 1 jersey.

Ray Clemence leaps to celebrate another goal at the other end. Playing for Liverpool, he sometimes found himself using more energy in this sort of activity than in defending his goal. In the 1978-79 season, he conceded only 16 goals in 42 League games, keeping 28 clean sheets.

Pat Jennings The largest hands in football

Pat Jennings is known for having the largest hands in football. Whether or not this is true, they must seem enormous to opposing players as he plucks their crosses out of the air, sometimes even catching the ball one-handed. The evergreen Irishman has never been the most orthodox of keepers, but he is one of the safest, and inspires the utmost confidence in his fellow players.

At his peak with Spurs, Jennings had few equals. And one of those, England's Gordon Banks, has gone on record as saying that Jennings was the 'perfect' keeper, the finest in the world in his era—no man could wish for greater or more sincere praise.

Jennings possesses all the goalkeeping skills in abundance. Standing 6ft (1.83m) and weighing 12st 6lb (79kg), he has lightning reflexes, breaking the heart of many a striker with point-blank saves. His positioning and judgement are faultless, and he comes out bravely to smother a shot or spread himself in front of an oncoming forward, as often as not blocking the ball with his legs. Above all, he has a wonderful temperament, never flustered and never flapping whatever the state of the game, and accepting physical challenge or adverse decisions without demur. He dominates his defence with quiet assurance, and distributes the ball thoughtfully and accurately. He has even been known to score—as he did with an enormous punt the length of the field for Spurs in the 1967 Charity Shield match against Manchester United, which bounced over Alex Stepney's head.

Gaelic Influence

Jennings' accurate and powerful kicking derives from the Gaelic football he played at school in Newry, where he was born in 1945. He learnt his soccer in the streets, and represented the Northern Ireland youth side in the Little World Cup, played in England in 1963. Less than a week after the tournament, Third Division Watford paid Newry Town £6,000 for him.

He played one full season with Watford, during which he won two international caps. His debut in April 1964 against Wales at Swansea was the start of a long run as Ireland's first-choice goalkeeper. Some 16 years later he was still No. 1 and had amassed over 80 caps, easily a record for Northern Ireland.

Spurs snapped him up for £27,500 in 1964, and this marked the beginning of a long and distinguished career in the First Division. In his 13 seasons at Tottenham, he won an FA Cup medal in 1967, League Cup medals in 1971 and 1973, a UEFA Cup medal in 1972, besides being voted Footballer of the Year in 1973, PFA Player of the Year in 1975, and the same year being awarded the MBE.

His 472 League games for Spurs was a club record, and when they decided to let him go in 1977, to give his stand-in Barry Daines a

Jennings saves a Liverpool penalty in March 1973 (left) and is voted Footballer of the year in May.

chance, the fans were upset to lose this most modest and popular of players. They were even more displeased that he should have been allowed to go to North London rivals Arsenal for £40,000—a 'gift' at current values.

At 32, Jennings began a new career with Arsenal, and in three years had another three FA Cup finals under his belt, one of them a winning one. In 1980, he kept a clean sheet for 120 minutes in the European Cup-Winners Cup final, only for Arsenal to lose on penalties. He was 'only 35' though, with plenty of time for further honours.

Stanley Matthews

Garrincha

Jimmy Mullen

Tom Finney

Once upon a time every team had two wingers, an outside-right and an outside-left. But with the advent of overlapping full-backs and 4-4-2 in the 1960s, the art of wing play began to die out, especially in the British game, where it was once supreme. Wingers such as Jackson and Morton of Scotland, Matthews and Finney of England, and in different ages Meredith and Jones of Wales provided the greatest thrills of the game.

There are few better sights in football than a speedy, skilful winger losing his full-back and making for the bye-line to cross the ball onto a team-mate's head, or cutting in to hammer a shot at goal. Although the tendency today is for all members of a side to get into crossing positions, it is a specialist's job, and the sooner wingmen come back into football, the better for the game.

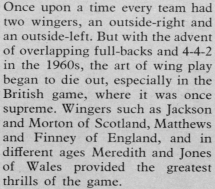

Johnny Hancocks

Billy Meredith

Billy Liddell

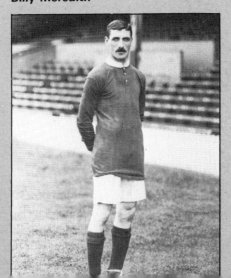

Cliff Jones

79

Hancocks & Mullen
Wing-to-wing play at Wolves

After the war, Wolves possessed a pair of devastating wingers, Johnny Hancocks and Jimmy Mullen. Manager Stan Cullis had developed a direct, no-nonsense style of play based on a powerful half-back line (Slater, Shorthouse, and Wright) that moved the ball about with the minimum of frills, two penetrating wingers capable of playing long balls across field to each other in order to stretch the opposing defence, and big, uncompromising strikers (Pye, Wilshaw, Swinbourne) who could convert their crosses.

In Hancocks and Mullen, Cullis had the ideal wingers for his effective, if controversial (some critics found it too crude) methods, for they could also shoot. The tiny Hancocks on the right—he stood only 5ft 5in (1.65m)—packed a tremendous shot in his size $5\frac{1}{2}$ boots, and in his 10 seasons with the club was never out of double figures. He scored 157 goals in 343 League games to add to the 8 in 30 games he played for Walsall, his only other club, in the season before the war. When Wolves won the Championship in 1954, he was their joint top scorer with 25, and he scored another 25 the following season, in only 32 games, to lead their scorers. He played just one more season, retiring in his mid-thirties.

Mullen was not such a prolific scorer, but found the net consistently. Wolves were his only club, and he played a few games for them as a 16-year-old in 1939. In 13 seasons after the war, he scored 99 goals in 437 League games. He retired in the 1958-59 season, having played enough matches to win his third Championship medal.

Both wingers played in the fine Wolves side that beat Leicester 3-1 in the 1949 Cup final, but they never played together for England. Hancocks won only three caps (two of them on the left wing), being at his peak when Matthews and Fin-

Johnny Hancocks

ney were around. He scored twice on his international debut against Switzerland in 1948. Mullen, who rarely seemed to be able to reproduce his club form for England, won 12 caps between 1947 and 1954. Nevertheless, he scored six goals for England, including two in the 4-4 draw with the Rest of Europe in 1953.

But it was as a pair that Hancocks and Mullen excelled. With their speed and accuracy of crossing, they tore opposing defences apart. The ball would sometimes travel between them from touchline to touchline twice in one attack, so that when it eventually arrived in the middle the defence tended to be caught square, making the strikers' job that much easier. It was these tactics that helped to kill off the third-back game and result in the introduction of a fourth player in the back line. When Hancocks retired, Cullis tried unsuccessfully to find a replacement. And although Wolves maintained their place in the forefront of English football to the end of the fifties, they could never recapture the wing-to-wing game of Hancocks and Mullen. It was the old, old story of fitting a style of play to the very special skills of certain players, but of being unable to find new players to fit in with the style.

Jimmy Mullen about to power the ball across to the opposite wing.

Sir Stanley Matthews
The Wizard of Dribble

Stanley Matthews won many awards in his long and amazing career: he became the first footballer to be knighted, when he made his final appearance a month before his 50th birthday; he was voted European Footballer of the Year at 41 and Footballer of the Year for the second time at 48; he won 54 England caps and played another 30 wartime and 'Victory' internationals; he won a Cup winner's medal in an emotional and dramatic game now known as the 'Matthews final'; and he earned nicknames such as 'the Prince of the Potteries' and 'the Wizard of Dribble'. But above all he won worldwide respect and admiration for his genius and his sportsmanship. Never once, in a career that spanned nearly 35 years, did he deliberately foul an opponent or retaliate (and there was certainly provocation enough) or dissent from a referee's decision. His name became synonymous with football wherever it was played.

Fitness First

What was the secret of this Peter Pan of football? How could a man of nearly 50 play in the First Division of the Football League in the 1960s? How could he take the ball up to a healthy young athlete half his age and still beat the man for speed?

The secret of Matthews's remarkable longevity was in the way he looked after his body, keeping it in perfect physical trim throughout his career. And he had his father to thank for it. Jack Matthews, known in his boxing days as the 'Fighting Barber of Hanley', was a fitness fanatic. He never drank or smoked in his life, and nor did Stanley. When Stanley was 10, his father made him join in the morning exercises with his elder brothers. The young Stanley called it the 'dawn torture', as every morning at six the sheets were

pulled off him for breathing in front of an open window and then a spell with a chest expander. And although he was a reluctant participant at first, it was a habit that he never lost.

His father also nurtured his sprinting ability by timing and

Right: The young Matthews tormented left-backs on Stoke's right-wing before the war. Below: As Blackpool's hero in the 1953 Cup final, he receives his medal from the Queen. Bottom: Back at Stoke, he continued to dazzle in his 40s.

training him for the 100 yards in the annual Stoke-on-Trent sports. He won this event four times, first as a 7-year-old with a 40-yard start and finally at 14 from scratch. And during his career, Matthews concentrated on 20-yard sprints in training. His speed off the mark became legendary. One moment he was there . . . and then he was gone. Once past a back, there was no way he could be caught.

Prince of the Potteries

Matthews was a native of Hanley, in the area of central England known as the Potteries. He signed for Stoke, only two miles from his home, at the age of 15, as an amateur and office boy, and two years later as a professional. They used him sparingly at first, but in his second season he helped them win promotion to Division I. In the First Division, Stoke were a middle-of-the-table side. They won no honours, but in Stanley Matthews they had a priceless asset. He was a great crowd puller, a marvellously exciting entertainer who was coveted by every other club in the country. He was truly the 'Prince of the Potteries'.

A Change of Style

Matthews married the Stoke trainer's daughter when he was 19 and settled down. He was very single-minded about his football career, a great thinker about his game, always looking for ways to improve it. He was at first a regular goal-scorer, cutting in towards goal to shoot—though his left foot was markedly weaker than his right, and he headed the ball so rarely that it would create a stir in the crowd. Then, suddenly, soon after the start of the 1936-37 season, he changed his style. He had thought about it, and decided that he would be more use to his side if he concentrated on making scoring chances for the inside-forward trio. And he stuck to this conviction to the end of his

At 42, Matthews was still performing his magic on England's right wing. He played superbly against Brazil in 1956, and this sequence shows him typically beating his man and drawing another before crossing.

playing days.

It was ironic that Matthews was often accused of selfishness, for his whole philosophy was built on creating goals for others. There were two periods in his career when he did not score a goal for five years!

Yet if he did have a failing it was his reluctance to part with the ball until he had beaten a man—

THE LONELY LEFT-BACK

Playing left-back against Matthews, you were the loneliest man on the field. All eyes were on you, waiting for him to make a fool of you. Some backs felt they could stop Matthews. After all, they knew exactly what he was going to do. He never cut inside, did he? But Matthews had confidence and he had perfect timing. He liked to receive the ball at his feet. He would control it, move it forward slowly, maybe put his foot on it. Once he had the ball, if you rushed in to tackle him you were 'dead'. (You wouldn't do that to ordinary wingers.) So you closed down on him and jockeyed back a bit; you let him bring the ball to you. He would take it straight up to you, caressing it gently, almost daintily. As he got almost within striking distance he would lean to his left. But he wouldn't be going inside, would he? No, of course not, he would take it outside as usual—but when you lunged for the ball it wasn't there any more, and nor was Matthews. No wonder they called him the 'Wizard of Dribble'. It was magic—with several performances every Saturday, year in year out. And the crowds never grew tired of it.

---

sometimes more than once. Beating the full-back was always a challenge to his skill, it seemed, and he was often criticized for allowing a defence time to recover, when a first-time pass might have been decisive.

Nevertheless, Matthews always maintained that when he got to the bye-line he had taken two, maybe three defenders out of the game, and it was impossible for his team-mates to be offside and it also allowed them to get into position. And furthermore, he argued, in this way he could destroy the confidence of his opponents. He was quite ruthless about this, and although he never lifted a finger in anger, he would destroy defenders psychologically. And the more he was fouled, the more he knew he had the opposition rattled.

International Career

At 19, Matthews made his international debut against Wales in September 1934, and scored once in an easy 4-0 victory, and he played a couple of months later against Italy in the notorious 'Battle of Highbury'. But it was another three years before he gained a regular place in the side, and all in all he had a chequered international career. More than once he was omitted because he was thought to be too individualistic. But how can you ask or expect a player of Matthews's genius to conform to a set pattern of play? Matthews did one thing brilliantly—he has been described, aptly and affectionately, as a 'one-trick magician'—he would beat a man on the outside, sprint for the line, and put over pinpoint crosses

HOW TO STOP MATTHEWS

Many backs had theories for stopping Matthews. Perhaps the best of these was Eddie Hapgood's, a great admirer of Matthews and England captain for most of Matthews's early career. Hapgood's answer was 'to make sure *he never got the ball'*.

This was easier said than done, of course, for Matthews did not just hang around on the right wing waiting for the ball. His positional play was masterly, and he used to pop up in all sorts of places to receive a pass. It is something perhaps not fully appreciated of the 'maestro' that his running off the ball was way ahead of his time.

Arsenal's Eddie Hapgood can't stop Matthews this time. Few backs could.

DO YOU THINK IT WILL SUIT ME?

As a young boy, Stanley Matthews's usual position was centre-half, and he once scored eight goals for his school from there. One day, at the age of 13, he was called to his headmaster's study and told, without warning, that he had been selected to play for England Schools against Wales. After he had recovered from the shock, the head dropped another bombshell: 'You have been chosen to play at outside-right.' Young Stanley's face fell: 'Outside-right, sir? That's not my usual position. Do you think it will suit me?'

to the feet or heads of his colleagues. He did it almost every time he got the ball; he did it better than anyone had ever done it before; and no winger since has equalled his skill.

Matthews clinched his England place in 1937 with a most uncharacteristic performance—he scored a hat-trick, all three with his left foot! It was against Czechoslovakia at Tottenham in December. Because of injuries, he played most of the game at inside-right. With just a few minutes remaining, he had already scored two, but the Czechs were level 4-4. The ground was heavy and it was getting dark, when he picked up the ball in midfield, took it on, and

slotted it past the keeper.

A year later, he had an equally brilliant game against Ireland. This time he scored only once, but he struck up a marvellous relationship with Willie Hall, the little Spurs inside-right, and made four of the record five goals he scored that day. England won 7-0, and Matthews ran half the length of the field in scoring the last goal himself, past a completely demoralized Irish defence.

During the war, Matthews formed another brilliant partnership, with Raich Carter, and played in 29 wartime and 'victory' internationals. But when football resumed, he lost his place to Tom Finney. Finney was a superb goalscoring winger, and Matthews was 31. How lucky England were to find such a replacement for Matthews; yet how frustrating, for Matthews was far from finished. Then, a brilliant solution was found—Finney was switched to the left wing. With probably the finest forward line they ever fielded—Matthews, Mortensen, Lawton, Mannion, Finney—England went to Lisbon and annihilated Portugal 10-0. Six times England fielded these five, winning five matches (Northern Ireland managed to hold them to a draw), and scoring 24 goals.

Matthews prepares to go for the line in the 1953 Cup final.

Although out of the side in 1950, Matthews was selected for the party that went to Brazil for the World Cup that year, the first time England had entered. He was not picked for the first two matches, and had to watch in mortification while England went down ignominiously to the United States. He did play in the next match, against Spain, but they lost this, too, and were eliminated.

Matthews played once more, at the beginning of the next season, but that seemed to be the end of his international career. But, again, Matthews was far from finished. Three years later, at the age of 38, he was recalled against the Rest of Europe. And he went on to play another 20 internationals after that! He took part in the 1954 World Cup; in 1955 he took the Scots apart at Wembley, and although Wilshaw scored four in England's 7-2 win, it became known as 'Matthews's match'; in 1956 he inspired England to a 4-2 victory over Brazil at Wembley, when at the age of 41 he worked all his old magic on Nilton Santos, one of the world's best backs; and he made his final appearance for England a year later in Copenhagen.

The Matthews Final

Matthews had the occasional dispute with Stoke City, but these were usually magnified out of all proportion by the press. Nevertheless, he put in a transfer request in 1938. This created an uproar in the city. Thousands stopped working to attend a protest meeting and parade the streets, demanding that he should not leave Stoke. He stayed for another nine years.

In May 1947, at Hampden Park, Matthews helped a Great Britain side beat the Rest of Europe 6-1, and a few hours later signed for Blackpool for £11,500. It was a substantial fee at that time, especially for a 32-year-old, but Blackpool got 14 seasons out of Matthews.

In his first season, they reached Wembley, where they lost a thrilling Cup final to Manchester United. Matthews's consolation was to be the first recipient of the Footballer of the Year award. It is every player's ambition to gain a Cup winner's medal, and Matthews was no exception, but Blackpool lost at Wembley again in 1951, to Newcastle. And when they found themselves there yet again in 1953, but 3-1 down to Bolton with only 20 minutes to go, it looked as if his last chance had slipped by. What happened next was sad for Bolton, who were depleted by injuries, but it was an emotional time for the whole nation, who were willing Matthews to get his coveted medal whether they were interested in football or not. And he didn't let them down. He proceeded to tear the Bolton defence apart with a display of all his guile and wizardry, swerving and feinting, turning his man this way and that, threading his way to the bye-line as he had done a thousand times before. The keeper fumbled his cross—he was mesmerized like the rest of his defence—and Mortensen scrambled the ball over the line. Matthews continued to panic Bolton and they conceded a free-kick just outside the box, which Mortensen hammered in for his hat-trick and the equalizer two minutes from time. There were only seconds left and Matthews had the ball again. He beat one man, then another. He

A fitting end to a fairy-tale career. Sir Stanley Matthews, 50-year-old Peter Pan of soccer, is chaired off by Lev Yachin and Ferenc Puskas after his testimonial in 1965.

made for the line. People were pinching themselves to make sure they weren't dreaming. He cut the ball back, hard and low, right to the feet of left-winger Perry, who joyfully swept it into the net. Matthews had his medal at last.

Epilogue

Blackpool were a good First Division side, and they finished as high as second in 1956, although they were never in with a chance of the League title. In 1961, when they just escaped relegation, Matthews was 46. Surely this was the end? He had had a wonderful career in football, and was probably the most famous English sportsman of all time. But, yet again . . . he was far from finished.

Blackpool let him go back to Stoke in 1961 for a nominal £2,500. His old club were languishing near the foot of the Second Division table at the time. But the Prince had come home, and the crowds flocked back in their thousands. He didn't disappoint them. Stoke stayed up that season and Matthews even scored a couple of goals—after four

barren seasons. The gates had trebled, and by his sheer presence Matthews lifted the whole side. The next season they finished top and were promoted. It had all depended on the last match, which they had to win, at home to Luton. They came out after half-time with a shaky 1-0 lead, but, sure enough, it was the old 'maestro' Stanley Matthews—he certainly had a good script-writer—who clinched it with a goal soon after the interval. It was his first goal of the season—and his last in professional football.

Nearly 50, he played a few more games for Stoke, in reputedly the hardest League in the world, the English First Division. He was made a freeman of the city, he was knighted, and great players from all over the world played in his benefit match in January 1965 at Stoke's Victoria Ground, where he had begun his illustrious career 35 years earlier.

Matthews tried management, briefly and unsuccessfully, with Port Vale, before settling down in Malta. There, he coached the local club Hibernians . . . and continued to play football.

		MATTHEWS SEASON BY SEASON			
Club	Season	League		England	
		Games	Goals	Games	Goals
Stoke City	1931-32	1	—		
	1932-33	16	1		
	1933-34	29	11		
	1934-35	36	10	2	1
	1935-36	40	10	1	—
	1936-37	40	7	1	—
	1937-38	38	6	6	5
	1938-39	36	2	7	2
	1946-47	23	4	3	1
Blackpool	1947-48	33	1	5	—
	1948-49	25	3	5	1
	1949-50	31	—	1	—
	1950-51	36	—	2	—
	1951-52	18	1		
	1952-53	20	4		
	1953-54	30	2	5	—
	1954-55	34	1	7	—
	1955-56	36	3	2	—
	1956-57	25	2	7	1
	1957-58	28	—		
	1958-59	19	—		
	1959-60	15	—		
	1960-61	27	—		
	1961-62	2	—		
Stoke City		18	2		
	1962-63	32	1		
	1963-64	9	—		
	1964-65	1	—		
		698	71	54	11

Welsh wing wizards

A contrast in styles

The Welsh have produced some fine wingers, but none better than Billy Meredith and Cliff Jones. Both represented Wales over long periods, Meredith on the right, Jones mainly on the left, Meredith from 1895 to 1920, Jones from 1954 to 1969. Meredith more often than not took the ball to the corner flag before crossing, while Jones was noted for his dazzling runs into the box and his flair for heading goals.

Billy Meredith starred for both Manchester sides over 30 years.

Billy Meredith

One of the finest outside-rights of all time, Billy Meredith (pronounced with the accent on the second syllable) rivals Stanley Matthews for longevity as well as for skills. He played in first-class football for 30 years. Born in 1875, he made his League debut for Manchester City in November 1894 and played his last match for them in March 1924. At 49 years 8 months, he was the oldest man ever to play in the FA Cup.

He played his last international when he was nearly 46. His 48 caps were all won against the other home countries.

Suspended with a number of other City players in 1905 for receiving illegal bonuses, he missed a season and then joined Manchester United, where he soon won one Cup and two League medals to add to the Cup medal won with City. He returned to City in 1921 to play out his last days. He played 670 League matches in all, scoring 181 goals.

But mere statistics, however impressive, do not tell the real story of Meredith. He was one of the great characters of football, bandy legged, moustachioed, and constantly chewing a tooth-pick on the field. A marvellous dribbler, fast and elusive, he was adept at hurdling the outstretched leg of a defender. He was famed, too, for a unique back-pass, effected so cleverly as he moved forward that it would deceive the back into going with him, while opening up the defence for his own wing-half.

Meredith always kept himself in perfect condition, yet throughout his career he never trained for more than two days a week and his only training method was ball practice.

Cliff Jones

Cliff Jones was a key member of Spurs' 'double' winning side of 1960-61. A natural on either flank, with fine ball control, he had the ability and willingness to attack defences. He often played when he was not fully fit, because he worried the opposition to the extent that they usually detailed two men to mark him. He was frequently injured, as his courage in the box resulted in many a knock.

Swansea-born, he joined Town straight from school, made his League debut for them in 1953 and his Welsh debut a year later. He was an established international when Spurs bought him for £35,000 in 1958, and he played in all five of Wales's World Cup matches later that year. He played on the right for the Spurs 'double' side, switched to the left for the side that retained the Cup in 1962, and was back on the right again when Spurs won the European Cup-Winners Cup the following year. He won a third Cup medal in 1967 as substitute, although he did not play. Spurs allowed him to go to Fulham in 1968-69 on a free transfer, and in his two seasons there he took his tally of caps to 59 (exceeded only by Ivor Allchurch for Wales). In all, he scored 182 goals in 511 League matches and 16 for Wales.

Jones is remembered most for his diagonal runs, as he beat defender after defender in full flight and cut in for goal or made for the bye-line, and especially for his soaring leaps at the far post to head spectacular goals.

Cliff Jones scores a typical goal for Spurs against Liverpool at White Hart Lane in 1967, arriving a split second before the dive of keeper Tommy Lawrence and the tackle of Emlyn Hughes.

Tom Finney

The Preston Plumber

Tom Finney's knack of dribbling with his left foot on the right wing, and his ability to transfer the ball from one foot to the other, posed all kinds of problems for full-backs. He was equally at home on the left.

Tom Finney, the 'Preston Plumber', was the winger who had everything. Equally at home on the left or the right, he finished his career as one of the finest of deeply-lying centre-forwards. He was a contemporary of Stanley Matthews, and arguments were forever raging as to their respective merits. The England selectors found the choice impossible, and it was then, in 1947 against Portugal, that they found the perfect solution by switching Finney from right to left. With the two best wingers in the world attacking along both their flanks, it is no wonder the Portuguese defence crumbled. And of England's 10 goals that day, Finney's stands out—a dazzling touchline run from inside his own half, before cutting inside to power his shot past the keeper, with a trail of beaten defenders in his wake. So bewildered was the Portuguese right-back against Finney that he had to be substituted—and he was their captain!

This was the effect Finney had on most backs that came up against him, many of whom would dearly have loved to be substituted had it

been possible at that time. Like Matthews, Finney could torment a back until one felt sorry for the poor fellow. With his perfect balance and ball control, he would take the ball up to his man before dummying and speeding past him. Also like Matthews, he would take the ball right up to the bye-line before cutting it back for his oncoming team-mates. But there was even more to Finney than this, for he could cut inside to shoot, whichever wing he was on, and could score goals with his head as well as with both feet. One remark-

able skill, and a favourite trick of his, was, while dribbling at speed, to transfer the ball from right foot to left and in the same movement send over an inch-perfect cross.

One-Club Man

Finney was born and bred in Preston, and North End were the only club he played for, although he turned down a lucrative offer from Italy in 1952. He began as an inside-left, having modelled himself on his boyhood hero at Deepdale, Alex James. He became a right-winger by accident. He seemed to be fated to play the eternal reserve for Preston's under-18 side, when at the last minute one day he was drafted in at outside-right to replace an injured player. He made such an impression that that's where he stayed.

It was during the war that Finney played his first top-class football. He starred in the Preston side that won the wartime league's Northern Section in 1940-41 and went on to complete the 'double' by beating the mighty Arsenal in the Cup. That was his first of many trips to

Finney had a marvellously accurate shot with either foot, and was a deadly penalty-taker. Here he equalizes for England against the USSR in the 1958 World Cup. He scored 30 goals for England.

Wembley, and he managed to keep his knees from knocking for long enough to give the best left-back in the country, Eddie Hapgood, a tough time, as he did in the replay at Blackburn, which Preston won 2-1.

His first representative honour was for the FA against the RAF in 1942, when he was one of only two uncapped players on the field. He was up against Hapgood again, and also in the RAF side was Stanley Matthews. It was a classic game (the FA won 4-3), and it marked the beginning of all those Finney v Matthews arguments. The comparisons and false rivalry have always annoyed Finney, who had the greatest admiration for Matthews, because they were two such different players.

After the war, Finney was the star of the Preston side, although the best they could do in the way of honours was to finish runners-up twice in the League and once in the Cup in the 1950s. He was perhaps the most popular of all the post-war players, wherever he went. He was the perfect sportsman, never intentionally committing a foul or questioning a decision. He looked frail, but had a wiry strength—he needed it, for he was frequently the object of unscrupulous tackles. Thanks to his determination and ability to regain fitness after injury, his ab-sences from club and country were kept to a minimum. Nevertheless, in 14 full seasons for Preston he never played more than 37 League games. And although his record 431 League matches for the club has since been broken, his League tally of 187 goals still stands.

But Finney *was* Preston. And when he retired in 1960—prematurely some thought, for his change of position to a foraging centre- or inside-forward had given him a new lease of life—the once-great club folded like a house of cards. They went down to the Second Division the very next season, and some twenty years later were still there, having spent some time in the Third. Yet even now, those privileged to have seen him will spring to life at the mention of Preston, for the name is still

This prize-winning picture of Finney, taken at Stamford Bridge in 1956, captures the grace and balance of the 'Preston Plumber', as he negotiates a pool of water and leaves the Chelsea full-back floundering.

synonymous with that of Tom Finney and it conjures up a picture of the patterns he weaved on the wing.

England Career

Although during the war Matthews and overseas service (Finney was posted to Italy) kept him out of the England side, he made his international debut in 1946, as soon as football was officially resumed, against Ireland. The exclusion of Matthews caused a forest of raised eyebrows, but Finney struck up an instant relationship with Raich Carter. He scored in five of his six games for England that season, and made many more for Lawton and Mannion. The last of these games was the one in Lisbon, when Finney was switched to outside-left with such devastating effect. Fin-

ney played regularly for England for the next 12 seasons, and of his 76 appearances he started 40 on the right wing, 33 on the left, and the other three at centre-forward.

Finney had another superb game on the opposite wing to Matthews in England's famous 4-0 victory over Italy in Turin, scoring both their second-half goals. And in 1951 against Scotland, an early injury to Mannion forced Finney to move inside and partner Matthews on the right wing for the first and only time. England's ten men eventually lost 3-2, but the pair of them created an unforgettable impression.

It was 1957 before Finney was again given the chance as a midfield forager, in the No. 9 shirt, having worn it twice the previous year as a regular centre-forward.

4-2 defeat by Uruguay in the 1954 quarter-final. His final tally of 30 goals for England was a record at the time, and no winger has approached it.

Honours

Finney's lack of the major footballing medals in no way diminishes his stature as one of the all-time masters. He was twice voted Footballer of the Year, in 1954 and 1957, and when the Professional Footballers Association inaugurated their awards in 1979, he was the first to get the special Merit award.

This was entirely appropriate, for as much as anything else Tom Finney was a player's player, and admired and respected by his fellow professionals as he was idolized by his fans.

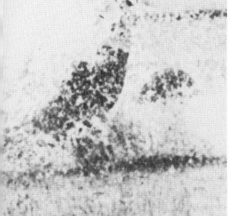

MORE POSITIONS THAN CLUBS

	Preston (League)		England		Positions	
Season	Games	Goals	Games	Goals	O-R	O-L
1946-47	32	7	6	5	5	1
1947-48	33	13	6	6	1	5
1948-49	24	7	6	3	3	3
1949-50	37	10	10	4	6	4
1950-51	34	13	4	2	3	1
1951-52	33	13	7	—	6	1
1952-53	34	17	8	3	8	—
1953-54	23	11	7	1	4	3
1954-55	30	7	1	—	—	1
1955-56	30	17	5	2	3	2
1956-57	34	23	7*	1	1	3
1957-58	34	26	7	2	—	7
1958-59	16	6	2	1	—	2
1959-60	37	17				
	431	187	76	30	40	33

* Includes three games in the No. 9 shirt.

Whatever he was asked to do for England, he did with skill, polish, modesty, and the minimum of fuss. His passing was immaculate, his shooting deadly accurate. He became England's regular penalty-taker, and of the four goals he scored in another splendid victory over Portugal in 1950 (5-3 in Lisbon), two were from the spot.

It was Finney in 1958 whose penalty earned England a late equalizer against the Russians in their opening World Cup match, despite an injury that kept him out for the rest of the tournament. Finney had played in both previous World Cups, scoring in England's

ACCOLADES FOR FINNEY

Eddie Hapgood: 'He's an outside-right and he does all his dribbling with his left foot. What can you do with a fellow like that?'

Jimmy Murphy (Matt Busby's right-hand man and one of the shrewdest judges of a footballer): '... the only player I've ever seen who has got the lot.'

Bill Shankly: 'Tom Finney was the best forward I ever saw in my life ... no player ever made more direct passes to a man to put the ball in the net. If I were pressed into it, I would say Tommy was the best player ever born.'

Jim Milne (Preston manager): 'He went into the tackle like a defender. ... Nothing frightened him. ... He was the greatest.'

Alf Ramsey: '... over a distance I doubt if there is another winger in the world to equal him for ball control while racing like a greyhound down the touchline.'

Joe Mercer (on a typical Finney performance, against Arsenal): 'The complete master of every situation ... making an outstanding left-back look ordinary ... he was unplayable. I never hope to see a better exhibition of wing play.'

Alec Jackson

The Laughing Cavalier

Left: Alec Jackson, a dashing, goal-scoring winger, lets one fly for Chelsea in 1930. Above: Pictured with Scotland and Chelsea team-mate Hughie Gallacher (left).

ALEC JACKSON: FACTS & FIGURES		
	League	
Clubs	Games	Goals
Aberdeen (1924-25)	34	7
Huddersfield (1925-30)	179	68
Chelsea (1930-32)	65	25
	278	100

A dashing right-winger with the grace of a gazelle, Alec Jackson is best remembered for the hat-trick he scored for Scotland against England in 1928. This was the match of the immortal 'Wembley Wizards', and Jackson, who had the happy knack of scoring from left-wing centres, got all three that day from floating crosses chipped over to the far post by his opposite wingman Alan Morton.

Standing only 5ft 7in (1.70m), Jackson was nevertheless the tallest of the 'Wizards' forward line. Some reports of that game made him the

man of the match, for although his goals were scored from barely a yard out (one a header, two touched in), his speed and skill on the wing and his powerful shooting were major factors in the destruction of England's defence.

Jackson emigrated to the United States as a teenager, and played there for a season before being persuaded to return to Scotland to join Aberdeen. He made such an impressive start that he won three caps in his first season and had several English clubs after him. Herbert Chapman won the race for

his signature, and Jackson's 16 goals in 1925-26 helped Huddersfield to their third consecutive League title. And that season he gave England a taste of things to come, scoring the only goal of the Scotland-England game.

With his all-round skills, dashing manner, and film-star profile, Jackson soon became a national figure and was nicknamed the 'Laughing Cavalier'. Chelsea paid £8,500 (a large fee in those days) for him in 1930, but after a dispute with the club two years later he drifted into non-League football.

Alan Morton

The Wee Blue Devil

To many Scots, Alan Morton was the finest winger of his generation, if not of all time. A star of the great Rangers sides of the 1920s, Morton was a direct, goalscoring left-winger with a powerful shot in each foot. He was renowned for his spectacular goals, and was one of the very few players in those days who could 'bend' the ball.

Like that other great Scottish idol Hughie Gallacher, Morton was small, standing only 5ft 4in (1.62m)—that is, when he was standing. For Morton was always on the move—in a direct line for goal. He had wonderful control, perfect balance, and was so fast off the mark that once past a back he could never be caught.

Morton perfected all aspects of his play. He was the master of the first-time pass; his ability to hit a moving ball with either foot and with the utmost accuracy opened up many a defence. He perfected what became known as the 'Morton lob', an undercut cross that floated to the far post tantalizingly out of reach of the keeper; this was a result of his extraordinary ability to pivot. And when he cut inside the back, he was dynamite.

A Part-Timer

Throughout his playing career, Morton continued to work as a mining engineer, often arriving at the ground to train immaculately dressed, complete with bowler hat and rolled umbrella. He was born in Glasgow, but the family—he was the youngest of five brothers—moved to Airdrie when he was a boy. He played for the Rest of Scotland in a schoolboy match against Glasgow in 1920. And although he played for them in a benefit match, Airdrie, to their undying shame, failed to recognize his talents. He eventually signed for Queen's Park, along with his brother Bob, in 1913.

On his first-team debut, he gave a hint of things to come by waltzing round Third Lanark's redoubtable keeper Jimmy Brownlie to score. He made his international debut against Wales in 1920, in the first full international after the war, having already played in representative matches.

When Morton signed professional forms with Rangers later in 1920, he was Willie Struth's first capture. There began an era unsur-

passed in Scottish football history, not only for the honours won but also for the quality of the football played. Morton struck up memorable partnerships with two inside-lefts, first Tommy Cairns and then Bob McPhail. In his 11 full seasons, Rangers won the Championship 9 times and the Cup twice, and he won a third Cup winner's medal in 1932, when he was coming to the end of his career. He never played in the reserves for Rangers, and in all matches scored 115 goals in 495 games.

The Wee Blue Devil

Morton played for Scotland from 1920 to 1932. To England he was the 'holy terror', and the English football writer Ivan Sharpe christ-

ened him the 'Wee Blue Devil', a nickname that stuck. England tried all kinds of right-backs against him and all kinds of tactics, but they could never contain, let alone subdue, him. His finest game was in 1928, for the so-called 'Wembley Wizards', when England were trounced 5-1 and he made all three of Jackson's goals with his crosses.

Morton announced his retirement soon after the start of the 1932-33 season, and was immediately co-opted onto Rangers' Board of Directors. He served them in this capacity until ill-health forced him to retire in 1968.

He died three years later, one of the most loved and respected of all Scottish footballers. He is remembered with great joy by those who had the privilege to see him, a tiny figure with long-striding legs, weaving and bobbing on the wing, beating his man with skill and grace, lofting over those floating centres or cutting inside to hammer those ferocious shots. He is remembered also as a perfect gentleman, both on and off the field. And above all, he is remembered, simply, as a genius in football boots.

MORTON'S MAGIC

Some of the goals Morton scored had a special magic about them. One, in particular, scored at Cathkin against Third Lanark, is often recalled. It was from a free-kick, way out on the left and not more than ten yards from the bye-line. No one knew about 'banana' kicks in those days—that is, except Alan Morton. He stepped up and hammered the ball across goal with the inside of his right foot. The keeper, Jimmy Brownlie, relaxed as the ball appeared to be passing the far post, when it suddenly swerved past his incredulous stare into the top corner of the net. Who said the Brazilians invented the banana kick?

Garrincha

'Little Bird'

England's Ramon Wilson (right) attempts to get to grips with Garrincha in the 1962 World Cup quarter-finals. But the 'Little Bird' was virtually unstoppable, and Brazil won 3-1.

The outstanding winger of two World Cups, Garrincha used his spectacular speed to get to the bye-line. From there he would arrow his lethal crosses into the path of Vava or Pelé, as he demonstrated so brilliantly in the 1958 World Cup. And he could score goals, too, as he proceeded to show with four in the 1962 tournament in Chile, with his head as well as his feet.

The extraordinary thing about Garrincha is that he was born a cripple. An operation left him with a distorted left leg and a bow-legged appearance. Overcoming his disability, he developed into a graceful athlete, with perfect ball control in full flight and a devilish 'banana' shot.

His nickname 'Garrincha', by which he was known throughout the world, came from his early pastime of hunting little birds—*garrinchinhas.* His real name was Manoel Francisco dos Santos. He joined the Rio club Botafogo in 1953 and won his first cap for Brazil in 1957. Perhaps because of his brilliant individuality he did not win a regular place, and his fellow players lobbyed for his return to the side in the 1958 World Cup finals after he had been omitted from the first two matches. So he played against Russia, and proceeded to set the World Cup alight, displaying all his wizardry in the remaining games and tying the Swedish defence in knots in the final.

In the 1962 World Cup, he took over when injury forced Pelé out of the tournament, ranging the field and hammering in shots from all angles. He, more than anyone, clinched a second winners medal for Brazil, and his four goals made him joint leading scorer. His performance against England in the quarter-finals was particularly outstanding. He headed the first goal despite the attentions of the much taller Maurice Norman, England's centre-half, made the second for Vava with a free-kick that Springett couldn't hold, and then scored with an extraordinary 'bender' from nearly 30 yards.

Injury in 1963 and domestic problems sadly curtailed Garrincha's career, and he was not the same man when he played in the 1966 World Cup in England. But with a goal from a swerving free-kick against Bulgaria, he brought back memories of the time when he was the best player in the world.

Francisco Gento

'Paco'

Known to the crowds as 'Paco', Francisco Gento was the flying left-winger of the all-conquering Real Madrid side of the 1950s. Playing among such stars as Argentina's Alfredo di Stefano, Hungary's Ferenc Puskas, and France's Raymond Kopa, he was nevertheless the crowd's favourite.

He played in all five of Real's triumphant European Cup campaigns from 1956 to 1960 and was there again in 1966 to win a record sixth European Cup medal. His overall record in the competition is remarkable. Real competed in the first 15 years of the European Cup and Gento was their left-winger throughout this period. In some ninety ties, he scored 31 goals. He built up a seemingly telepathic understanding with the great Di Stefano, whose passes he would take in his stride. What a stride he had! He was the fastest winger of his day, and with his electric acceleration could give opponents yards start and still fly past them.

In the first European Cup final, in 1956, it was Gento, put away on the left by Di Stefano, who found Rial unmarked for an easy score to win the match 4-3 against Reims. The following year against Fiorentina, Gento chipped over the keeper 15 minutes from the end to give Real a 2-0 victory. And in the 1958 final against Milan, with the score 2-2 and with players around him flagging in extra time, he first dribbled past three opponents only to

hit a post, and then cut along the bye-line to score the winner from the narrowest of angles 12 minutes from time.

Gento continued to dazzle defences over the years with his speed and made countless goals for others. When Di Stefano left in 1964, he took over the captaincy of Real. He also captained Spain, winning 44 caps and scoring 6 goals.

Real had signed Gento for £7,000 from Santander when he was 20. It was a cloak-and-dagger transfer, for they whisked him off to a disused garage for talks after watching him play, obtained his signature in Madrid four days later, and played him in the first team three days after that. He was a fine sportsman and popular wherever he played, but in Madrid he was the idol, worshipped even above the likes of Di Stefano and Puskas. A short, swarthy man, he won the hearts of the fans with his delightful personality, his mazy runs, uncatchable bursts of speed on the wing, and his precision crosses.

In his 18 years with Real, Gento won a long and impressive list of honours. Apart from his six European Cup medals, he won two runners-up medals and played in the side that won the first World Club Championship, against Penarol of Uruguay in 1960. He won 10 Spanish·League Championship medals.

The 1970-71 season was Gento's last, and it was the first time that Real were not competing in the European Cup. Nevertheless, they reached the final of the Cup-Winners Cup and Gento played in the drawn first game against Chelsea, although he was substituted. He came on himself as substitute for the last 15 minutes of the replay, to wear the white strip of his beloved Real for the very last time. It was not a story-book ending, for Real failed to get the equalizer they were striving for. It marked the end of an era in more ways than one, for it was the first time in 20 years that they had failed to win a major trophy. But it was fitting that Gento should make his farewell playing 'in Europe'.

Real Madrid's flying left-winger Gento leaves his marker stranded.

Billy Liddell

The Flying Scot of 'Liddellpool'

In the immediate post-war years, Liverpool had a Scottish left-winger, Billy Liddell, to compare with England's Matthews and Finney. In style, there could not have been a greater contrast. With Liddell, there was not the finesse of Finney or the teasing runs of Matthews. Liddell would tear through defences with strength, speed, and marvellous acceleration, hurdling and side-stepping tackles as he made straight for goal to unleash his right-foot thunderbolts or for the bye-line to hit his low driven crosses or float pinpoint centres onto the head of Balmer or Stubbins. But like his English counterparts, Liddell was known up and down the land for his sportsmanship and fair play. He played it hard, but there was never any animosity between Liddell and the opposing defenders, and in his whole career he had his name taken only once.

Liddell was born in Townhill, near Dunfermline, in 1922, son of a coalminer and the eldest of six children. He won his first representative honours for Scotland as a schoolboy, and Liverpool signed him from Lochgelly Violet, on a tip from their right-half Matt Busby, as a 16-year-old. He signed as a professional in 1939, and made his debut in wartime football. In only his second match, he scored a hat-trick against Manchester City—with Frank Swift in goal. He joined the RAF, and first played for Scotland in a 1942 wartime international.

Liddell was 24 when League football resumed after the war, and he starred in the side that won the first post-war Championship. Over the next few years, Liverpool declined, although they did reach the 1950 Cup final. Liddell was the one bright spot, fearlessly taking on defences on his own, holding the side together—to such an extent that the club was often referred to as 'Liddellpool'. 'Give it to Billy'

Billy Liddell, the one bright star of Liverpool's troubled days in the early 1950s, was a dangerous goalscoring winger.

was the familiar cry in those troubled times, for whatever the state of the game, there was always the chance of a goal when Liddell got the ball. He put the fear of the devil into opposing defenders. But even Liddell could not stave off relegation in 1954—Liverpool's defence was so shaky that they switched him to full-back! In eight seasons in Division I, Liddell had scored 97 goals in 300 games and four times led the Liverpool scorers—not bad going for a winger.

Division II saw another switch for Liddell, this time to centre-forward. By then in his thirties, Liddell proceeded to take those suspect defences apart—30 goals the first season, 27 the next—he was their leading scorer for another four seasons. But Liverpool's defence still let them down, and they would finish third or fourth in the table every time. When Liddell retired in 1960, he had taken his goal tally to 216 in what was then a record 492 League games. In the 12

seasons to 1957-58, he played in all 40 of their Cup-ties, scoring 12 goals. He lost his place in 1958, but when they were ignominiously knocked out of the Cup by non-League club Worcester City in 1959, he was restored to the team and at 37 scored 14 goals in their remaining 19 matches.

Liddell won 28 full Scottish caps, scoring 6 goals, and played in both of Great Britain's matches against the Rest of Europe, in 1947 and 1955—Stanley Matthews was the only other player to do so.

Throughout his career, Liddell had been a part-time player, having qualified in accountancy after leaving school. He had also latterly been a magistrate, did a great deal of youth and social work, and wrote a newspaper column. He became a bursar at Liverpool University.

THE HARD MEN

To many, the hard men of soccer are cast in the role of villains. Often lacking in the finer arts of the game themselves, they are the 'destroyers', the men whose job it is to subdue the skills of others, to win the ball for their own ball-players. And so it should be. Would the artistry of such as Pelé or Cruyff have been appreciated as much if all they had to contend with was powder-puff tackling?

Hard men are an intrinsic part of the game—so long as they keep within the laws. Normally, the hard man of a team is employed in midfield, as a so-called 'anchorman'. Also known as a 'spoiler' or 'marker', he is often delegated to stick to the most dangerous opponent and to provide cover and support for his own more creative team-mates in midfield.

Hard men are usually players' players, winning the gratitude and praise of their colleagues and the respect of their opponents. Men such as Wilf Copping, Nobby Stiles, and Norman Hunter played invaluable parts in the success of their teams, and Dave Mackay was really special because he combined fine footballing skills with his toughness and courage.

Sadly, however, some sides feel the need to pack their defence with hard men, spoilers bent on intimidation, who play the man rather than the ball. And they are being allowed to get away with it. Some of Italy's exhibitions, for example, in the 1980 European Championships were quite disgraceful—yet they were accepted with scarcely a complaint. It is up to the law-making bodies to ensure that this sort of behaviour is stamped out and that soccer does not become a game where hooligans are allowed to flourish.

Some of soccer's tough guys:
Top left: Norman Hunter of Leeds. Top right: Nobby Stiles, England's little terror of the mid-sixties. Centre: Arsenal's Peter Storey. Bottom: Dave Mackay of Spurs having to be restrained by an opponent.

95

Arsenal's Destroyers
Copping & Storey

Wilf Copping

Wilf Copping of Leeds United, Arsenal, and England was the archetypal hard man of football. Rugged, craggy, blue-chinned—he made a point of never shaving before a match—he must have presented a fearsome sight to opposing inside-forwards.

His motto was 'First man int' tackle never gets hurt', and he was in his element when the fur was really flying. He might have been lacking in the finer arts of the game, but he had the heart of a lion and never knew when he was beaten. Tommy Lawton, who had his nose broken twice in one season in clashes with Copping, nevertheless described him as 'one of the cleanest, though toughest, players I have met', and this is borne out by the fact that Copping was never sent off nor cautioned in his whole career.

A Yorkshireman, born in Barnsley, Copping spent four years with Leeds before moving to Arsenal in 1934 for £8,000. Arsenal's

manager Herbert Chapman had seen him in Rome the previous year rolling up his England sleeves and getting stuck in against Italy. 'That's the chap for me,' said Chapman, and he didn't rest until he brought the aggressive wing-half to Highbury. It was against Italy in 1934, in the notorious 'Battle of Highbury', that Copping played the game for which he is always remembered. England held out for a 3-2 victory, and as his club-mate right-back George Male said, 'he was practically playing them on his own at the finish'.

Peter Storey

Not even the most partisan of Arsenal fans would place Peter Storey very high in a soccer 'hall of fame'. When it came to the skills of the game, Storey was not over-endowed. Yet Alf Ramsey saw qualities enough to reward him with 19 England caps, and his club chairman went on record as saying that Storey was his kind of player —'player', not 'footballer', mark you.

And this was the key to Storey's success—for it must be deemed successful for a player of limited abilities to represent his country and play a leading part in his club's League and Cup 'double' triumph. For Storey was a great competitor. He made up with determination, concentration, and sheer grit what he lacked in skill and technique. On the debit side, he tended to carry this too far—attempting to 'pinch' yards at throw-ins, failing to retreat at free-kicks, and using all the sly ruses at his command to gain an often unfair advantage—certainly not the sort of example for young footballers to follow. But he never flinched from a tackle, and contrary to certain widely held opinions he was not a dirty player: crude, perhaps, but not for him the sly foul. Most of his transgressions were due to clumsiness.

It was once said of Storey that he never knew what to do with the ball when it came to him without an opponent on the other end of it. His passing ability was not a strong point. He was a great ball-winner, but if he couldn't lay the ball off immediately he found it difficult to be constructive. Similarly, his running off the ball was superb, but then he would often create goal-scoring chances for himself and almost as often fluff them.

Storey had made some 200 appearances for Arsenal at right-back when, at the start of the eventful 1970-71 season, he was pushed into midfield owing to injuries. And although his England debut later that season was at right-back, he played most of his internationals as the midfield ball-winner. His initial selection for England brought much criticism down on Ramsey, for it was regarded as a negative move. As most of those who played alongside him would confirm, however, he was a wonderful man to have on your side, always helping out and covering, always there when the going got rough.

He was to score some vital goals for Arsenal, none more so than the two he got in the Cup semi-final against Stoke in 1971. With Arsenal two down, he produced the finest shot of his career to volley home from the edge of the box. It was left to him, the coolest man on the ground, to take the last-minute penalty-kick and score the equalizer against Gordon Banks.

Hero or villain? Men like Storey will always be controversial. But not everyone can be a Pelé or a Best. Peter Storey proved that there is always a place in football for a stout heart. And as he showed in that dramatic semi-final, 'every dog has his day'.

Right: The rugged Wilf Copping. Left: The ref keeps a watchful eye on the spreadeagled Storey.

Dave Mackay

The greatest heart in football

A hard man and not one to stand any nonsense, the square-jawed Mackay threatens Billy Bremner as the referee races in to make peace.

Dave Mackay was a hard man all right. He tackled like a tank and invariably came away with the ball. He covered every blade of grass on the field, and never gave up trying. His will to win was matched only by his hatred of defeat. But there was more, very much more, than just sheer aggression to Mackay. There was dedication and determination, the courage to return, after breaking his leg twice—the second time, in his comeback match—to even greater deeds. There was ability in abundance—fine ball control, creative first-time passing, exceptional positioning and anticipation, and a ferocious shot. And there was his ability to inspire others around him, to get his colleagues playing.

Mackay had four distinct careers. With Hearts in the fifties, he won every Scottish honour; then he was the man that made the Spurs 'double' side tick; in the late sixties, after his remarkable comeback, he dragged a faltering Spurs side to Wembley for their third Cup victory of the decade; and finally, as advancing age threatened his midfield dynamo role, he converted to the back four and led a struggling Derby side to the First Division. Mackay also won 22 Scottish caps, over a period of eight years from 1957 to 1965.

Born near Edinburgh in 1934, Mackay set his heart on a football career early on in life. He played for Scotland Schools, and in junior football for Newtongrange Star, before signing for Hearts. He soon forced his way into the first team as a robust attacking left-half, and was the 'engine room' of the side that gave the club its greatest era, challenging the supremacy of Celtic and Rangers. He won League Cup medals in 1955 and 1959, a Cup medal in 1956, and above all a Championship medal in 1957-58. What a season that was, as Hearts surpassed anything even the Glasgow giants had ever achieved, scoring a record 132 goals in only 34 matches. With Mackay providing the midfield power, Wardhaugh and Bauld up front had countless field days, and Hearts finished 13 points ahead of Rangers, having lost only one League match all season.

In 1959, Spurs manager Bill Nicholson persuaded Hearts to part with Mackay for £30,000, then a record fee for a half-back. With Danny Blanchflower and his fellow Scot John White, who arrived shortly afterwards, Mackay made up the perfect half-back line. His physical 'presence' blended marvellously with their skills and finesse, as Spurs went from triumph to triumph—the 'double' in 1961, the Cup again in 1962, and the European Cup-Winners Cup in 1963. Mackay missed the latter final through injury, and later that year broke his left leg in a European tie at Old Trafford.

He was already a legend as the owner of 'the greatest heart in football', and his comeback served only to underline this. It was nine months before he fought his way back to fitness—nine months of gritty endeavour. Then, in his very first match, a try-out at White Hart Lane with the reserves, he broke the same leg again. Nearly 30, he was written off even by some of

In September 1964, nine months after breaking his leg, Mackay breaks it again in his come-back match. . .

Norman Hunter

'Clog and smile'

those with first-hand knowledge of his vast store of courage. And it is probably one of the most heroic tales in football that Mackay not only played again, as fearless and buoyant as ever, but led Spurs to Cup victory in 1967.

He played one more season for Spurs, before a series of minor injuries that restricted his appearances persuaded the club that they could do without him. Brian Clough was on their doorstep in a flash, and Spurs generously let him go to Derby for a small fee so that he could negotiate a lucrative contract.

Whatever Derby paid him, he was worth it. As a second stopper, he revitalized them, leading from the back, firing them with his own

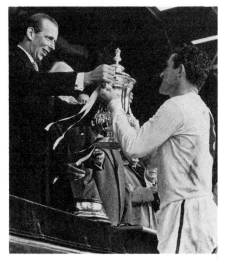

. . . but you can't keep a good man down, and here he is at Wembley after leading Spurs to Cup victory.

unrivalled competitive spirit. They topped the Division II table his very first season, and Mackay, somewhat belatedly, was voted Footballer of the Year (jointly). And in Division I, he laid the foundations of the side that would win the Championship in 1972, the year after he left. By then, he was player-manager of Swindon, and in 1972 he took over as manager of Nottingham Forest before returning to Derby as manager in 1973. Despite guiding them to the Championship in 1975, he was sacked in 1977, and later managed Walsall for a spell. Knowing of Mackay's determination and resilience, however, it would be premature to write him off.

While it was not perhaps the most felicitous of slogans for a footballer to inspire, 'Norman Bites Yer Leg' was a measure of the esteem—even affection—the Leeds fans had for Norman Hunter. Not that Hunter, who shared the central defensive duties with Jackie Charlton in the side that threatened to dominate English football in the late 1960s and early 1970s, would ever dream of perpetrating such ungentlemanly conduct—well, not deliberately, that is.

It is fair to say that Hunter was typical of Don Revie's uncompromising Leeds side—hard, determined, disciplined, but also extremely skilful. He was known primarily, of course, for his tackling, but his distribution and control were more than adequate and he would beat a man neatly to make more space for himself. He always seemed to use his educated left foot, but there was nothing wrong with his right, as he demonstrated with the two goals he scored for England, both tremendous right-foot drives.

Hunter, who was born in Northumberland in 1943, grew up in Yorkshire, and was an attacking wing-half before Leeds put him in the back four. He made his League debut in 1962, and in just over 14 seasons played 543 League games for them, making an essential contribution to their domestic and European successes over this period.

Alf Ramsey found a use for him in the England side as early as December 1965, when he came on as a substitute in Madrid against Spain. But his appearances were limited because of the consistency of Bobby Moore, and he eventually found himself filling a midfield role, as anchorman, and won a total of 28 caps.

Always a controversial character, Hunter tended to adopt an innocent, conciliatory attitude when referees came down on him for an obvious foul—his 'clog and smile routine' as one correspondent so aptly put it.

Leeds transferred him to Bristol City for £40,000 in 1976. Three years later, at 36, he went to Barnsley as player coach, taking over as manager in 1980.

Norman Hunter bows his head in contrite apology. The referee returns the smile, but it won't stop Hunter's name going in the book.

Nobby Stiles

The toy bulldog

A controversial hero of England's World Cup success in 1966, Nobby Stiles was regarded as a ruthless destroyer in some quarters, and there was much pressure on Alf Ramsey to drop him half-way through the tournament. But Ramsey stood firm. Stiles repaid him by snuffing out Eusebio in the semi-finals without a hint of any rough stuff, and he played a major part in the final, too. The sight of this tiny 'toothless terror', socks down to his ankles, skipping gleefully around the Wembley pitch after England's victory is one of the indelible memories of the 1966 World Cup.

That Norbert Stiles, known affectionately in Manchester as the 'Toy Bulldog', should terrify six-foot strikers was one of the biggest ironies in the game. Short-sighted —he wore contact lenses to play— balding, with a 'gappy' grin, he stood only 5ft 6in (1.68m). But he was a terrific little battler with a tigerish tackle, and he did a wonderful job for England. He was the first of the out-and-out ball-winners, sweeping up in front of his back four, a role demanding boundless energy and determination and the tactical ability to read the play.

Stiles's determination has never been in question, and the story of his rise from myopic weakling to World Cup hero is straight out of the pages of schoolboy fiction, and an inspiration to any youngster who feels he hasn't the physique to become a star. As a boy, he had been knocked down by a bus and almost killed. There was a chance that he would lose his sight, but in the event it was just 'permanently impaired'. To make up for his deficiences, he threw himself into sport with an unquenchable spirit, a burning desire to prove himself as good as the others.

It was his will to succeed and non-stop aggression on the field that attracted Manchester United to him, and he joined them in 1957 as a 15-year-old groundstaff boy. A less likely candidate for United and England stardom it would be difficult to imagine, for he could not have been more than 5ft (1.52m) tall and 6 stone (38kg) in weight. Yet within three years he had made his first-team debut. He played wing-half or inside-forward, and initially was in and out of the first team, missing the 1963 Cup final.

But in the 1964-65 season, he

'David and Goliath' . . . little Nobby tackles big Joe Royle.

A proud World Cup winner.

won a regular place as a defensive wing-half and a Championship medal at the end of it, together with his first four caps. He played the same role for both United and England, winning the ball and then usually finding Bobby Charlton with it. Stiles went from strength to strength—after the World Cup there was another League title, and then in 1968 United's historic European Cup victory.

Stiles won 28 England caps altogether. It was a tackle on a Frenchman that caused such a furore in 1966, even though the referee did not consider it a bookable offence. A FIFA judge at the match, however, decided it warrented a public 'FIFA caution'. The 'Stiles must go' brigade had a field day, but Ramsey simply said: 'If Stiles doesn't play, then England don't play.' And that was the end of the matter. Stiles might have had his critics, but he was never a dirty player; he never committed a vicious foul.

He went to Middlesbrough in 1971 for a couple of seasons, and then joined Preston, mixing coaching and playing until he hung up his boots in 1975. He continued as coach, and was appointed manager in 1977, achieving promotion to Division II in his first season.

THE HISTORY MAKERS

'Policeman' Herbie Roberts (left)

Herbert Chapman—third-back game

Beckenbauer—attacking sweeper

Sir Alf Ramsey—'wingless wonders'

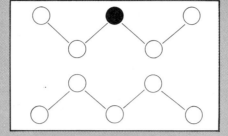
The W-M formation

Football is a continually changing game. New ideas and strategies are tried, and other tactics are devised to combat them. And every now and then a player, perhaps, or a manager will come up with a revolutionary piece of thinking that completely changes the face of football.

The offside game perfected by full-back Bill McCracken in the 1920s forced a change in the law, which in turn led to the development of the third-back game. The deep-lying centre-forward tactic employed by the Hungarians of the 1950s played havoc with the inflexible system of marking common in British football at that time, and England's massive defeats resulted in a complete rethink of tactics and of training methods. The dearth of top-class wingers in England in the mid-1960s led to 4-4-3, then 4-4-2, and almost to the demise of wingers altogether.

Catenaccio, sweepers, total football—all are terms associated with tactical innovations. Coaches are constantly searching for something new, some magic formula to bring success. Let us hope that the next history-makers do something to restore to the game some of the artistry and thrills that have been missing in recent years.

Geoff Hurst—target man.

Bill McCracken—'offside game'

Don Revie—'Revie plan'

Bugs Bunny—US razzamatazz

101

The Third-Back Game

W-M and the stopper centre-half

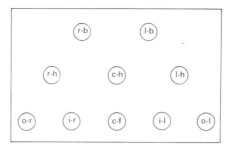

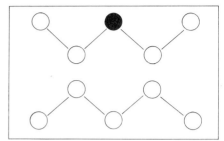

The most dramatic change in football tactics this century took place as a result of a change in the offside law in 1925. Before then the law required *three* men to be between the goal line and the ball receiver. Full-backs had begun to exploit this law before World War I by moving up to put the opposing attackers offside. Newcastle's Irish international right-back Bill McCracken perfected the ploy (which had its origins at Notts County), and others followed suit. After the war, legislators became increasingly disturbed that the continual whistling for offside was spoiling the game as a spectacle and reducing the number of goals scored. So the law was altered, rightly or wrongly, to require only *two* men between goal line and attacker.

The immediate result of the change was an upsurge in goalscoring: the top sides began logging up totals in the 90s and even the 100s over the 42-match season, rather than in the 60s and 70s as before. In the 1926-27 season, Camsell hit 59 goals for Second Division Middlesbrough, and the following term Dean recorded his famous 60 for champions Everton.

To counteract such dangerous thrusts down the middle, the 'stopper centre-half' or 'third back', as it is more properly called, was introduced. The centre-half had hitherto enjoyed a roving role in front of his two backs, but now his job was to police the middle. This changed the whole pattern of the game.

The 'third-back game', as it came to be called, was developed by that great innovator Herbert Chapman, manager of Arsenal. The idea was first suggested by inside-forward Charles Buchan after a 7-0 thrashing at the hands of Newcastle in October 1925, although Newcastle themselves were probably playing a version of the game at the time with Charles Spencer in the 'policeman' role. Chapman, however, was

always several moves ahead of the field, and he set about developing this tactic into a complete strategical plan. And what was more important, he set about finding the players who could fill the new roles that were required.

He groomed a raw youngster, Herbie Roberts, into the perfect stopper. He acquired two flying wingers, Joe Hulme on the right and Cliff 'Boy' Bastin on the left, and a 'battering ram' centreforward in Jack Lambert to provide the three-pronged attack. He used his backs rather than his winghalves to mark the opposing wingers, and brought his wing-halves in to take care of the opposing insideforwards. He pulled his own insideforwards back behind the three 'strikers', as they would now be called, one just behind the forwards, to score goals, the other just in front of the defence, to act as linkman. For the former role he bought David Jack, for the latter Alex James—and this was his trump card. He converted James—a goal-getter at Preston and at first reluctant to change his style—into the greatest schemer the game has ever known.

Arsenal's switch and—because of their unprecedented success—its resultant popularity exposed perhaps for the first time the basic problem of soccer tactics. For tac-

tics work only when the talents necessary to put them into action are available. In a way, it's the talents that come first. Too many imitators followed Arsenal's style blindly, without regard to the players on their books and the skills they possessed. Stopper centrehalves were not difficult to manufacture, but fast goalscoring wingers didn't grow on trees and there wasn't another player in the land who could convert defence into attack with the speed and cunning of the mercurial James. As a result, with most imitators it was the 'safety first' element of the system that predominated, and the emphasis in the British game was placed increasingly on defence.

What evolved from Chapman was the breakdown of the theory that teams could be divided into two types of players, attackers who attack and defenders who defend. Arsenal had wing-halves and inside-forwards who did both. It was called the W-M system, because the line-up took the shape of these letters, one above the other. It marked the end of the 2-3-5 formation, and was the forerunner of the modern systems. But they were a long time coming, perhaps because Chapman died in 1934 at the height of Arsenal's successes, and he had no need for further changes.

Arsenal manager Herbert Chapman (right) developed the third-back game in the late 1920s. For some 40 years teams had lined up with two backs and three half-backs (above left). Chapman groomed Herbie Roberts as a 'stopper', or third back, and created the W-M formation (above right), with three full-backs.

Four-Two-Four

The deep-lying centre-forward

Above: Hungary's deep-lying centre-forward Nandor Hidegkuti scores in the 1954 World Cup. The 'Revie plan', with Don Revie (right) in the key role, was Manchester City's later version of the tactic . . .

The introduction of the 4-2-4 formation is often attributed to the dazzling Brazilian side who used it so spectacularly when winning the 1958 World Cup. But it was being played just as brilliantly and successfully by the Hungarians in the early 1950s, before the 'numbers game' was introduced into soccer tactics.

Until the 1950s, the British had regarded themselves as the masters of soccer, invincible at home. The third-back game had stood the test of over 20 years, and there was no thought of changing the tactical system. Even England's setback in the 1950 World Cup was ignored. But in 1953, the Hungarians came to Wembley and won 6-3—the first foreign side to defeat the English on their own soil.

There were a number of reasons for this famous victory. Their superior teamwork, ball skills, and fitness were enough in themselves, but they also exposed England's basic tactical shortcomings. Their centre-forward, Nandor Hidegkuti, played behind his two inside-forwards as a midfield forager. So there were twin spearheads, reversing the traditional 'W' formation to

produce, with the wingers also not as advanced, an 'M' attacking line-up. Poor Harry Johnston, the England centre-half and no mean strategist himself, didn't know what to make of it. The opposing No. 9 (Hidegkuti) was playing in midfield and he had no one to mark. Johnston's colleagues, who included Alf Ramsey and Billy Wright, were just as nonplussed. The Hungarian forwards tore their defence apart, and they did it again the following year in Budapest,

with a crushing 7-1 victory.

The first British side to adopt these tactics were Manchester City in the mid-1950s. Known as the 'Revie plan', it was nevertheless a carbon copy of the Hungarian prototype, with Don Revie the creative deep-lying centre-forward operating in midfield with right-half Ken Barnes. It was incredible that they got away with this ruse for so long. But so narrow was the tactical thinking in those days that the No. 9 on Revie's back confused opposing centre-halves, who followed him so deep that they left an enormous hole in their defence for the inside-forwards to exploit.

Another tactic to expose the W-M system of the third-back game was the wing-to-wing passing of Wolves wingers Hancocks and Mullen. The 'pendulum' system operated by the three at the back could not cope,

and it became obvious that another central defender was required.

It was soon after the 1958 World Cup that British clubs began experimenting with what soon became known as the 4-2-4 system. Yet it did not last long. For the Brazilians themselves, who had adopted it before 1958, were already making changes. In the World Cup, 4-2-4 had served them well, with key men Didi and Zito working the midfield. But in the final, Sweden put them under so much pressure in the opening stages that the midfield pair were unable to set up attacks. So left-winger Zagalo withdrew into midfield, and for a period they were playing 4-3-3. It was this formation they used to retain the World Cup in 1962.

The trouble with 4-2-4 was that it left the midfield weak. Few teams had the players to operate it successfully. And it also restricted

. . . yet Tommy Lawton (centre, striped shirt) was playing a similar role for Second Division Brentford in the early 1950s.

players to defined roles in specific areas of the pitch. So 4-3-3 became the norm, as the battle for the midfield stepped up. Employed by ordinary players, however, it tended to make the game less attractive. But it was not nearly as negative as the system that had been developing in Italy—'catenaccio', with its defensive 'sweeper'.

The Sweeper

The 'sweeper' emerged as the central figure of the 'catenaccio' defensive system, which originated in the 1950s and was developed by the Italians into a suffocating blanket of negativity. The Italians, however, did not invent the sweeper, the player who covers behind the back men and 'sweeps up' anything that gets past them.

The first system to use four last-line defenders was the Swiss 'verrou', a feature of which was the 'bolt' defence. The 'bolt' was a centre-back who covered the three defenders in front of him. In other words, he was the first sweeper. It was an Austrian international, Karl Rappan, who introduced this system, as a coach in Switzerland in the 1930s. He worked miracles with the Swiss national side, steering this amateur and undistinguished footballing nation to the finals of four World Cups.

The verrou system had many variations. And it required great versatility on the part of certain players, especially the centre-half, who would assume an attacking role when his side had possession, with the centre-back (the sweeper) covering for him. As a result, it was never widely accepted.

The direct predecessor of catenaccio was probably the sweeper system developed by some South American countries in the early 1950s. Uruguay used it in the 1954 World Cup, with Santamaria (later of Real Madrid fame) excelling in the sweeper role. It was certainly not a negative formation, as Uruguay's results demonstrate— 2-0, 7-0, and 4-2 wins over Czechoslovakia, Scotland, and England, respectively, before going down 4-2 after extra time to the great Hungarians in the semi-finals.

The diagrams (right) show the sweeper in various formations. The West Germans developed the creative sweeper, using highly skilled players in the role, from Franz Beckenbauer to Bernd Schuster (top).

Catenaccio

In the 1950s, the big Italian clubs imported a great deal of foreign talent, including goalscoring stars such as Gunnar Nordahl of Sweden, John Charles of Wales, and Jose Altafini of Brazil. As a result, some of the weaker clubs found themselves being hammered by huge scores, and began to pack their defences, double-marking the opposing forwards and using seven

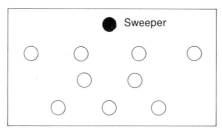

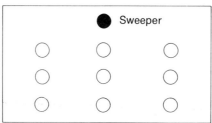

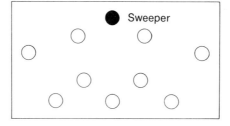

or even eight men permanently in defence. The system became known as 'catenaccio', Italian for 'bolt' or 'padlock'.

There are several variations, from 1-3-3-3 and 1-4-2-3 (the '1' at the back being the sweeper, or 'libero') to the extreme 4-4-2, where in this case the second '4' are the marking defenders, the first '4' all providing cover! In the 1960s, catenaccio achieved a large measure of success for Italian clubs. The chief disciples were Nereo Rocco, who guided AC Milan to European Cup success in 1963, and Helenio Herrera, who did the same for Inter Milan in 1964 and 1965.

Creative Sweeper

The Italians have continued to use the sweeper in a negative role in club football, but the Germans, who began to use man-for-man marking in the early 1960s, produced a more creative sweeper, culminating in the positive, attacking role played by Franz Beckenbauer in the 1970s. The sweeper breaking past his defence with or without the ball became a familiar sight on the Continent, with others emulating Beckenbauer, such as the West German Stielike and Holland's Krol.

It was sometimes thought that England used a sweeper in the late 1960s, in Moore and then Hunter. But their function was to cover the central defender, guarding space to his left, with no rigid marking duties.

The latest trend is to employ a sweeper behind two marking central defenders, with the two backs zonal-marking on the flanks—as used by West Germany in the 1980 European Championships. This combines the Continental 'man-for-man with sweeper' defence with the British zonal defence, and if the sweeper is going to appear on the British scene in any great numbers, it will probably be in this form.

Wingless Wonders

An endangered species

Blame for the virtual disappearance of wingers in England from the late 1960s is often laid at Sir Alf Ramsey's door. After all, he won the World Cup for England in 1966 without a wingman in sight, and the clubs all began to copy his successful 'formula', whether it was 4-3-3 or 4-4-2.

Ramsey appreciated the need to strengthen the midfield, as the Brazilians had done by using Zagalo as a 'withdrawn winger', thus converting their successful 4-2-4 formation into an equally successful 4-3-3. Ramsey's problem was finding a winger who could satisfactorily fulfil this role.

It is fascinating to look at the England line-ups just prior to their 1966 success. In the six matches before the World Cup, Ramsey used various wingers—Connelly, Paine, Tambling, and Callaghan—sometimes one, but twice he used two in the same team. In the last of these matches, he used Alan Ball in the withdrawn winger role, but

Ball, of course, was a recognized midfield man. Even in the three World Cup group matches, Ramsey was still trying to find room for a winger—he used a different one in each game! Then, in the quarter-final, he reverted to the wingless formation, and retained it for the semi-final and final.

What Ramsey did was to make the best use of the players available. He cannot be faulted for that, and coaches at all levels would be well advised to copy—you adapt your tactics to suit your players, not the other way around.

Ramsey's team thrived on hard work—the term 'work-rate' was later very much overused, to the detriment of skill—and they all worked for each other. The midfield partnership of Stiles and Bobby Charlton was a tremendous success. Stiles was virtually a sweeper in front of his back four, winning the ball and giving it to Charlton. Charlton was the perfect deep-lying centre-forward, spraying

long passes about the field or taking the ball through for one of his thunderbolt shots. Of the other midfield players, Peters was appearing in front of goal from nowhere and Ball was making wide runs and covering an enormous amount of ground. The full-backs Cohen and Wilson were making use of the spaces on the flanks with overlapping runs. And the two big strikers were taking through-balls and laying them off as support arrived. Hurst was the first of the 'target men', whose function was primarily to do that.

It was unfortunate that teams up and down the country copied Ramsey's Wingless Wonders. It was too easy to make work-rate and superior fitness the goal, and to fill the midfield with 'spoilers' who did not have the necessary skills to operate creatively in a confined space. As a result, the game became dull and negative—and the true winger could well be classified as an 'endangered species'.

THE VANISHING WINGERS

April 2, v Scotland

Ball Stiles Charlton
Hunt Hurst **Connolly**

June 29, v Norway

Stiles Charlton
Paine Greaves Hunt **Connelly**

July 11, v Uruguay (WC)

Ball Charlton Stiles
Greaves Hunt **Connelly**

May 4, v Yugoslavia

Charlton Peters
Paine Greaves Hurst **Tambling**

July 3, v Denmark

Ball Eastham Stiles
Greaves Hurst **Connelly**

July 16, v Mexico (WC)

Stiles Charlton Peters
Paine Greaves Hunt

June 26, v Finland

Ball Charlton Peters
Callaghan Hunt Hurst

July 5, v Poland

Ball Stiles Charlton Peters
Hunt Greaves

July 20, v France (WC)

Stiles Charlton Peters
Callaghan Greaves Hunt

Line-up for last three matches, July 23, 26, 30,
v Argentina, Portugal, and West Germany, respectively

Banks
Cohen Charlton J Moore Wilson
Stiles
Ball Charlton B Peters
Hurst Hunt

The above nine line-ups show the formations (excluding the back four and the keeper) Ramsey tried in the six matches immediately prior to the 1966 World Cup and the formations he used for the three group matches. Recognized wingers are indicated in heavy type.

Alan Ball (right) made use of the space on the right wing with runs from midfield.

American Experiments

The razzamatazz of American soccer

Cheerleaders and scoreboard acclaim the entry of the 'gladiators', who run the gauntlet one by one.

There were several attempts to establish soccer in the North American continent before the 1970s. All fizzled out because of the deeply ingrained American allegiance to their own particular code of football, which is more like rugby than soccer. Then, in the mid-1970s, the great Pelé was lured out of retirement to spearhead a massive onslaught on the sporting tastes of the American public, and suddenly soccer began to flourish.

The North American Soccer League (NASL), an amalgamation of two previous competitions, was founded in 1968. It stumbled along from year to year, like its predecessors, introducing all manner of gimmicks. But the charisma of one man did more for American soccer than all the shoot-outs and cheerleaders, the flashing scoreboards and rule changes. Pelé arrived in New York in 1975 and captured the hearts of the nation. The New York Cosmos, with Pelé, began to attract huge crowds—fifty, sixty, even seventy thousand. Most important of all, soccer began to flourish at the grass roots. Youngsters were being attracted to the game, and they had their heroes to identify with—Pelé, Chinaglia, Beckenbauer, Cruyff, Rodney Marsh, Gerd Müller, Gordon Banks, Best, Ball—the world's finest talents were enlisted to spread the gospel.

At first, teams were made up largely from imported players. But gradually these are being phased out to make way for home-grown talent. When North America can stand on its own two feet, and produce its own stars, then—and only then—can it be said that soccer has come to stay.

The Americans have tried to produce a soccer package that will appeal to a wide family audience—all-seater stadiums (the norm, anyway, in the USA), on-field entertainment before the game and during the interval, after-match interviews with the players, first-class amenities, club facilities for youngsters, and so on. Although much of this is typical American razzamatazz and nothing to do with the game itself, it should make certain old-established footballing countries sit up and think about

In case you missed it, that hurt!

improving the lot of the poor, neglected football fan.

The gimmickry resorted to in an attempt to improve the game, however, is another matter. The chief innovations in American soccer are the 35-yard offside line and the shoot-out, both introduced in 1973. The new lines are drawn 35 yards from each goal-line, and players can be offside only behind those lines. While this has tended to reduce the midfield congestion, it has also created large gaps between the back line and the strikers.

The shoot-out is a tiebreaker, and results from the decision to do away with drawn games. If the scores are tied after 90 minutes, a sudden-death 'overtime' period of $7\frac{1}{2}$ minutes each way is played, the first team to score winning the game. If there is no score in overtime, the shoot-out comes into operation. Basically it is like the penalty tie-breaker used in European competitions, with five players from each team all having attempts—but they don't take penalties. The player taking the attempt starts with the ball on the 35-yard line and has 5 seconds to score, with only the goalkeeper to beat. He may dribble the ball as far as he likes and the keeper may come off his line.

FIFA gave the NASL permission to try these experiments, but until they bring their game into line with the rest of the world the Americans are going to find international competition difficult. On the other hand, the world can learn something from the Americans. Their insistence on producing a positive result from every game might appear naive, but the means they have devised is at least an improvement on the farcical penalty deciders in use elsewhere, as a spectacle and a test of skill.

The shoot-out. A player has 5 seconds to score—usually by shooting past the advancing keeper.

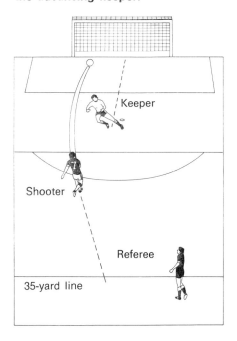

THE LAWS

The laws of association football are organized under 17 headings, each comprising specific laws or groups of laws as well as International Board decisions. The latter are in turn augmented by items of 'advice'—to referees, to players, and in some cases to secretaries.

The International Board (or to give it its full name, the International Football Association Board) is the sole law-making body of the game. It was formed in 1886 and comprised two members from each of the national associations of the four 'home countries', and later augmented to include two representatives of FIFA. Today, each of the five bodies is allowed four delegates, but the British associations have one vote each and FIFA has four. The Board meets annually in June. Laws can be changed only at this meeting of the Board, and then only by agreement of three-quarters of the representatives present and entitled to vote.

Football first became organized in the English public schools in the early 1800s, and most of them possessed written sets of rules by about 1840. Naturally enough, the games varied from school to school, but they were all known as football (until 1863). The various sets of rules were first co-ordinated at Cambridge University in 1848. When the Football Association was founded in 1863, it used the current Cambridge rules as well as earlier versions on which to base its first laws.

There were initially 14 laws (reduced to 12 by 1870), compared with the 17 of today, and although none of the original ones remain unaltered, the basic principles of many of them have been retained.

The chief changes in the laws have been made to counteract practices introduced by players that, while they did not break the letter of the law, were contrary to the spirit of the game. As a result of the various additions and amendments, the laws had become so haphazard by the 1930s that the International Board decided to have them tidied up and redrafted. The new laws were accepted in 1938.

The time is now ripe for another complete overhaul.

Above: The man in the middle.

Referee Jim Finney enlists police help to enforce a sending-off.

Pity the Poor Ref
The Man in the Middle

The laws of any game should serve a number of purposes. They should define the game precisely. They should provide appropriate penalties for unfair play. And they should be regularly adjusted to keep pace with the spirit (or lack of it) in which the game is played.

Unfortunately, the laws of association football do not fulfil any of these criteria. Firstly, they do not define the game adequately. The laws dealing with offside and

The poor referee is like a football being belted to and fro between the players, who abuse the laws, and the administrators, who refuse to change them.

foul play, in particular, are open to too wide a range of interpretation. Secondly, the penalties for foul play often allow the offending side to gain an advantage by breaking the law. And thirdly, there is a marked reluctance on the part of the law-makers to make any alterations at all, even though the game has become so 'professional' that many players and teams regard

sportsmanship as old-fashioned and will stop at nothing in order to win.

The laws were last redrafted some forty years ago by the then Secretary of the Football Association, Sir Stanley Rous. This, indeed, was a giant step forward, and in his various capacities since then (including President of FIFA), Sir Stanley has nurtured and protected the laws as a mother would her baby. Sir Stanley has done so much for football and self-lessly given so many years to the game that it seems churlish to criticize him. But as far as the laws are concerned, he developed a blind spot. Or perhaps he refused to admit that sport is no longer played exclusively by sportsmen, but has been infiltrated by 'sporting mercenaries' whose motto is 'win at all costs'.

To restore the game to the great

108

contest and spectacle it once was, you must first admit that winning does matter. Then you must ensure that the only way to win is to win fairly. The laws as they stand cannot do this.

Some Simple Flaws

Perhaps the best way to demonstrate that the laws are not all they should be is to look at one or two minor adjustments that are crying out to be made, but are never considered.

For example, Law 16 states that if the ball is not kicked out of the penalty-area from a goal-kick the kick must be retaken. The flaw in this is often shown up when the keeper attempts to pass the ball to a team-mate just outside the box. If, say, an opponent anticipates this move and threatens to reach the ball first, all the defender has to do is touch the ball before it travels out of the box. The kick must be retaken, and any danger is averted.

The solution to prevent this little piece of nonsense is to penalize any player who deliberately plays the ball from a goal-kick before it has cleared the penalty-area by awarding the other side an indirect free-kick. This glaring fault in the laws is so easy to remedy that it is in itself an indictment of the school of thought that insists there is nothing wrong with the laws.

Another serious omission is to be found in the law relating to the throw-in. This states that 'part of each foot shall be either on the touch-line or on the ground outside the touch-line'. This can (and indeed *has*) been interpreted to mean that a throw is fair so long as *part* of each foot is on the ground and either on the touch-line or outside it, allowing, presumably, another part of each foot to be over the touch-line. But this is not so. If any part of either foot is over the touch-line when a throw is taken, it is a foul throw. This could be made perfectly clear in the rules by use of a diagram, or simply by the addition of the words 'but not over it' to the passage quoted above.

There surely can be no argument against these slight adjustments, so failure to implement them must be put down to sheer negligence, or just plain inertia, on the part of the law-makers.

The Poor Referee

The referee is 'the man in the middle' in more ways than one. Like a football being kicked to and fro, he finds himself between the administrators of the game and the players. The players (or at least some of them) squeeze every advantage out of the laws that they can, and the law-makers fail to equip the

The behaviour of some players is enough to enrage the mildest of referees.

referee with the necessary 'tools' to do his job satisfactorily. It is the unhappy lot of the poor referee to interpret and administer an ambiguous and antiquated set of rules, contend with a growing army of cheats on the field, and put up with abuse from the fans, the loudest of whom are usually the most ignorant. Who'd be a referee?

What the Referee Needs

The referee needs more scope to ensure that the penalty always fits the crime. For example, a common form of cheating, often euphemistically called 'gamesmanship' in football circles, is for a player taking a throw-in to advance as far as he can along the touch-line from the spot where the ball went out of play—i.e. to 'pinch' as much yardage as he can get away with. Because of the nature of the game

and the diagonal system of control that the officials operate, they cannot always be close enough to prevent this. All the referee can do is make the player retake the throw from the proper spot. If he persists in this subterfuge, the referee might book him. That, really, is his only effective weapon. But, as with many other cases of booking, it is using the proverbial sledge-hammer to crack a walnut. It would be so much easier and fairer if the referee were empowered to award the throw to the other side if a player deliberately took it from the wrong spot. That would soon put a stop to these tricks.

In fact the law does not even have to be changed, for it stipulates that the ball 'shall be thrown in from the point where it crossed the line', and that if the ball 'is improperly thrown in the throw-in shall be taken by a player of the opposing team'. Surely, not taking the throw from the point where it crossed the line constitutes an improper throw. Q.E.D.

Other forms of cheating could be eradicated by empowering the referee to award 'yardage' at free-kicks, to award penalty-kicks for offences committed outside the penalty-area, and to award goals for misdemeanours that prevent a certain score. These are examined on the next page, which looks at free-kicks.

109

Foul play and free-kicks
Fitting the punishment to the crime

There are 10 offences punishable by direct free-kicks (or penalties if the offence takes place in the penalty-area) and about 20 punishable by indirect free-kicks. The latter are not grouped together anywhere in the laws of the game. Several are listed in Law 12 (Fouls and Misconduct), together with the direct free-kick offences. But they are also scattered about the other laws and found under International Board decisions. This is not altogether satisfactory, but it makes for interesting quizzes on the laws!

What is entirely unsatisfactory, however, is that the punishment does not always fit the crime. The booking of a player is no consolation to the other side if by his unfair actions he has robbed them of a goal. Even a sending-off will not necessarily compensate the sinned-against side. There are certain alterations in the rules that would allow justice to be done instantly, curb foul play and cheating, and be beneficial to the game as a whole.

Advantage
Which law explains the so-called 'advantage rule'? No, it's not the law on Fouls and Misconduct, but the law on Referees. The relevant section states that the referee (among other things) shall: 'Refrain from penalizing in cases where he is satisfied that, by doing so, he would be giving an advantage to the offending team. And the 'decisions' include one to the effect that the referee cannot revoke his decision to apply the advantage clause (even if he has not indicated it by gesture). The law does not stipulate how many micro-seconds the poor referee has in which to make up his mind, but it is often impossible to apply the law satisfactorily. There is no reason why soccer cannot take a leaf out of rugby's book and allow the referee to award a free-kick if the sinned-against side lose possession. Why

not give them two bites of the cherry? It would certainly help to cut down foul play.

Wall Cheats
The offending side nowadays acts as if it has a divine right to form a defensive wall before a free-kick near the penalty-box is taken. As a result, at least one player will be delegated to delay the taking of the kick, while his team-mates arrange themselves in a 'wall' in front of the ball to their keeper's satisfaction. To delay the kick still further and gain an extra advantage, they will form the wall perhaps 6 yards from the ball instead of the requisite 10. It really is an extraordinary scene, with the referee motioning the defenders to move back, but not wishing to move from the place where the kick is taken for fear the kicker will take it when he is not looking or perhaps move the ball forward a few inches. He is empowered only to book a player for delaying tactics or for not retreating the proper distance. Often, when a player has received a booking, another player will be used to delay the next kick. Occasionally a referee might be courageous enough to take the names of all the players in a wall, but then he will probably be reprimanded by the authorities for overstepping his duties.

The remedy—the very simple remedy—is to take another leaf out of rugby's book and empower the referee to advance the kick 10 yards if the offending side do not immediately retire the proper distance. And if that takes a direct free-kick into the penalty-area, then a penalty would be awarded. There is no doubt at all that this would eradicate such delaying tactics from the game. It would also serve to cut down foul play, because teams would be more reluctant to give away free-kicks when they realized they would no longer be able to reduce their effectiveness.

More Power to the Ref
Why award penalties only for offences committed in the penalty-area? Quite often such a good chance of scoring is not merited, say for a minor handling offence in the corner of the box. On the other hand, offences outside the area are often more serious and prevent near-certain goals.

There is no good reason why referees should not be empowered to award indirect free-kicks, direct free-kicks, and penalties according to the seriousness of the offence, rather than the type of offence or where it took place. A deliberate foul or handball just outside the box to prevent a player homing in on goal should be punishable by a penalty.

And what about the offence that prevents a certain goal—the deliberate handball on the line, for example? Why not empower referees to award a goal in such cases (and also when an outside influence, such as a spectator, is involved), if in his opinion the ball would have crossed the line or a player, say, would have been free to walk the ball into the net? After all, a referee often *disallows* a goal on a matter of his opinion. 'Ah,' the law-makers will say, 'this was tried in 1881 and found unacceptable to the clubs'. True, but what they omit to add is that the referee was first mentioned in the laws only a year earlier, so it is not surprising that clubs at that time resented any new powers he might have. Things have changed.

Would these extra powers make the referee less acceptable? The answer is almost certainly not, because he would be making decisions relating to fairness, justice, and the spirit of the law—i.e. fitting the punishment to the crime. The game would flow more freely, with foul play and cheating curtailed, skill would be allowed to flourish, and fans and players alike would get more enjoyment from the game.

Offside

Interpretation

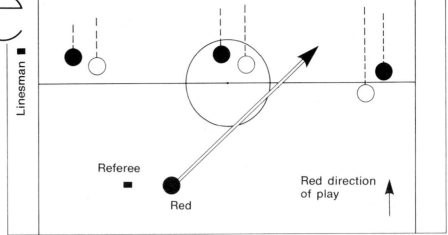

Contrary to a widespread belief, the offside law is neither difficult nor complicated. It is perhaps not so easy to explain in words, but the use of diagrams makes it crystal clear. Anyone who plays or watches football should have no trouble in understanding offside. The controversy surrounding the law is due entirely to the interpretation of one aspect of it.

Basically, the law states that a player is *in an offside position* 'if he is nearer to his opponents' goal-line than the ball, unless (a) he is in his own half, or (b) there are at least two of his opponents nearer their own goal-line than he is'. But a player shall be *declared offside and penalized* only if, at the moment the ball is played by (or touches) one of his team-mates, he is, 'in the opinion of the referee', (a) interfering with play or an opponent or (b) *seeking* to gain an advantage by being in that position. So being in an offside position is not an offence in itself.

Oddly enough, there is no mention in the law itself of the player in an offside position actually playing the ball. This is left to the International Board decision, which follows the law and states: 'Offside shall not be judged at the moment the player in question receives the ball, but at the moment when the ball is passed to him by one of his own side. . . .'

Once you have grasped the basic elements of the law (in addition, a player cannot be offside direct from a goal-kick, corner-kick, throw-in, or dropped ball), the only problem is the interpretation of *interfering with play or an opponent* and *seeking to gain an advantage*. It is the referee's opinion that counts here.

A Simple Example

Let us now take a simple and very common example encountered in play (see the diagram). The ball is in the Reds' half and the Reds are mounting an attack. They have three forwards in the Whites' half —one in the centre and one on each wing. As a Red midfielder is about to play the ball, the White defenders all move upfield (except the keeper) to put the Red forwards in an offside position. But the Red midfielder plays the ball through to the right wing, where his team-mate, who had just managed to stay onside, is able to collect it.

What happens? Well, almost certainly the linesman will put his flag up, signalling offside, because of the player or players in an offside position. It is not up to the linesman to decide whether or not they are interfering with play or seeking to gain an advantage, because he is not often in a position to do so. This leaves the referee with an extremely difficult decision, which he must make immediately. Does he blow up for offside or does he let play continue? First he must ask himself whether the man receiving the ball was offside. From his angle it is impossible to tell. Then he must decide whether any player in an offside position was interfering with play, etc.

Unfortunately, nowadays, most referees will blow up for offside in such a situation. This is, in effect, evading the issue, for, acting on the only certain piece of information he has—i.e. at least one player is in an offside position—he decides to give the defence the benefit of the doubt. In other words, *in his opinion,* a player in an offside position was interfering with play or seeking to gain an advantage. You can't argue with that!

A simple example. The Red man on the right is onside. Are his team-mates seeking to gain an advantage?

A Simple Solution

Surely it is not beyond the inventiveness of the law-makers to find a solution to this referee's dilemma. All it requires is a simple means of communication between linesman and referee to indicate whether or not the man receiving the ball was in an offside position. It is ironical that only after the referee has blown for offside does the linesman signal (by the position of his flag) where the offence took place (if indeed it was an offence).

'Playing offside' is a perfectly fair tactic, even if it was not originally in the spirit of the game. But more and more over the past 15 to 20 years, as the tactic has proliferated, referees have tended to err in favour of the defence. They ignore the 'interfering with play and seeking to gain an advantage' aspect (how can a player near the touchline, for example, who has just been deliberately made offside by his opponents, be interfering with play or *seeking* to gain an advantage?).

These 'lazy' offside decisions do much to ruin the game as a spectacle. It is not easy for an attacking side to beat the 'offside trap'. It requires fine teamwork, timing, and accuracy. Done properly, it can be quite spectacular. But it is infuriating and frustrating for both players and spectators when a perfectly fair move is pulled up short by a referee who is incorrectly interpreting the law.

'LITTLE MASTERS'

Some of the world's finest footballers have been small men. Lack of inches does not seem to affect ability, and in many cases can be turned to a player's advantage. A low centre of gravity gives more mobility in tight situations, especially in front of goal.

Some of the players featured in other sections of this book could equally well go under the heading of 'Little Masters', notably Alex James, the finest of schemers, Hughie Gallacher, goalscorer supreme, and the other 'Wembley Wizards'. Other small players with big reputations include Jimmy Greaves, Denis Law, Johnny Giles, Nobby Stiles, and Johnny Hancocks.

In this section, though, we look at some of the small stars that are difficult to put a conventional label on—not schemers, or wingers, or goalscorers primarily, but masters of their craft, nevertheless, always on the move, always buzzing, making others play.

The little men who become giants on the football field, from the top right, clockwise: Osvaldo Ardiles, Billy Bremner, Alan Ball, Kevin Keegan, and Diego Maradona.

Diego Maradona

Gift from the gods

Only very rarely in football does a player come along who belongs, not to a club or a country, but to the world—a player so talented and such a joy to watch that he inspires admiration universally, irrespective of chauvinistic allegiance. The crowds turn up to see his performance, and any partisan feelings are forgotten. Pelé, of course, was such a star, and so was Stanley Matthews and, in his brief career, Duncan Edwards. And today, football is fortunate to have another 'gift from the gods'—Diego Maradona.

One of soccer's 'mighty atoms', Maradona stands only 5ft 5in (1.65m), but he packs massive strength into his frame, and weighs around 12 stone (76kg). He was playing in Argentina's first division at 15 and won his first cap when only 16, in February 1977. A year later, Maradona was in Argentina's 25-strong squad in training for the 1978 World Cup, and was bitterly disappointed when Cesar Menotti omitted him from the final 22 because he felt he was too young to be exposed to the passions of the World Cup.

Nominally an inside-left, with the No. 10 on his back, Maradona has been compared with Pelé, but his game is more like that of that other Argentinian superstar Di Stefano. He is the orchestrator of the side. He makes the other players play, always available for quick one-twos all over the pitch, controlling the flow of the game with an awareness that has been described as 'built-in radar'. And like Di Stefano before him, he can also score goals—often spectacular ones, running half the length of the pitch or more, going past opponents as if they were statues, and slamming in 25-yarders or sending the keeper the wrong way.

He was leading League scorer in Argentina in 1978, with 22 goals in 40 matches, a third of his side's total. He had, almost single-handed, taken the unfashionable Argentinos Juniors into a respectable fifth place in the 21-team league. In August 1979, he starred in the World Youth Cup, in Tokyo, scoring in Argentina's 3-1 defeat of Russia in the final, and he was voted South American Footballer of the Year. He was a sensation wherever he went. At Hampden Park, he destroyed the Scots with a magical display not only of ball control, passing, and acceleration, but also of his Houdini-like ability to emerge from the 'chains and padlocks' put on him by opponents. At Wembley he had even rabid England fans willing him to score as he squirmed spectacularly away from three defenders and just put the ball wide.

The fifth child of eight, Maradona came from a very poor family, and their welfare has always been his prime concern. It is always difficult for clubs like Argentinos to keep their players, and in 1980 Barcelona were locked in a struggle with the Argentina FA after a £3 million deal had been blocked. Menotti intended to build Argentina's defence of the World Cup round the little wizard. So it was a relief when Buenos Aires Bocas Juniors stepped in and Maradona joined them on a year's loan for £2 million plus several players!

Maradona eludes the Dutch defence.

Billy Bremner

Billy **Bremner** had too much talent to be classified as an out-and-out hooligan. But all too often his 'win at all costs' philosophy overflowed into violence. And his volatile temperament cost him numerous fines and suspensions. Yet he was a brilliant footballer, the motivator of the powerful Leeds side that emerged in the late 1960s, and an inspiring captain. Footballer of the Year in 1970, he had a wonderful big-match temperament—the bigger the occasion, the better he would play. He also captained Scotland, and won a record 54 caps before the Scottish FA banned him from international football for life in 1975, for off-the-field incidents.

Bremner was a tiny terror on the field, standing 5ft 5½in (1.66m) and weighing 9st 13lb (63kg). Apart from an initial spell on the wing, he played throughout his career in midfield. With his chalky-white face and flaming red hair, he was a conspicuous figure on the pitch, and always in the action, whether in defence or attack. As a ball-winner, there was none better, and many a big opponent recoiled in disbelief when he first felt the ferocity of the little man's tackle.

Stirling Steel

Bremner developed his 'steel' in his native Stirling, where he lived in a tough district and learnt early how to take care of himself. His belligerence, unfortunately, spilled onto the football field.

At 13, he was playing in under-21 football, and later represented Scotland Schools. Several clubs came after him, but he settled for Leeds. He made his first-team debut at 17, in 1959-60, the season Leeds were relegated to Division II. And although he won a regular place, he was unhappy at Elland Road and pleaded to go back to Scotland. Eventually, Don Revie, who had stepped up from player to manager, persuaded him to stay.

Revie's Masterstroke

Bremner's behaviour on the field was highly irresponsible. If he wasn't overdoing the physical contact, he was arguing with the referee. He was fond of dishing out the rough stuff, but was the first to whine when the other side meted out similar treatment. His fiery temper was continually getting him into trouble, usually in the form of suspensions, as he piled up the bookings at an alarming rate.

Revie decided that the best way to deal with the problem was to make

Bremner captain! And it worked. Not that Bremner became an angel overnight, but he channelled his competitiveness and vigour more towards the needs of his team. Leeds were a competitive side, anyway, and with Bremner driving them on they became at one stage almost unbeatable.

Bremner wasn't just a ball-winner. With Johnny Giles, he formed an unrivalled midfield partnership. Going forward, Bremner was magnificent, his passing superb. And he was regularly among the goals. If Leeds were be-

hind or struggling to break a deadlock, Bremner would play up front, and time and again he would score or make the all-important goal.

Bremner led Leeds to all their triumphs—the Championship in 1969 (with a record 67 points and only two defeats) and 1974, the Cup in 1972, the League Cup in 1968, and the European Fairs Cup in 1968 and 1971. In one spell, from 26 October 1968 to 30 August 1969, they ran up a record 33 First Division games without defeat. Yet this great period of supremacy was marked more by their near misses —they were runners-up 11 times in major competitions.

Despite the presence of other great players, it was Bremner who personified Leeds. And although they were never a popular side they played some marvellous football. But Bremner and Leeds blotted their copy-books too often to rank among the soccer immortals, and it was perhaps a retribution of the gods that they fell short so often.

Captain of Scotland

Bremner made his international debut in 1965 against Spain, and first captained Scotland in 1970. His international career came to a sad and abrupt end in 1975, at 33, after a European Championship match in Denmark, when he and four of his team were banned for a series of escapades at a night-club and at their hotel.

Bremner left Leeds in 1976 to become player-manager of Hull, before taking over as manager of Doncaster in 1978. He could look back on a distinguished playing career with mixed feelings. His fanatic determination had won him many honours, but also brought him much shame. Had he been able to temper it with a little old-fashioned sportsmanship and self-control, who knows what heights he—and Leeds—could have reached.

Alan Ball

Ball of fire

To the time he became player-manager of Third Division Blackpool in 1980, Alan Ball had played 633 League games for Blackpool, Everton, Arsenal, and Southampton and 72 matches for England, and in none of these and his numerous cup-ties and other games did he give less than 100 per cent effort. A master of the first-time pass, he came to prominence in the 1966 World Cup as the little red-haired dynamo who didn't stop running. It was his extra-time chase to the right wing in the final against West Germany, followed by a cross to Hurst, that made England's controversial third goal, the one that finally knocked the stuffing out of the Germans.

With Ball's sizzling style of play and his fiery temperament, it is hardly surprising that 'Ball of Fire' became a stock phrase for headline writers. He was always quick to erupt on the field, but team-mates as well as opponents have suffered his wrath, for he expects all-out effort from his colleagues, too. His tongue has frequently got him into trouble with referees, and most of his fines and suspensions have been for dissent. But he never allowed his extreme competitiveness and sheer hatred of losing to overflow into dirty play—he would go in as hard as the next man, but always with the aim of getting the ball.

As a boy, Ball was coached by his father, Alan Ball Sr, a former player and sometime manager. He signed amateur forms with Bolton, their local team, but even as a youngster Alan Ball Jr was a firebrand, and a bust-up with the club spelt the end of their brief association. He signed for Blackpool, and made his First Division debut at 17, in August 1962, and won a regular place the following season. Despite his size—5ft 6in (1.68m) and 10st 5lb (66kg)—he had complete confidence in himself, although his cockiness did not always endear him to opposing fans. He won

Under-23 honours—and a sending-off against Austria for throwing the ball at the referee—and soon forced himself into the senior side, winning his first full cup against Yugoslavia in 1965.

Blackpool could not hold onto him after his superb World Cup performances—at 21, he was the youngest player in England's team—and he went to Everton for a record £110,000. He was their leading scorer in his first two seasons there (with 20 in 1967-68), and won a Championship medal in 1969-70.

His great influence on other players made him a natural choice as captain, although often a controversial one, because he was always getting involved in flare-ups and showed a tendency to berate his colleagues in that squeaky voice of his. But he would do anything to get his team-mates playing better, and his running, great determination, and strong personality lifted them when their heads were down. His running off the ball was tremendous, and he was constantly available for passes out of defence, and always knew where to put the ball, usually with a first-time pass. He hated to lose the ball and would tackle back with great ferocity.

In December 1971, Ball went to Arsenal for £220,000, another record fee. Arsenal had just done

the 'double', but despite all Ball's enthusiasm, the best they could do in his five seasons at Highbury were runners-up medals in both League and Cup. In 1973-74 he was their top scorer with 13 League goals, and took over the club captaincy. But when Terry Neill became manager in 1976, the two did not see eye to eye over tactics, and Ball was soon on his way to Southampton. There, he again became captain, and made a fine midfield general, taking Southampton to Division I in 1977-78, his first full season. While with Southampton, Ball spent a couple of summers playing in North America, and in 1979 skippered Vancouver Whitecaps to their NASL success.

At 35, Ball could not cover the same amount of ground as in his younger days, and although he might be just as adept at starting moves, he was unlikely to be there at the finish, too. But he was still a force, using his vast experience and one-touch skills to galvanize those around him. It took the offer of a manager's job to lure him away from the challenge and thrill of First Division football in 1980. Blackpool had sunk a long way since he left them 14 years earlier, but he did not last long, and before the season was over he found himself back at Southampton.

115

Kevin Keegan

Action Man

England side, and a perfect model for any aspiring young footballer. He believes in nothing less than total commitment, and total involvement in every game in which he plays. Without it, as he says, his game crumbles. In other words, to produce his fine skills, to score his spectacular goals, requires maximum effort. Not for him the leisurely, strolling, approach. He must be the busiest player on the field—and he usually is, whether playing in midfield or up front.

Yorkshire-born, Keegan spent his early life in Doncaster, but it was for Fourth Division Scunthorpe that he signed as a 16-year-old apprentice. He made his first-team debut in 1968, and three years later Bill Shankly shrewdly brought him to Liverpool for £35,000.

Several leading clubs had watched Keegan, but failed to see his potential. Such was Shankly's confidence in him, though, that he put him straight into the first team, at the start of the 1971-72 season. Twice League champions in the

Keegan airborne—in his Liverpool days against Everton (left) and for England against Northern Ireland (below).

The supreme example of the modern all-action, all-purpose forward, Keegan is the first to admit that his game is built on his work-rate. Yet he is full of all the footballing skills. Standing only 5ft 7in (1.70m), but with powerful thighs and wiry strength, he has an explosive right-foot shot and his timing, courage, and jumping ability make him exceptionally dangerous in the air. With his darting runs, turning on the ball, acceleration, and close control, he can open up the tightest of defences, and his positional sense and eye for an opening make him both a maker and a taker of snap chances.

As a captain, Keegan leads by example. He is an inspiration to the

A lethal shot. Keegan pierces the Brazil wall with a free-kick (above) and celebrates (right).

mid-sixties and beaten Cup finalists in 1971, Liverpool were in the process of rebuilding. In his six years at Anfield, Liverpool became the leading club side in Europe, and it was Keegan who was the inspiration. He took the transition from Fourth to First Division football in his stride, and with his flair, his awareness, and his non-stop running he lit the fuse that exploded Liverpool to the very top. Every honour came their way, and Keegan's—the League in 1973, 1976, and 1977, the Cup in 1974, and three European competitions, the UEFA Cup in 1973 and 1976 and the European Cup in 1977.

Added to this, Keegan was voted Footballer of the Year in 1975-76, and had established himself in the England side. But this had not been easy. After his England debut against Wales at Cardiff in November 1972, he played only one more game before finally becoming a regular in May 1974.

Keegan had made it clear, before he went to Hamburg in June 1977 for £500,000, a British record, that he wanted to broaden his footballing experience abroad. It was a brave decision. Certainly, he would be paid more in West Germany, but such was his and Liverpool's success that most people thought he was crazy to risk failure, as so many

other British 'exports' had experienced before.

At first, life was extremely difficult for Keegan in Germany, and not for the first time did he need all his courage, determination, and physical and mental resources to survive. But he did more than that. He overcame the initial animosity of his fellow players, the disadvantage of not being able to speak the language, and the fierce tackling from behind that strikers have to suffer in the Bundesliga. He won the hearts of the German fans, the respect of his fellow players, and even more honours. Voted European Footballer of the Year in both 1978 and 1979, he won a championship medal with

the Hamburg team in 1979.

Again, Keegan made it clear that he would be moving on at the end of the 1979-80 season, but he caused a sensation when he chose to return to England with unfashionable First Division side Southampton, when he could have gone virtually anywhere.

The end of the season was disappointing for Keegan. Hamburg lost to Nottingham Forest in the European Cup final and England failed to impress in the European Championships, Keegan himself having to battle against injury. However, nothing could dampen his spirits or his passionate ambition to lead England to success in the 1982 World Cup.

Osvaldo Ardiles

Ossie the Spur

After some outstanding performances for Argentina in the 1978 World Cup, Osvaldo Ardiles transferred his industrious talents to England, and not only won the affection of the partisan Spurs fans, but became a firm favourite in English football.

There were many who regarded Ardiles as the finest Argentinian on view in the World Cup, despite the fluent skills and dramatic goals of the flamboyant Kempes. For Ardiles was never out of the action, doing what he does best—winning the ball by anticipation, making himself available to team-mates,

From World Cup victory in Argentina, Ossie Ardiles made a highly successful transition to English football with Spurs.

running at the opposition with the ball, and setting up brilliant one-twos with his colleagues.

What endeared him most of all to everyone who watched the World Cup was his complete sincerity as a footballer. Not for him the gamesmanship or sly fouls some of his compatriots were accused of, or the blatant clogging he often had to face from other sides. The little Ardiles—5ft 6in (1.68m) and 9st

10lb (62kg)—was in there battling for every ball, but battling fairly. And he takes the knocks that come his way without a thought of retaliation.

Twenty-five at the time of the World Cup, Ardiles, with 45 caps, had been a midfield force in the Argentina side for some time. He was born in Cordoba, and joined the local club Instituto as a youngster. In 1975 he was snapped up by Huracán.

He took a great deal of punishment in the World Cup, but this only demonstrated his resilience and fighting qualities. Against Poland, he made a lovely goal for Kempes, travelling almost the length of the pitch with the ball before slipping it to the man who won all the glory. Despite being carried off with a twisted ankle just before half-time against Brazil, amd missing the game with Peru, Ardiles was back for the final, although he again had to go off, after 66 minutes.

Spurs manager Keith Burkinshaw brought off a sensational coup when he persuaded Huracán to part with Ardiles soon after the World Cup. He was lucky, too, to get another international, Ricardo Villa from Racing Club, at the same time, for Ardiles would not have moved on his own. At about £700,000 the pair, they were the bargain of the season.

A law student in his spare time, Ardiles settled down more quickly and more decidedly than Villa in English soccer. His sheer class was like a breath of fresh air in the Football League. He tired towards the end of his first season—not surprisingly in view of the terrible winter in 1978, the severity of the English programme, and his World Cup exertions the previous summer. But he came back with the same sparkle, and continued to delight and entertain, not only with his skills but by the consistency and character of his performance.

'TOTAL FOOTBALLERS'

There's really no such animal as a 'total footballer', but it's the perfect term to describe the very special players in this section. Yet most of them bear little resemblance to the others, either in style or in play, except perhaps that in his own way each is unique—John Charles, the Welsh giant equally at home as centre-half or centre-forward; Duncan Edwards, in control of the game wherever he played; Alfredo di Stefano, patrolling the pitch between goalmouths and in complete command; Franz Beckenbauer, set-

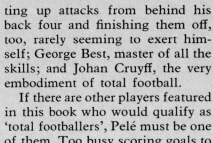

Above: George Best

ting up attacks from behind his back four and finishing them off, too, rarely seeming to exert himself; George Best, master of all the skills; and Johan Cruyff, the very embodiment of total football.

If there are other players featured in this book who would qualify as 'total footballers', Pelé must be one of them. Too busy scoring goals to give his defensive qualities much chance to be noticed, he would have shone in any position—and it is said that he would have made a world-class goalkeeper.

Below: John Charles

Above: Duncan Edwards

Below: Alfredo di Stefano

Below: Johan Cruyff

Below: Franz Beckenbauer

Johan Cruyff
Number 14

The Dutch team that Cruyff starred in during the early 1970s were the first to play what became known as 'total football'. And it was their captain, Johan Cruyff himself, who symbolized the resurgence in Europe at that time of adventurous, exciting football.

Cruyff was the 'superstar' of the seventies, taking over from Pelé as the idol of the fans. He inspired his club, Ajax Amsterdam, to a hat-trick of European Cup victories. He took the Dutch national side—who were never before regarded as a force in world football—to the verge of World Cup triumph. And he graced the game with sparkling skills on the ball, explosive finishing, and an inventiveness that so

often produced the spectacular. He was the most complete footballer since Di Stefano, and one of the most athletic players the game has ever known.

When Cruyff moved, he always appeared to have the speed of a greyhound, as he flashed past defenders leaving them flat-footed. Yet he was not a particularly fast runner. It was his speed of thought and speed off the mark, together with a beautiful body swerve, that made him so elusive.

Standing 5ft 11in (1.80m), but with a spare frame, Cruyff does not give the impression of power. But he possessed immense stamina to go with his delicate skills, so he was always in the game.

Below left: Dutch superstar Johan Cruyff beats West Germany's Bertie Vogts in the 1974 World Cup final. Above, left to right: Cruyff put Ajax on the European map before moving to Barcelona in 1973, and later playing in the United States.

Where did he Play?

It is almost impossible to answer the question: 'What position did Cruyff play?' Ajax first used him as a striking centre-forward. In 1966-67, his second full season with them, he was Holland's leading league scorer with 33 goals. But even then he was making many more for his colleagues, squirming free of the tight marking to play one-twos or dropping right back to collect the ball and take opponents out of the game.

And just as often he would drift out to the wing, where his ability to beat a man on either side left him free to make for the bye-line or cut in and shoot.

His passing was always incisive. For club and country, he was always at the hub of things, making the others play. And he was a superb finisher, with either foot or with his head. He delighted in taking the ball on the volley, the higher the better.

Lack of Control

One of the few criticisms of Cruyff as a footballer was his inability at times to control his tongue. Like all great players, he suffered frequent

provocation, and took plenty of knocks. He had a tendency, especially early in his career, to retaliate. But more usually he would give vent to his feelings verbally. As a result, he often found himself in trouble with referees. He won his first cap at 19, in 1966, but in only his second international was sent off. And he nearly went too far again in the 1974 World Cup final, when, as captain, he was booked for arguing with the referee as the teams were leaving the field at half-time.

Achievements

Cruyff was born in Amsterdam in 1947. He joined Ajax, where his mother was a cleaner, while still a schoolboy. He made his first-team debut at 17 and became a regular the following season, 1965-66, helping Ajax win the League title. He became captain in 1972. In his eight full seasons with Ajax, they won the League six times, the Cup four times, and the European Cup three times.

More than anyone else it was Cruyff who put Ajax on the European map. As early as December 1966, he was destroying the Liverpool defence in the European Cup. In 1969 Ajax were the first Dutch club to reach the final, losing 4-1 to AC Milan. They made up for this by winning the trophy three years running (1971-73), and in their 1972 victory over Inter, Cruyff scored both goals.

In 1973, Cruyff was transferred to Barcelona for a world record £922,300—about £400,000 of which went to Cruyff himself. He had a galvanic effect on the ailing Spanish club, taking them from near the bottom of the League to their first title in 14 years.

Cruyff's international career spanned only 48 games, chiefly because of disputes with the Dutch FA. They could ill afford to upset their priceless jewel, who never shone brighter than in the 1974 World Cup. Already the star of the tournament and a marked man in the final from the very kick-off, he nevertheless picked up the ball in his own half before a German had touched it, showed it to them, and then proceeded to dart and jig right

through their defence until pulled down in the penalty box. Neeskens gave Holland the lead from the spot, but later decisions went against them and it was sad that Cruyff and Holland failed to do full justice to their marvellous football.

It was significant, however, that Cruyff won the European Footballer of the Year award (for an unprecedented third time), rather than the German captain Franz Beckenbauer, who had carried all before him that year.

Cruyff helped his country qualify for the next World Cup before retiring while still in his prime, although he later took up lucrative contracts to play in the United States. He was sorely missed in Argentina in 1978.

Cruyff (background), the star of the 1974 World Cup, scores brilliantly from a narrow angle against Argentina.

John Charles

John Charles strikes for goal in Juventus colours. He became a great hero in Italy.

Most big central defenders enjoy the occasional sortie upfield to use their height to advantage in the opposing penalty area, especially at set pieces such as corners and free-kicks. Many stoppers have played up front in an emergency, and some have converted successfully to centre-forward. John Charles did this to spectacular effect in the 1950s, and was equally good in either role, the best in the world perhaps in his era. And he was just as capable of playing full-back or in midfield, too. To complete the picture of versatility, he also succeeded in starring in two widely contrasting soccer spheres—the Football League, with its emphasis on stamina and speed, and Italian football with its packed defences and more leisurely pace.

The Gentle Giant

John Charles is remembered as 'The Gentle Giant'. He had probably the most impressive physique of any footballer of his generation, standing 6ft 1½in (1.87m) and weighing nearly 14st (89kg), yet he never used his weight or strength unfairly. No referee ever had cause to admonish him, let alone book him or send him off—and this, despite the fact that throughout his career he was the victim of considerable maltreatment. Defenders would resort to any means to stop him, using all the dirty tricks they could get away with, knowing full well that he would never retaliate. The only time he ever became aggressive was in a notorious international with Austria at Wrexham in 1955. And it was not his own injury that made him lose his customary poise, but that of his brother Mel, shamefully hacked down and carried off the field in the last quarter of an hour. In the remaining 15 minutes, John Charles gave as good as he got. His philosphy, however, remained that there was no place in football for violence.

The Transformation

Charles was born in December 1931 in Cwmdu, near Swansea. He exhibited a natural gift for football at an early age, and at 12 played for Swansea schoolboys. He joined Swansea Town (now City) at 14 as an amateur, but was snapped up by Second Division Leeds United and signed professional forms with them at 17. He made a quiet first-team debut at the end of the 1948-49 season, still only 17.

By now he was filling out, maturing as both a man and a footballer, and the following season he not only established himself as Leeds' centre-half, playing in every match, but also won his first international cap, against Northern Ireland at Wrexham on 8 March 1950. At 18 years 71 days, he was the youngest player ever to represent Wales. Although the game was drawn 0-0, his inexperience showed, and it was another three years before he won a regular place—and that was after his transformation into a striker.

It was Leeds manager Major Frank Buckley, of Wolves fame, who decided to experiment with Charles up front in the 1952-53 season. Charles was immediately among the goals—30 in 21 matches —so he stayed at centre-forward. The next season he set a club record with 42 goals in 39 League games. Yet Leeds finished only 10th, with an 89-81 goal record. Promotion would surely have come sooner had they been able to play Charles at centre-half and centre-forward simultaneously! It came eventually in 1956, when Charles, after another spell at the back to bolster the defence, returned to centre-forward to score 30 League goals.

Defences in the upper echelon of

Charles pictured in Leeds strip before he left for Italy.

the Football League found Charles just as much of a handful, and in the very first season he finished leading scorer in Division I with 38 goals out of his team's 72. It was the only season he ever played in England's First Division, for at the end of it he left to find further fame and considerable fortune in Italy.

Charles rises superbly to head the equalizer for Wales against Hungary in the 1958 World Cup.

The King

Charles was just establishing himself in the forefront of British football when he was whisked away in the summer of 1957 to play for Turin club Juventus. The fee—£65,000 (including £10,000 for Charles)—was a British record. Charles was tailor-made for Italian football. His strength enabled him to withstand the strongest challenges, and the slower pace allowed him to give full play to his range of ball skills. He was powerful on the ground, expert at winning the loose ball in a packed penalty area and screening it with his massive frame before unleashing a shot with either foot or laying the ball off to a colleague. And in the air he was well nigh unbeatable—in the Dean and Lawton class. But perhaps his greatest asset in Italy was his calm authority, his imperturbability. He was a wonderful stabilizing influence on the hot Latin temperament around him, always keeping cool in the emotional atmosphere and in the face of childish outbursts and histrionics. And the crowds loved him for it. He was soon the 'King' of Italian soccer, turning the struggling Juventus once more into the country's leading side. He struck up a fine partnership with another 'import', the scheming inside-forward Omar Sivori from Argentina. Charles was ever-present in his first season, scoring 28 goals in 34 matches, and Juventus won the title. In his five seasons with them, they won the League three times and the Cup twice,

including a 'double' in 1960.

Off the field, he was revered by the public, never out of the headlines, and treated like a film star. He settled down marvellously, without a hint of the difficulties encountered by other British players in Italy. His club rated him the most valuable player in the world. His goal tally would have been even more impressive than the 93 he scored in 155 League games had not Juventus used him somewhat cynically at times, switching him to centre-half as soon as he scored his almost inevitable goal, in order to protect their 1-0 lead.

> ### THE SWITCHING CHARLES'S
>
> **Before going to Italy in 1957, John Charles played 21 consecutive games for Wales. It is interesting to see how he was switched around from inside-right (8) to centre-forward (9) to centre-half (5), in the days when the numbers on players' backs signified the position they played, and the shirt a player was handed served as the 'tactical talk'. These are the numbers he wore (1953-57): 8, 8, 8, 9, 9, 9, 5, 5, 5, 9, 9, 5, 5, 5, 5, 8, 9, 9, 5, 5, 9. His younger brother Mel was often in the same side, and he too played in those three positions plus right-half (4) for Wales. The brothers looked alike, with similar build, and often switched positions during a game. It must have been terrifying for opposing defences to see two Charles's bearing down on them.**

Anticlimax

Charles's career fizzled out in anticlimax. Feeling a little homesick and concerned about his children's education, he made what he later described as a big mistake, and left Juventus. In 1962 he returned to Leeds (by then back in Division II), but he could not settle in Yorkshire again nor in English football. Too much was expected of him too soon, and the quicker pace of the game and lack of support made adjustment slow. After just a few months, he returned to Italy, this time with Roma. But now he could not recapture his Italian form either, and at the end of the season

was transferred to Cardiff. He stayed there for just over two seasons before joining non-League Hereford in 1965, later to become player-manager. He left them in 1971, shortly before they attained League status, and he eventually disappeared from the soccer scene.

Playing for Wales

Because of his self-imposed exile, Charles's appearances for Wales were restricted to 38, in which he scored 15 goals. He regarded playing for Wales as the greatest honour in the game, and it was one of his biggest regrets that he could not obtain his release from Juventus very often.

He would play anywhere for Wales. He began as centre-half as a much-publicized youngster, but nerves ruined his debut in 1950 and another game the next year did little to retrieve his reputation. But after two years in the international wilderness he returned in 1953 with two goals against Northern Ireland, and after that only injury or club calls kept him out of the side.

Charles managed to get released for the 1958 World Cup and led Wales courageously through to the quarter-finals, the high point in the football history of the Principality. In two matches against Hungary, he was the victim of a concerted plan to put him out of the game. They finally crippled him in the play-off, but he returned to make an equalizer and then, bravely hobbling about the field, kept the opposition busy while his teammates stormed through to a famous victory.

But the game Charles is perhaps remembered for more than any other is an international against Northern Ireland in 1956. He crowned a brilliant all-round performance by breaking out of defence and beating man after man as he progressed the length of the field before laying on a goal for a colleague. In defence or attack, John Charles was the complete footballer, an immovable object and an irresistible force. But, above all, he was a fine sportsman and the gentlest giant that ever appeared on a football field.

BECKENBAUER'S HONOURS

World Cup 1974 (1st), 1966 (2nd), 1970 (3rd)
European Championships 1972 (1st), 1976 (2nd)
European Cup 1974, 75, 76
European Cup-Winners Cup 1967
Bundesliga 1969, 72, 73, 74
West German Cup 1966, 67, 69, 71
NASL 1977, 78

International caps 103
European Footballer of the Year 1972, 76

Franz Beckenbauer

Kaiser Franz

Captain of West Germany, Franz Beckenbauer won just about every honour in the game. And he could play equally well in defence, in midfield, or up front. He was a complete footballer in every sense, and such was his mastery of the game that he rarely raised a bead of sweat.

His elegant, almost casual, style of play has often been mistaken for arrogance, but it is his masterly reading of the game that enables him to conserve his energy. His anticipation is so good that he rarely has to make a tackle.

Beckenbauer created a new role, a new position on the field—that of attacking sweeper. The nearest approach to this is the old attacking centre-half, but in modern times only 'the Kaiser' has had the supreme footballing ability to fill such a role. He master-minded the West German and Bayern Munich triumphs of the 1970s, always choosing the right time to counter-attack, always ready to come up himself, and frequently making or scoring vital goals. The successes of both club and country were due largely to his fine leadership and his remarkably accurate passing, with either foot. A speciality that he developed was the 'bent chip'.

Kevin Keegan relates how he was detailed to 'mark' Beckenbauer when England played West Germany at Wembley in 1975. This, he discovered, was impossible; every time he closed him down, expecting him to pass back to the keeper, he found the ball whistling past him in a neat arc. That's how Beckenbauer would start his side's attacks.

As a schoolboy, Beckenbauer was a centre-forward, scoring as much as a hundred goals one season. He joined Bayern Munich early in 1964 and first played in the Bundesliga as an outside-left, but soon developed as an attacking midfield player. Helmut Schoen brought him into the World Cup squad as a 19-year-old, and he earned his place for the 1966 tournament with some fine performances in the qualifying matches. In England he scored four goals in helping Germany to reach the final. But against England, Schoen put him on Bobby Charlton, and although his marking was effective, Germany missed his creative talents and went down 4-2.

Four years later, in Mexico, it was Beckenbauer who turned the game against England, scoring when Germany were 2-0 down and

The 1974 World Cup triumph.

then driving them to extra-time victory. But he suffered disappointment again, when Germany went out to Italy in the semi-finals, courageously playing much of the game with his right arm in a sling but unable to prevent the Italians winning an exciting match 4-3.

Finally, in 1974, Beckenbauer won the World Cup medal he so richly deserved. And what a triumphant year that was. He led Bayern Munich to their third consecutive League success, their first European Cup victory (the first of a hat-trick), and then, in Munich, led his country to world honours.

Beckenbauer retired from international football in 1977 with 103 caps, a German record. He transferred his talents across the Atlantic, where he won further honours with the New York Cosmos. Then, in 1980 at the age of 34, he surprisingly decided to return to Germany and join Hamburg. But such are his talents that there is no reason why he should not enjoy success for many years to come.

Below: Beckenbaur (left), arm in a sling, looks on helplessly as Italy score the winner in the semi-finals of the 1970 World Cup.

Alfredo di Stefano

The complete footballer

Born in Argentina in July 1926, Alfredo di Stefano became the complete footballer. He is best known for the years he spent in Spain, with Real Madrid, when he made them the undisputed 'kings of Europe'. Nominally a centre-forward with a No. 9 on his shirt, he was more than just a striker, more than a deep-lying centre-forward, more than a scheming midfield player, more than a sweeper. He was all of these at the same time.

He was a superb finisher who scored over 400 goals for Real, including 49 in the European Cup; he made countless goals for others; he possessed a matchless tactical brain, always in control of his side's strategy; and his defensive covering and tackling were faultless. But what, more than anything else, set Di Stefano apart from lesser mortals was his passing—his ability to accept and make passes at bewildering speed. He would take complete control of a game, patrolling the area between the opposite goalmouths, moving into position, calling for the ball, controlling it in a flash each time, and spraying inch-perfect passes, before moving into position for the return.

Argentina Abandoned

Di Stefano signed as an amateur for River Plate, his father's old club, at 16, moved to Huracan for a year on loan, and returned to River Plate where he made his first-team debut in 1944. He soon became the idol of the fans, and in 1947 won a championship medal and was the League's leading scorer with 27 goals. He also won seven caps for Argentina.

But in 1949, together with under-paid footballers from many parts of the world, he 'defected' to the rebel Colombian League, where he received 15 times what he had been getting at home. He signed for Los Millionarios of Bogotá, and stayed

Alfredo di Stefano in the famous all-white strip of Real Madrid.

there over three years, helping them to two title wins.

When Colombia rejoined FIFA in 1953, the clubs had to release all the players they had poached from other leagues. Di Stefano decided not to return to Argentina but to go to Spain. When he got there, however, he found himself in the curious position of being claimed by two clubs, Real Madrid and Barcelona. One had paid a fee to Millionarios, the other to River Plate, who still officially held his registration. The Spanish FA ruled that he

should play alternate seasons for the two clubs, but after a season with Real they came to an agreement by which he stayed in Madrid.

It was not long before the 28-year-old was winning a championship medal in his third country and embarking on a career in club football without parallel. In 11 years, he won 5 European Cup winners medals and 2 runners-up medals, 8 League medals and 1 Cup medal, and was the League's leading scorer on 5 occasions: 1954 (29 goals), 1956 (24), 1957 (31), 1958

(19), and 1959 (23). He continued to score prolifically in the 1960s, but was content to make more goals for the Hungarian exile Ferenc Puskas, with whom he struck up a perfect footballing relationship. In all, in 510 games for Real, Di Stefano scored 428 goals, and when he later went to Espanol in 1964 to finish his playing career, he scored another 19 goals in 81 games.

International Career

Di Stefano holds the remarkable distinction—although it is one of his lesser achievements—of having played for three countries. Before he left Argentina he won seven caps, and he also represented Colombia while he was there, although they were not members of FIFA at the time and their internationals were not officially recognized as such. He took out Spanish nationality and made his international debut for them in 1957, winning a total of 31 caps and scoring a record 23 goals. Yet he never achieved the heights for Spain that he did for Real, perhaps because he was not 'in charge' of the national side, which boasted another 'orchestrator' in Barcelona's Luisito Suarez. Di Stefano was notorious for his dislike of competition, as

several of Real's imports found to their discomfort. France's Raymond Kopa, for example, found himself banished to the wing, and Brazil's Didi barely saw first-team service at all during the season he spent with Real.

One honour escaped Di Stefano completely during his illustrious career, that of playing in the World Cup finals. His only opportunity came with Spain in 1962, but injury prevented his taking part, although it was felt that the more likely reason was another conflict of egos, this time with Spanish team manager Helenio Herrera.

The European Cup

When the European Cup was first held, in 1955, it did not receive universal support. A competition for the champion clubs of Europe, it might not have survived but for Real Madrid and Alfredo di

Stefano. For, led by Di Stefano, Real Madrid proceeded to dominate the competition in style. Such was the quality of their football, such was the charisma of their victories, that the future of the competition was assured. They were masters of Europe, and every club wanted to beat them. It was six years before their fellow-countrymen from Barcelona knocked them out of the competition, however.

From the very first, Di Stefano made his name synonymous with the European Cup. In the 1955-56 final, with Real two down to Reims of France, Di Stefano took hold of the game and established himself as one of the outstanding players of all time. Beating two players in midfield, he put Marsal away and then stopped, losing his markers, before accelerating away again to lash the return pass into the net. He was the driving force behind Real's other goals as they equalized, fell

EUROPEAN CUP SCORING RECORD		
Season	**Games**	**Goals**
1955-56	7	5
1956-57	8	7
1957-58	7	10
1958-59	7	6
1959-60	6	8
1960-61	2	0
1961-62	10	7
1962-63	2	1
1963-64	9	5
Total	58	49

behind and then scored two to snatch a brilliant 4-3 victory.

Every year it was the same, with Di Stefano leading Real to victory after victory, making and scoring goal after goal. In those five glorious seasons, Di Stefano scored 36 goals in European Cup competition, in 35 games. He scored in every final, culminating in a hat-trick in the famous 1960 defeat of Eintracht Frankfurt 7-3.

During this time, he was twice voted European Footballer of the Year, in 1957 and 1959, and he led Real to victory in the first World Club Championship in 1960. He also led the Rest of the World attack against England in 1963 in the FA Centenary match.

Below: Di Stefano (left) races in but is foiled by England's keeper Gordon Banks at Wembley in the FA Centenary match in 1963. Di Stefano captained the Rest of the World side.

127

George Best

Fallen idol

George Best was an enigma for much of his playing career, and his career remained an enigma even when he stopped playing—although one could never be sure that the unpredictable Irishman had really hung up his boots for good.

As a player, Best was magic. Was he a winger? Was he a striker? Or was he something else—Superman, maybe? It really doesn't matter, because he was a footballing genius, an artist whose canvas was the pitch and who painted his pictures in a style all his own.

He was the first 'pop idol' of soccer, and in the end the pressures proved too much for him. Suffocated by fans, hounded by the media and surrounded by 'hangers-on', he eventually toppled from his pedestal. When George Best left Manchester United, that was the end of his footballing career. True, he made comebacks—from Fulham to Fort Lauderdale, from Los Angeles to Edinburgh—but everything after United was a downhill stumble. Whoever he played for and wherever he played, the class still showed, glimpses of greatness still shone through from time to time, but they served only as a reminder of the glorious days with United, when George Best played the kind of football you only dream about.

Best in full flight during his great days at Old Trafford, and (right) in America—the end of the trail.

Discovery of Genius

The first Manchester United heard of George Best was a letter from their scout in Ulster, Bob Bishop: 'I think I have found a genius.' But when this 15-year-old 'waif' arrived at old Trafford in 1961, he looked far from a footballer, standing only 5 feet (1.52m) and weighing a puny 8 stone (50.8kg). He was so homesick and shy that within a couple of days he was back in Belfast. But his father persuaded him to return and he was soon demonstrating his genius on the training ground, drifting past first-team stars as if they were kiddies in the park. Matt Busby instructed his

Above right: Manager Matt Busby admires the Footballer of the Year trophy Best won in 1967-68. Right: Two weeks later, and Best scores in the European Cup final.

coaching staff: 'Leave this lad alone . . . let him develop naturally.'

That was the only time in his whole career that Best showed anything less than complete confidence in himself. He was never cocky, but he had nerves of steel, and no matter how big the occasion he took it in his stride. Coach Jimmy Murphy reckoned he had 'ice in his veins'.

He made his debut at 17 against West Bromwich at old Trafford in September 1963 and won a permanent first-team place later that year. He won his first cap for Northern Ireland against Wales at Swansea in April 1964, a month before his 18th birthday. Already he was attracting the attention that would eventually prove his downfall. Dark-haired, filling out now to a deceptively strong 5ft 8½in (1.74m) and 10st 3lb (64.9kg), he had that 'little boy lost' look about him on the field, yet managed to run rings round everyone who had the misfortune to

come up against him. That's the stuff that heroes are made of, and Georgie Best became the hero not only of schoolboys up and down the land, but of schoolgirls too. He became a cult figure and was as well known to people who'd never seen a football match as he was to the thousands who flocked to Old Trafford and grounds all over the country to marvel at his skills. In the days of 'Beatlemania', he was soccer's answer to the pop stars.

'El Beatle'

It was in March 1966, in the Stadium of Light, Lisbon, that George Best, his black locks lapping his ears, first made his impact on world football and earned the name 'El Beatle' from an admiring Portuguese Press. The occasion was the second leg of the European Cup quarter-final against Benfica. United had reached the European Cup for the first time since the Munich disaster by winning the

League title in 1965, Best's first full season, in which he played in all but one game. But they came to Lisbon with only a slender one-goal lead over Europe's most successful side since Real Madrid's hey-day.

With Benfica's formidable home record in Europe, and up against the likes of Eusebio and Coluna, Busby told his side to play a holding game for 20 minutes. But Best, as Busby was to joke later, 'must have had cotton wool in his ears', for he took the Benfica defence apart and scored twice in the first 12 minutes. The first was a perfectly timed header from a Dunne free-kick, the second a mazy run after picking up a Herd header from a Gregg punt upfield—a superb goal which was a portent of things to come. United ran out 5-1 winners after perhaps the finest display by a British club side on foreign soil. But United went out of the Cup in the semi-final (for the third time), largely perhaps because of an injury to Best which kept him out of the second leg against Partizan Belgrade and for the rest of that season.

Back to fitness next season after a cartilage operation, Best played in all 42 League games and won his second Championship medal. So United were in the European Cup again in 1967-68, and it was Best's goal that gave them a 1-0 lead to take to Madrid in the semi-final, and his dribble to the bye-line and cut-back for Foulkes to knock in the winner after Real had taken the lead on aggregate. The final was at Wembley, against Benfica, who pulled back a United goal to take the match into extra time. In the first minute, Kidd headed on a long Stepney clearance and Best pounced on the ball, sweeping past his 'watch-dog' Cruz in the same movement and making for goal from near the half-way line. If you could pick a man for such a one-to-one situation in extra time in the final of the European Cup, you could do no better than pick George Best. And sure enough, with 100,000 delirious fans roaring him on, he neatly side-stepped the keeper and slid the ball home.

United went on to win 4-1, the first English side to win the Euro-pean Cup, and it crowned a wonderful season for Best, who was their top League scorer with 28 goals and voted Footballer of the Year, and at the end of 1968 European Footballer of the Year, too.

A sad, but common, sight in the early 1970s—Best being booked for arguing. A prime target for the crude spoilers of soccer, he never got the protection that was his right.

The Troubles

Best was also joint leading scorer in the First Division that season, which for a winger is an exceedingly rare achievement. And although he didn't quite reach 20 again, he was United's leading scorer for the next four seasons.

But all was not running smoothly for the gifted Irishman, on or off the field.

Like all great attacking stars, on the field Best was the target for the nasty men of soccer, the players who compensate for their own lack of skill by resorting to foul, often dangerous, means. Best suffered more than his share of the hacking and kicking, the tripping and needling, the body-checks and the shirt-pulling. It was amazing the knocks he took. He never shirked a tackle, but he felt—quite rightly—that he wasn't getting adequate protection from referees. Thus he himself started to get into trouble with referees, and was sent off more than once—always for retaliation or dissent—suspended, and even charged with bringing the game into disrepute. Well, perhaps Best's is not the finest example for young players to follow, but this latter charge against players of his quality is one of the ironies of soccer. For the very men that bring the charge—the administrators of the game—are the guilty ones, for their sheer negligence in allowing the 'hooligans' of the football field to prosper.

Off the field, too, Best was knee-deep in trouble. While still a young man, he had made a fortune from the game, but the lifestyle he chose—or, rather, fell into—was more that of a pop star than a professional footballer: the flash sports cars, the nightclubs, the boutiques, and the inevitable bevy of girls queuing up to throw themselves at him. Although he continued to make back-page news, he was making far too much front-page news with his escapades. He was proving too much of a handful for Matt Busby, who thought of him as a son, so what chance did Busby's successors stand? He disappeared for days on end, he didn't turn up for training, he ran away to Spain. He was always punished for his misdemeanours at Old Trafford and he was always contrite, but in the end the pressures were too much, the excesses inexcusable.

Best played his last game for United on January 1, 1974. After that it was mainly downhill progress, with the occasional step up. He played, at various times and for various periods, for Stockport in the Fourth Division, Cork Celtic in Eire, Los Angeles Aztecs in California and Fulham in the Second Division, getting involved in a dispute between the last two as to who held his registration, and then Fort Lauderdale Strikers in Florida and Hibs in Scotland. He was paid well for his services and he always gave of his best on the field, but his bouts of heavy drinking played havoc with his fitness. It is a sad, sad story, and it is perhaps not over yet. But the story of George Best, footballing genius, ended a long time ago.

Duncan Edwards

There are many who say that Duncan Edwards was England's most complete footballer. Some rate him as the finest player of all time, and while that is arguable, who could deny that he would have become just that, had he not died so tragically in the Munich air disaster. In his short career, he was already universally acknowledged as one of the masters of the game. In any discussions of an England all-time XI, the name of Duncan Edwards is usually agreed for left-half without argument. Yet he was only 21 when he died.

Edwards was born in Dudley, Worcester, on October 1, 1936. He was always a big lad, and was a legend even as a schoolboy international, with every club in the League after him. He signed for Manchester United as soon as he was 16, made his League debut at 16½, and was the youngest ever player to represent England—18 years 183 days—when he made his debut at Wembley in April 1955, in England's 7-2 thrashing of Scotland. Altogether he won 18 caps and scored 5 goals for England.

For Manchester United, he was the outstanding member of the 'Busby Babes', one of the finest club sides in the history of British football, and potentially the greatest ever. He won two championship medals with United, in 1956 and 1957, and a Cup runners-up medal in 1957, when he went to centre-half and played so superbly in United's gallant 10-man struggle.

That was just one of his remarkable qualities—he could play in any position. Wherever he played—half-back, centre-half, full-back, inside-forward, or centre-forward—he was outstanding, always the man in control of the game. He was renowned for his long, raking pass from one side of the field to the opposite wing. He had immense power in the tackle, and was rarely dispossessed himself. He was equally powerful with either foot, and scored many of his goals from distances of 20 to 40 yards. One memorable example was the one he

EPITAPHS FOR A GIANT

Sir Matt Busby: 'He seemed too good to be true. . . . Whatever was needed he had it. . . . He was prodigiously gifted in the arts and crafts of the game. His temperament was perfect. . . . Goodness only knows what impact he would have made on the game had he been spared. Any manager asked what he would like for Christmas would have said: "I would like a Duncan Edwards, please." '

Jimmy Murphy (United coach): 'There was only one Duncan Edwards.'

Bobby Charlton: 'He was a hard, unrelenting player in the tackle —harder than Dave Mackay, but with this toughness he combined the fairness and shrewdness of Danny Blanchflower. He had a shot which could beat the greatest goalkeeper in the world and yet when the pressure was on in his own goalmouth he would be there helping to clear the lines. He was never caught out of position. . . . English football will produce other talented players but there will only be one Duncan Edwards.'

Johnny Haynes: 'I would doubt if there ever has been a player quite like Duncan Edwards in football. . . . His greatest asset was his strength, not so much physical strength but a kind of dynamic strength which kept him endlessly on the move, covering, shadowing, backing up attacks, plunging through to finish off an attack with scoring shots. . . . His defensive play was quite outstanding, his heading superb . . . a joy it was to play with this man, the most indomitable player I have known.'

scored against Germany in Berlin in 1956. England were being over-run by the world champions, when he came out of defence, powered through the middle of the field, swerving past defenders, until from 25 yards he hit a glorious shot to put England on their way to a

The masterful young Duncan Edwards in action for England.

famous 3-1 victory. That was the day the Germans christened him 'Boom-Boom'.

He had a huge appetite for the game. In the 1956-57 season he played 95 matches—for United, England, and the Army. Having captained England Schoolboys and Under-23s, he would surely have led England, too, for many years. And despite all the adulation, he was modest and unassuming, always willing to help lesser mortals, a model professional in every way. When he died, it was not only United's and England's loss, it was also a tragic loss to the world of sport.

Memorial in a Dudley church.

GREAT TEAM PERFORMANCES

Matches are remembered for various reasons. They do not necessarily have to be cliff-hangers or produce the purest exhibitions of football. Some teams have made their permanent mark in soccer history for displays of courage in the face of adversity, such as the battered England's triumph over Mussolini's Italy in the 'Battle of Highbury', or in the face of heavy odds, such as the giant-killing feats of Colchester and Walsall. For pure football, though, the Hungarians of the early fifties stand out, and at club level the Real Madrid side of the late fifties—with Ferenc Puskas remarkably starring in both these great sides. These were teams that produced countless brilliant performances over a number of years. But perhaps the finest exhibition of soccer ever seen was put together by a side that 'clicked' just once— an ill-prepared bunch of little Scots who, back in 1928, won immortality as the 'Wembley Wizards'.

The 1953 Hungarians (top) and the England defence they mesmerized (left). Below left: 'The Battle of Highbury'. Below: Crawford gets Colchester's first against Leeds.

Kings of Europe

What was the greatest club match in football history? Most experts will put forward, without hesitation, the 1960 European Cup final between Real Madrid of Spain and Eintracht Frankfurt of West Germany. There have been closer matches, true, and there have been more exciting clashes. But for sheer quality of football, for dazzling teamwork and sparkling individual displays, the game that confirmed Real Madrid as 'Kings of Europe' stands out.

Real had dominated European competition since the inception of the European Cup in 1955. They had won the trophy each year, and were now in their fifth final. They had built a reputation as a team that went for goals. They never much cared about giving goals away, because they were always confident that they could score more. They had a remarkably high level of technical skill, and built up attacks in the classical manner of a deceptively slow, elaborate approach followed by an explosive finish. And at the heart of everything was the Argentinian 'maestro' Alfredo di Stefano. He was the man who had been the inspiration of their four previous victories, the great orchestrator of the side.

The side had been built up by their president, and former player, Santiago Bernabeu. First he built their superb new stadium, and then he went about recruiting players from all over the world, the great stars who would fill it. Di Stefano was his first signing, followed by names such as Franciso Gento, the flying left-winger from Spanish club Real Santander, Raymond Kopa from France, Jose Santamaria from Uruguay, Luis del Sol

Di Stefano, having as usual lost his marker, converts a cross from Canario for the equalizer, the first of his three.

from Betis Seville, and the overweight self-exile of the Hungarian Uprising Ferenc Puskas.

This was Puskas's first final, although he had played a part in the previous campaign. He had struck up a marvellous partnership with Di Stefano, and at Hampden Park in 1960 the pair of them were sheer magic.

Eintracht, though, were no pushovers, as demonstrated in the semi-finals, in which they hit six goals against Scottish champions Rangers in each leg. They had a remarkable duo of veterans in the 33-year-old scheming inside-forward Pfaff and the 35-year-old right-winger Kress, who put them ahead after 18 minutes. This wasn't the first time Real had been down in the final, and as usual it was Di Stefano who replied, lashing home a cross from Brazilian right-winger Canario eight minutes later. Three

minutes after this he took advantage of a defensive slip to put Real ahead.

Di Stefano was dominating the match, patrolling his usual beat between penalty spots, calling for the ball, laying it off, demoralizing the Germans. Then Puskas took the stage, scoring just before half-time from the bye-line, and in the second half from a penalty, with a header from a perfect Gento cross, and then with a brilliant pivot from just inside the box.

The Germans scored twice more, but in between Di Stefano treated the crowd to an exhibition of interpassing as he took the play from his own defence to his opponents' goal before slamming in a majestic seventh goal.

As the heroes of Madrid paraded the cup at the finish, the normally partisan Scottish crowd stood to give them a deafening ovation.

Puskas slots in a penalty with the greatest of ease to score the second of his four.

The Magnificent Magyars
The end of an era

England (2)3 Hungary (4)6
Sewell, Morten- Hidegkuti 3,
sen, Ramsey (pen) Puskas 2, Bozsik

Wembley, 25 November 1953, att. 100,000

England: Merrick; Ramsey, Eckersley; Wright, Johnston, Dickinson; Matthews, Taylor, Mortensen, Sewell, Robb.
Hungary: Grosics; Buzansky, Lantos; Bozsik, Lorant, Zakarias; Budai, Kocsis, Hidegkuti, Puskas, Czibor.

Hungary (3)7 England (0)1
Lantos, Puskas Broadis
2, Kocsis 2,
Toth, Hidegkuti

People's Stadium, Budapest, 23 May 1954, att. 92,000

Hungary: As above, except Toth for Budai.
England: Merrick; Staniforth, Byrne; Wright, Owen, Dickinson; Harris, Sewell, Jezzard, Broadis, Finney.

The two teams come out at Wembley, England led by Billy Wright (right) and Hungary by Ferenc Puskas. Behind the Hungarian captain are Gyula Grosics (keeper), Gyula Lorant (stopper), and Nandor Hidegkuti, the deep-lying centre-forward who scored a hat-trick.

England's first home defeat by foreign opposition (apart from little Eire's largely forgotten 2-0 win at Everton four years earlier) was achieved by perhaps the finest national side the world has seen. The speedy, fluent, confident Hungarians gave a display that would have shattered any team. England, ill-prepared, possibly over-confident after so many invincible years, were not in the same class. Not that they played badly. Their first two goals were brilliantly taken. But the Hungarians were so superior in almost every aspect of the game that the margin must have been greater had they not slackened off in the last half-hour, after building a 6-2 lead.

The average insular Englishman's pre-match assessment was 'No European nation has beaten us here, and none ever will'. After all, hadn't England beaten the Austrians in 1932 when the so-called *Wunderteam* were thrashing the strongest sides in Europe? Surely the Hungarians were coming to Wembley to learn a lesson, to find out how football was really played?

That the Hungarians were virtually unknown in England was due to an equally insular Press, who had largely ignored their remarkable record of success during the preceding years. Just how good was this record? In over 50 matches since the war they had averaged four goals a game, and it was five years since they had failed to score in an international. It was 22 matches and three and a half years since they had been beaten.

England Receive a Lesson

From the first minute of the match, when Nandor Hidegkuti slashed a 20-yard rising shot beyond Gilbert Merrick in goal (who said the Continentals couldn't shoot!), the Hungarians delivered a lesson—a lesson in ball control, in teamwork, in tactics, and in finishing. They tore England's fine defence to shreds

—and let there be no mistaking it, England have had few finer defences, with an outstanding half-back line of Billy Wright, Harry Johnston, and Jimmy Dickinson.

Wright himself summed it up perfectly: 'The Hungarians proceeded to produce some of the finest, most brilliantly applied football it has ever been my privilege to see. The ball did precisely what they wanted. They mixed the long pass with the short with unbelievable accuracy and imagination. They were relentless. They were superb.'

The temperament and the confidence of the Hungarians were first class, too, for they were put to the test shortly, when England equalized after 13 minutes. Johnston intercepted, burst out of defence, and fed Stan Mortensen. He took the ball on before putting Jackie Sewell through, unchallenged, to score. It was a classic move and it gave the England fans great heart—but not for long.

What happened next marked the end of an era. In a devastating onslaught on the England goal, Hungary scored three times in a seven-minute spell. The first, after 20 minutes, came from the left. Puskas put Zoltan Czibor away on the wing, his cross was met by the incomparable head of Sandor Kocsis, whose deflection was converted by Hidegkuti from close in. Then came the goal that is still talked about today. Kocsis put Czibor away on the right this time, and after rounding Bill Eckersley the speedy winger sent a low cross to the near post. Puskas had Wright tackling thin air as he rolled the ball back with his studs and rifled the ball inside Merrick all in one beautiful, flowing movement. Then a Puskas deflection from a Bozsik free-kick made the score 4-1.

Mortensen scored a typical bustling goal to make it 4-2 at half-time. But in the second-half an unstoppable drive from Bozsik and a volley that gave Hidegkuti his hat-trick put the result beyond doubt. A Ramsey penalty for England was little consolation.

The tactic of playing Hidegkuti as a deep-lying centre-forward had confused the England defence and caused them problems that they never solved. But it was plain for all to see that England were also years behind the Hungarians in the very basics of football—ball control, technique, and accuracy.

Lesson No. 2

In case anyone was misguided enough to think that the Wembley result was a fluke, the Hungarians repeated the lesson some six months later in Budapest, when they humiliated England 7-1. Unfortunately for England, this lesson, like the first, went largely unheeded. They still continued to approach their games in an almost amateur manner—ill-prepared, tactically naive, and with a stubborn belief that in the end English football would triumph.

As for the Hungarians—those magic and magnificent Magyars—they went on in game after game to produce dazzling football of breathtaking quality, and, with one exception, to dominate world foot-

Puskas (10) celebrates his classic goal with the English defence bemused.

ball until the break-up of the team after the Hungarian Uprising of 1956. That exception, sadly, was the World Cup of 1954, when they lost in the final to Germany. The best side did not win that day. The Hungarians had already beaten the Germans 8-3 in a group match, but an injury to Puskas had put him out until the final, for which he was not fully fit, and they failed to sustain an early two-goal lead. However, Hungary's record speaks for itself. This was their only defeat in 51 matches between June 1950 and November 1955, during which time they scored 220 goals against 58. And they scored in every game!

Sandor Kocsis, clean through, about to hit No. 4 in Budapest.

135

Wembley Wizards

The Wee Blue Devils

England   (0)**1**   **Scotland**   (2)**5**
Kelly   Jackson 3,
                         James 2

Wembley, 31 March 1928, British International Championship, att. 80,868.

England: Hufton (West Ham); Goodall (Huddersfield), Jones (Blackburn); Edwards (Leeds), Wilson (Huddersfield), Healless (Blackburn); Hulme (Arsenal), Kelly (Huddersfield), Dean (Everton), Bradford (Birmingham), Smith (Huddersfield).
Scotland: Harkness (Queen's Park); Nelson (Cardiff), Law (Chelsea); Gibson (Aston Villa), Bradshaw (Bury), McMullan (Manchester City); Jackson (Huddersfield), Dunn (Hibs), Gallacher (Newcastle), James (Preston), Morton (Rangers).

Jimmy McMullan leads his team out onto the slippery Wembley turf for what was to be Scotland's greatest victory over England since the Battle of Bannockburn. Following him out are Alec Jackson who scored three of the goals, and centre-forward Hughie Gallacher.

Scotland's 5-1 thrashing of England at Wembley in 1928 was their most famous victory, and it has remained so for over half a century. Two years later England beat the Scots 5-2 at Wembley, and they humiliated them by scores of 7-2 in 1955 and 9-3 in 1961. But none of these games made the same impact on football history. Why is it then that the victory of the team forever known as the 'Wembley Wizards' that rainy day in March 1928 has been immortalized? It wasn't that England were a great side at the time; far from it. And it wasn't that it was a thrilling see-saw match; it was, in the event, an extremely one-sided match. No, the answer lies in the quality of the Scottish football, the sheer exuberance of their play. The artistry of their forwards and half-backs produced football the like of which, some say, has never been seen since.

'Pray for Rain'

The Scots, as usual for that time, were ill-prepared for the match. Indeed, it is true to say that they were not prepared at all. The announcement of the side had been greeted with astonishment, and no little dismay, in Scotland. Eight of the side were playing for English clubs, some of their transfers having caused much bitterness in Scotland, where the feeling was that the home game was being denuded of its stars. Some Scottish favourites had been passed over, notably the Celtic 'goal machine' Jimmy McGrory, replaced by Hughie Gallacher—admittedly the regular centre-forward, but he had not played for two months. The forward line was the smallest in the history of Scottish soccer, right-winger Alec Jackson being the tallest at 5ft 7in.

On the Friday evening the players gathered at the Regent Palace Hotel in Piccadilly Circus, where they occupied a corner of the lounge amid the hubbub of excited fans consuming their normal ration of pre-match alcohol. Their only 'team talk' took place on the landing on the way to bed, when their captain Jimmy McMullan suggested they 'pray for rain'. How many of them did just that is not recorded, but the next day it poured!

The 'Wee Blue Devils'

The rain made the well-grassed Wembley pitch slippery, and this gave the little Scots an advantage over their bulkier opponents. Yet it all could have been so different, for England almost scored in the first few seconds, when Billy Smith cut in from the left and hammered a shot which hit the post and rebounded into play.

Only a couple of minutes later, however, Scotland gave notice that this was to be their day of days, with a beautifully fashioned goal, the ball going from man to man without an England player getting a sniff of it. It was that great attacking wing-half McMullan who started the move, holding the ball in midfield, calming the pace of the game, and setting up a string of passes, with Jimmy Gibson and Alex James. James found Alan Morton on the left. He beat Goodall, made for the bye-line, and centred, and there was Alec Jackson steaming in to head home Scotland's first after three minutes.

Both keepers performed well to prevent further goals until nearly half-time. Then James got the ball from Gibson, feinted to shrug off an English challenge in that inimitable way of his, and cracked the ball on the volley from 25 yards for what he later described as the best goal he ever scored.

Scotland went in at half-time with a deserved two-goal lead. McMullan and Gibson had taken control of the midfield, Jackson was exuding confidence on the right, Gallacher was tying up England's central defence and giving his inside-forwards the time and space they needed, and James was wreaking his usual havoc with his little shuffles and feints.

And then in the second half Scotland really turned it on. They completely dominated the game and made England look like helpless, stumbling schoolboys. Only fine goalkeeping kept the score down. James hit the cross-bar, and in one amazing incident Gallacher slipped on his face as he was about to touch the ball home from a yard out. But the goals came. Morton, who had had a relatively quiet first half, came into his own, exhibiting his unique wizardry on the left. He made two more goals for Jackson—Scotland's third, in the 65th minute, a carbon copy of the first, headed in from a bye-line cross; and the last, five minutes from the end, this from another cross which Jackson volleyed home, again from close in. James, whose cross-field ball to Jackson had time and again opened up the English defence, scored the fourth himself, pouncing on a loose ball as Gallacher was tackled and smashing the ball home, laying out a defender on the way. England scored their goal in the last minute with a free-kick from over 20 yards out by Kelly. It was no consolation.

The Plaudits

Years later, the critics—English critics, at that—were still raving about Scotland's performance.

Gallacher (left) is just wide with an attempt from close in as the battered English defence look on helplessly.

That doyen of football writers Ivan Sharpe summed it up like this: 'England were not merely beaten. They were bewildered—run to a standstill, made to appear utterly inferior by a team whose play was as cultured and beautiful as I ever expect to see. . . . It was a triumph for the Scottish style. . . . Never has sheer ball-skill and artistry gained greater triumph. . . . There were times in the second half when the play was the purest and finest ever seen.'

And Ralph Finn was inspired to a lifetime of soccer writing when he saw the game as a 16-year-old: 'I owe them [the Wembley Wizards] such a lot. They opened my eyes to real football, showed me how it should be played and that it could be played. They took me from that insular, narrow-minded partisanship which sees no merit in anything outside of one's immediate neighbourhood, and, by teaching me first to appreciate Scots Soccer, led me on to delight in good football wherever it was played and whoever played it.'

Sadly, the Scots have never played like this again. It was a one-off performance when five or six of their greatest players 'got it together', in the modern idiom, and inspired the rest to play above themselves, the result being a perfect exhibition of football. Few sides, if any, have been able to match it since.

WALES THE WINNERS

The Wembley game, strangely enough, had no bearing on the International Championship, except that England 'earned' the wooden spoon, finishing without a point for the first time. The great Wembley Wizards were only third, having drawn with Wales and, only a month before their Wembley triumph, lost at home to Ireland. Wales topped the table:

	P	W	D	L	F	A	P
Wales	3	2	1	0	6	4	5
Ireland	3	2	0	1	4	2	4
Scotland	3	1	1	1	7	4	3
England	3	0	0	3	2	9	0

The Battle of Highbury

'By our War Correspondent'

The international between England and Italy in November 1934 has gone down in soccer folklore as the 'Battle of Highbury'. One of the most violent matches, up till then, seen on an English football pitch, it had one newspaperman signing his report 'BY OUR WAR CORRESPONDENT'. And after the game, the Football Association seriously contemplated withdrawing from competition with foreign sides.

The Build-up

Italy had just won the World Cup, for which England had not entered. But England, with characteristic arrogance but a certain amount of justification, regarded themselves as world masters of the game, and no foreign side had been able to disprove this boast on English soil (nor would they for another 19 years). So this meeting, it was widely felt, was for the unofficial title of world champions. In Italy the match was billed as 'The most important football match to be played anywhere in the world since the Great War'.

In addition, Fascism was flourishing in Italy at that time, and their dictator, Mussolini, was bent on boosting the morale of the people. A victory for Italy over England in the home of football would be a great triumph. It has been said, although it was never substantiated, that Mussolini promised the players magnificent bonuses if they won, and this was played up in the English Press.

The Italians had prepared for the match together, secretly, in a country resort. The England team, as was usual in those days, had no preliminary get-together, nor did they even have a team manager or coach. And because of injuries with their clubs on the previous Saturday, two of the selected eleven had to be replaced.

The two men drafted into the side at the last moment were both

England (3)3   Italy (0)2
Brook 2, Drake   Meazza 2

Highbury, 14 November 1934, att. 50,000

England: Moss; Male, Hapgood (Arsenal); Britton (Everton), Barker (Derby), Copping (Arsenal); Matthews (Stoke), Bowden, Drake, Bastin (Arsenal), Brook (Manchester City).

Italy: Ceresoli (Inter); Monzeglio (Bologna), Allemandi (Inter); Ferraris (Lazio), Monti, Bertolini (Juventus); Guaita (Rome), Serantoni (Juventus), Meazza (Inter), Ferrari, Orsi (Juventus).

The calm before the storm: Hapgood (right) greets the Italian captain, the ruthless Monti.

Arsenal players winning their first caps, right-back George Male and centre-forward Ted Drake. This meant that seven Arsenal men were playing 'at home', so to speak, an all-time record for England. On the right wing was Stanley Matthews, making only his second international appearance.

The Match

From the kick-off it was apparent that this was going to be a rough game, and the Italians conceded a penalty before the match was a minute old. Eric Brook, the Manchester City left-winger, took it, but Italy's acrobatic keeper, Ceresoli, made a brilliant full-length diving save. This inspired the Italians to become even more excited. But perhaps the incident that sparked off the 'battle' more than anything else occurred a minute or so later, when their captain, Luisito Monti, hurt his toe in a challenge on Drake. An Argentinian who seemed hell-bent on living up to an already frightening reputation, Monti was convinced this was a deliberate foul. And although he was eventually persuaded to leave the field, he managed to hobble around on what was a broken toe and stir up his team-mates to the excessive violence that took place.

The action, on and off the ball, packed into the next few minutes was astonishing. First, England scored. Matthews received the ball out on the right, and could see Allemandi, Italy's left-back, pounding towards him. By this time he knew what to expect, but instead of taking evasive action, he took the ball straight up to him, sent him the wrong way with a typical dummy, and sped past him on the outside. Having drawn other defenders out of position, Matthews then sent a spinning cross to the far post, where it was met by the blond head of Brook, who atoned for his penalty miss.

Shortly after this, an England player had his legs scythed from under him a few yards outside the box. As Brook shaped to take the kick, Ceresoli, having saved a penalty from the same man, imperiously waved his defenders out of the way. He couldn't have seen the ball as Brook blasted it into the net.

The first serious England casualty was Hapgood, who received a cynical Italian elbow in his face which broke his nose. Shortly after he was carried off, Monti left the field, and then Drake broke away and slammed home a stunning third goal. The game was only 15 minutes old, and England were three up and two players had left the field.

England centre-forward Ted Drake (extreme right) looks menacing as Ceresoli saves. Drake's charging of the keeper, though fair, made him the prime target for Italian violence, and he was later carried off.

Hapgood returned with his nose patched up, but before half-time Drake, who had had the temerity to charge the Italian keeper (a fair tactic, but one that was deplored on the Continent) and had been the object of much of the violence, was also carried off.

The second half continued where the first left off, although the Italians took time off from physical aggression midway through the half for Meazza to score two brilliant goals. That left England to fight a rearguard action, and who better to do it than left-half Copping, who never shaved before a match, and the tough Brook. Bruised and battered, they gave as good as they got, and with Moss, Male, and Hapgood performing defensive heroics, England held out.

The Aftermath

The England dressing-room after the match was like a casualty station. Hapgood and Brook, who had finished the match with an arm strapped up, were dispatched to hospital. Drake, Copping, Moss, Bastin, and Bowden were being patched up.

As for the Italians, they regarded the match as a moral victory. Their team manager, Vittorio Pozzo, blamed their defeat on Monti's injury, although he was later to express, not for the first time, his great admiration for English play and players.

Perhaps we should let the referee have the last word. A Swede, appointed apparently because he spoke neither English nor Italian, he said that he had to warn two of the Italian defenders repeatedly. Then came a masterpiece of understatement: '. . . whether they understood me or not, I do not know. I hope they did.'

Trainer Tom Whittaker working on the wounded after the match—from the left: Wilf Copping, Frank Moss, Cliff Bastin, and Ted Drake.

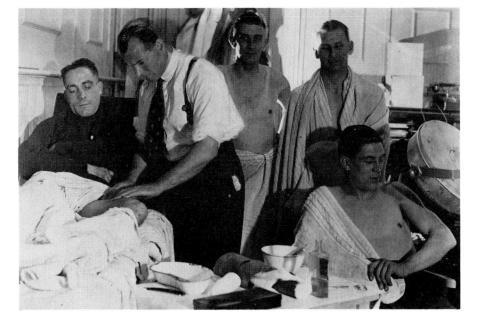

The Giant-Killers

Every dog has his day

Ray Crawford hooks the ball past Sprake while lying on the ground.

Colchester (2)3 Leeds (0)2
Crawford 2,   Hunter, Giles
Simmons

Layer Road Ground, 13 February 1971, att. 16,000

Colchester: Smith; Hall, Garvey, Kurila, Cram; Gilchrist, Gibbs, Simmons; Lewis, Crawford, Mahon.
Leeds: Sprake; Reaney, Charlton, Hunter, Cooper; Bates, Giles, Madeley; Lorimer, Clarke, Jones.

Some of the finest team performances in football have been the giant-killing exploits of lowly clubs that are a regular feature of knockout competitions. This is particularly true of the FA Cup, the history of which is littered with the bodies of famous clubs humbled by teams from lower divisions or even by non-League sides.

The FA Cup has the reputation of being a great 'leveller', inspiring small fry to play above themselves, and bringing the top clubs down to their opponents' level. Non-Leaguers that have won Cup fame include Yeovil, whose sloping ground went into football folklore when they beat First Division Sunderland 2-1 in 1949, and Hereford, who in 1972 held Newcastle away and won the replay 2-1.

Perhaps the greatest team performance in the category of Cup giant-killing, however, was that of Fourth Division Colchester United in 1971. Having reached the fifth round by virtue of victories over two non-League sides and clubs from the lower divisions, they were drawn at home to Leeds. Leeds had built a reputation for ruthless invincibility. In 1969, they had won the League with a record 67 points and only two defeats. In 1970, they were runners-up and also beaten

cup finalists. Now, in 1971, with two-thirds of the League programme over, they were leading the table by three points and were hot favourites to win the Cup.

The Leeds side was crammed with internationals. They were renowned as being professionals through and through. Colchester, on the other hand, were a team built round rejects in their thirties, pieced together virtually from other clubs' discards. Only centre-forward Ray Crawford, at 34, could look back on a successful career.

It was Crawford who first rattled Leeds. He harassed centre-half Jackie Charlton into a host of errors as Colchester ran and ran in an attempt to unsettle the favourites. After 18 minutes he headed a brilliant goal from a long, dipping free-kick, and shortly afterwards shattered their composure further with his second—hooked in while lying on the ground!

Two down at half-time, Leeds came out determined to take control. But Colchester played inspired football, and after 10 minutes Dave Simmons swept through and headed past the hesitant Sprake for a 3-0 scoreline that shook the country as it flashed onto television screens up and down the land. Finally, Leeds recovered. They

scored twice, after 61 and 75 minutes, but keeper Graham Smith came to flagging Colchester's rescue with a series of heroic saves.

Colchester's victory, above all, was a tribute to veteran manager Dick Graham, who had welded a collection of 'misfits' and 'no-hopers' into a team that for one afternoon outplayed one of the strongest sides in football history.

WALSALL

The name of Walsall became synonymous with giant-killing when they shamed the mighty Arsenal in 1933. In 1931, Arsenal had won the League with a record 66 points and in 1932 had narrowly missed the League and Cup double. Drawn away to Walsall in the third round of the Cup, they were again comfortably leading Division I. Walsall were an almost anonymous Third Division side whose place in the table depended on whether they were playing in the North or the South section of the division.

Yet they defeated the greatest side in the land. The scoreline 'Walsall 2 Arsenal 0' sent a shockwave through the footballing world that has been reverberating ever since. Walsall had become the 'Waterloo' of soccer. And although there have been comparable shocks since then, Arsenal have never lived down the day they 'met their Walsall'.

THE WORLD CUP

The FIFA World Cup

Every four years, the world's leading footballing countries compete for the FIFA World Cup. With over 140 countries affiliated to FIFA, the entrants have to play in groups to qualify for the finals, which often provide a feast of football watched by hundreds of millions of fans on television, in almost every country of the world. Brazil have provided many of these soccer feasts, and by winning in 1970 for the third time took permanent possession of the original cup, the Jules Rimet Trophy. They have always been worthy winners, but other fine sides, such as the Hungarians of 1954 and the Dutch of 1974, have failed at the final hurdle.

Not all of the world's greatest footballers have been fortunate enough to parade their skills on the World Cup stage. Those that have include Brazil's Pelé and Garrincha, Germany's Beckenbauer and Müller, Holland's Cruyff, and Portugal's Eusebio.

Some of the most memorable moments have been produced by the unlikeliest sources, such as the North Koreans of 1966 and the American side that beat England in 1950.

And the World Cup has thrown up some unlikely heroes, too, among them Just Fontaine of France, scorer of a record 13 goals in the 1958 finals, and Geoff Hurst, who hit a hat-trick for England in the 1966 final.

1978—Argentina at last

Above: Gerd Müller—14 goals
Below: Jairzinho—goal a game

Above: Just Fontaine—13 goals
Below: Geoff Hurst—hat-trick

141

Hurst's Hat-trick

The target man strikes

To score a hat-trick in a World Cup final is a unique achievement in the first fifty years of the World Cup. Yet the man who accomplished this out of the ordinary feat, Geoff Hurst, was never a prolific goal-scorer. He was playing in his first season as an international, had won his place in England's World Cup side owing to an injury to another player, and had eventually been a controversial choice for the final. Nevertheless, Hurst was something special, for he was the first of the 'target men', an unspectacular role which involves a great deal of unselfish running for others. In that 1966 World Cup final, Geoff Hurst got his just reward.

A reserve wing-half at West Ham in the early sixties, Hurst could see little future for himself until manager Ron Greenwood decided to convert him into a striker—but one with a difference, for he was to create a new role. It was a role, however, that was not appreciated by the fans, and the big man was regarded as a bit of a 'cart-horse'. One of the few to appreciate Hurst, though, was England manager Alf Ramsey, and when he picked him for the England squad it was as much of a surprise to Hurst as it was to everyone else.

Hurst rises to nod home Bobby Moore's free-kick for England's equalizer.

Hurst made his debut for England at Wembley in February 1966 against West Germany, retained his place (and scored) against Scotland two months later, but had a poor time in England's pre-World Cup tour to Scandinavia. When the World Cup started, Jimmy Greaves and Roger Hunt were the strikers, with Bobby Charlton playing a deep-lying centre-forward.

Then came Greaves's injury, a badly gashed shin. So Hurst found himself playing in the quarter-finals, against Argentina. He scored the only goal of the game, a typical 'West Ham goal', ghosting onto a cross from club colleague Peters on the near post and placing his header across the keeper into the far corner of the net. In the semi-final, against Portugal, he made Bobby Charlton's second goal.

Greaves was now fit, though, and the ever-modest Hurst spent the days fearing he would be omitted from the final. He need not have worried, for had Ramsey seen fit to restore Greaves—one of the greatest goalscorers of modern times—to the side, it must surely have been to the exclusion of Hunt or Ball. (There are still those who say that if anyone deserved to score a hat-trick in a World Cup final, it was Jimmy Greaves, and it would be difficult to disagree.)

The Final

England's opponents in the final were West Germany, and it looked like being a close match, with England marginal favourites, chiefly because of their 'home' advantage. There were 93,000 at Wembley, the pitch was in fine condition, and the weather was a little showery.

West Germany shocked England with a goal in 12 minutes: an untypical Wilson error, and Haller slotted the ball home. But seven

Hurst lashes in England's controversial third goal from close in.

142

minutes later Bobby Moore took a quick free-kick that caught everyone napping—everyone, that is, except his alert club-mate Hurst, who ran onto it and headed past Tilkowski. The Germans had the better of the remainder of the first half, but after the interval England got on top. After a lot of pressure they took a deserved lead in the 78th minute, when Tilkowski could only parry Hurst's shot from a Ball corner and Peters volleyed past him from close in.

The Germans appeared to be on their knees and it looked all over, when out of the blue Weber scrambled an equalizer following a disputed free-kick. Hurst must have been as sickened as any of his team-mates at having victory snatched

away in the dying seconds—but what followed earned him a very special place in soccer history.

In the 10th minute of extra time, the indefatigable Ball, after a long chase to the right wing, pulled the ball back to the ever-available Hurst, who hooked it hard against the underside of the bar. Did it cross the line? Hunt thought so, spinning round and leaping for joy. Weber, who had headed the ball over, and his team-mates thought differently. The referee wasn't sure, but his Russian linesman was, and a goal was given. It is still argued about to this day.

The Germans had nothing left. But this time Hurst made sure. Picking up a long clearance from Moore near the half-way line, he made for goal, with a defender in despairing pursuit, and as he reached the box he hit a glorious

WORLD CUP SCORING FEATS

Although Hurst was the first man to score three goals in a World Cup final, two others have scored three in World Cup finals, both Brazilians—Pelé, inevitably, and Vava. Both scored two in Brazil's spectacular 5-2 victory over Sweden in the 1958 final, and Vava scored his third four years later, when Brazil beat Czechoslovakia 3-1 in Chile. Pelé missed that match through injury, but got his third in 1970, 12 years after his first two, in Brazil's fine 4-1 triumph over Italy.

The most goals scored in one World Cup is 13, by Frenchman Just Fontaine in 1958. In the group matches he scored three against Paraguay, two against Yugoslavia, and one against Scotland; another two against Northern Ireland in the quarter-finals, one in the semi-final with Brazil, and then four, all in the second half, in the third-place match with West Germany.

Leading World Cup scorers:

Gerd Müller (W. Germany)	14
Just Fontaine (France)	13
Pelé (Brazil)	12
Sandor Kocsis (Hungary)	11
Helmut Rahn (W. Germany)	10
Teofilo Cubillas (Peru)	10

drive into the roof of the net. What a way to finish a World Cup!

Hurst went on to play 49 games for England and score 24 goals, no mean total. Yet despite his consistency, his continued selection met with criticism from many quarters. He was a model professional, a players' player, but few people outside football understood the contribution he made to the games he played in and to the game as a whole. He will, of course, always be remembered for his World Cup hat-trick, but it is the largely unnoticed things—the little runs hither and thither, the non-stop harrying of defenders, the constant availability for a pass, the ghosting onto the near post—that have made the most significant impact on football.

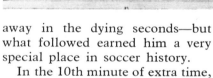

Fans are already on the pitch (above, arrowed) in the dying seconds as Hurst homes in on goal and slams his third (below).

A Tale of Two Penalties

The 1974 World Cup Final

The final of the 1974 World Cup was not a classic, but it had a dramatic opening, with a Dutch goal in 78 seconds—before a West German player had even touched the ball.

The Germans, reigning European champions and playing in front of their own crowds, had been strong favourites to win the competition from the start. Marshalled at the back by the great Franz Beckenbauer and spearheaded by Gerd Müller, whose ability to convert the half-chance was already legendary, they were a versatile footballing side.

The Dutch, with some brilliant individuals but an erratic international record, had started as dark horses but had gradually established themselves as the most colourful and entertaining footballing side in the finals. They had the incomparable Johan Cruyff and the all-action Johan Neeskens, and they had the rapidly growing reputation as a team of all-rounders who played 'total football', with the accent on attack.

They kicked off, and began passing the ball among themselves in their own half. Suddenly Cruyff was in possession and racing through the German lines like a thoroughbred, with his designated 'shadow', the tenacious Berti Vogts, struggling like a selling-plater in his wake. Cruyff carried the ball some 50 yards and danced into the penalty area. Uli Hoeness, the only man who could match Cruyff's pace, had chased back to help his startled defence, but his challenge was clumsy, and down went Cruyff. English referee Jack Taylor pointed to the spot. Neeskens cracked in the penalty, and the Dutch were ahead with barely a minute gone.

The German game began to get physical, and Taylor showed Vogts the yellow card for persistent fouling after only four minutes. Neeskens, though, chopped Hoeness down twice in the next minute and got away with it. Then, suddenly, the Dutch became the villains of the piece. Wim van Hanegem was booked for pushing Müller in an off-the-ball incident spotted by a linesman. Soon after this, Bernd Holzenbein was put away on the left. As he moved into the Dutch penalty area, Wim Jansen came across to challenge and Holzenbein went sprawling. It was by no means a clear-cut foul, but the referee had no hesitation in awarding another spot-kick. Paul Breitner made no mistake and the Germans were level, after 25 minutes.

The second German goal also came soon after a Dutch booking—Neeskens was finally shown the yellow card for bringing down Holzenbein and almost trampling on him. The man who made the goal was Rainer Bonhof, who was becoming more and more impressive in midfield. He beat Arie Haan near the right-hand bye-line and crossed square to the lurking Müller, who hooked the ball low just inside the far post. It was a typical opportunist Müller goal, a couple of minutes before half-time—and enough to win the World Cup for West Germany.

The Germans remained on top for about five minutes of the second half, but thereafter it was nearly all Holland, who went close several times. Most experts agreed that the better side lost, and there was a feeling that the Germans had cunningly taken advantage of their own early setbacks. For although referee Taylor could hardly be faulted for any of his decisions, the Germans had gradually capitalized on his understandable willingness to accept opportunities to redress the balance regarding his marginal decisions.

The game is barely a minute old when Neeskens scores from the spot.

Eusebio v North Korea

The North Koreans were the unknown quantity of the 1966 World Cup. They had beaten Australia twice, 6-1 and 3-1, to earn a place in the finals, but no one really took them seriously. The average height of the entire squad was only 5ft 5in, so they were quoted at 1,000-1 at the outset.

They won respect in their first group match, despite their 3-0 defeat by the hefty Russians. A 1-1 draw with Chile and then a sensational 1-0 win over the Italians put them into the quarter-finals, and people were beginning to notice this superbly fit, well-drilled side of clever little ball-players who had already won the hearts of the Ayresome Park crowd. But now they were up against the all-conquering Portugal, victors over Brazil.

Within a minute of the kick-off, though, at Goodison Park, the little men with the strange-sounding names were a goal up. Within 25 minutes they were three up. Their non-stop chasing and clever individual work was tearing holes in the always suspect back four of the Portuguese. As the news was flashed around the world, it seemed that a new football force had emerged from the obscurity of the Far East.

But that was when Eusebio decided to take matters into his own hands. Going deep to collect the ball, he began to run it at the Korean defence. His first goal came after 27 minutes—an exchange of

THE BLACK PANTHER

Eusebio's performance in the 1966 World Cup—unlike that of the North Koreans—was not just a flash in the pan. For he was the star of the fine Benfica side that took over Real Madrid's mantle in the European Cup in the early 1960s. Born in Mozambique and nicknamed the 'Black Panther', he was a lithe, graceful footballer, powerful in the air and with an explosive right-foot shot. He used his tremendous speed and body swerve to cut through opposing defences. He scored two goals when Benfica beat Real Madrid 5-3 in the 1962 European Cup final, and won three runners-up medals in the next six years. His 46-goal tally in European Cup competition is second only to Di Stefano's. A member of the Rest of the World team against England in 1963, he was voted European Footballer of the Year in 1965.

passes with Simoes before lashing the ball into the net. He retrieved the ball himself and ran with it back to the centre circle—a process that was to be repeated two minutes before half-time, when he scored from a spot-kick awarded for a foul on the giant Torres. Then, 15 minutes after the interval he completed his hat-trick with a ferocious shot from Simoes's cross, having put the left-winger away himself.

That was virtually the end of the gallant Koreans. If ever one man had taken complete charge of a game, this was it. It was Eusebio versus North Korea, and they just

didn't know how to stop him. And there he was again, the 'Black Panther' from Mozambique, jinking through their defence, just about to shoot, when he was tripped. So he had to score his fourth from the spot again. Torres added a fifth for good measure just before the end.

The Portuguese team eventually finished third, after losing to England in the semi-finals, and Eusebio was easily the tournament's top scorer with 9 goals. The North Koreans disappeared into obscurity once more. Will we ever see the like of them again?

Left: Eusebio strikes and reduces the North Korean lead to 3-1. Right: They finally find a way to stop him! He scored from the spot.

Argentina at last

From 1930 to 1978

For nearly half a century Argentina lived in the shadow of their great South American rivals, first Uruguay and then Brazil, who between them won the World Cup five times from 1930 to 1970. In the first World Cup, held in 1930, it was Uruguay who beat them 4-2 in the final.

From the very start of their World Cup history, Argentina were caught up in controversy. In their first match, against France, their attacking centre-half Luisito Monti took time off from incapacitating opponents to score the only goal of the game after 81 minutes. But when, after only 84 minutes, the referee blew up for time, with France in a possible scoring position, pandemonium broke out. He eventually admitted his mistake and had to recall the teams from their dressing-rooms to finish the match.

Farcical refereeing also pervaded Argentina's next game, in which five penalties were awarded—and Monti wasn't even playing! How many resulted in goals is not recorded, but Argentina beat Mexico 6-3. Guillermo Stabile, who had not played in the first match, scored a hat-trick, and he scored another two in the 3-1 defeat of Chile that qualified Argentina for the semi-finals. That game was marked by a brawl between the teams—sparked off, naturally, by a blatant Monti foul—that was eventually broken up by the police. Yet no one was sent off.

Argentina went on to thrash the United States 6-1 in the semi-finals, before meeting Uruguay in the final. Boatloads of Argentinian fans crossed the River Plate from Buenos Aires to Montevideo, and all were searched for arms, both on arrival and at the stadium, which was packed with nearly 100,000 spectators two hours before the kick-off.

Uruguay opened the scoring but Argentina equalized, and 10 minutes from half-time Stabile put them ahead with his eighth goal of the tournament, a record unsurpassed for 24 years. But in a surprisingly sporting game, Uruguay scored three without reply in the second half. After the match, though, Argentina complained of Uruguayan 'brutality' and one-sided refereeing, and a crowd stormed the Uruguayan consulate in Buenos Aires—presumably to compensate for their team's good behaviour in the final.

So this was the start of Argentina's stormy career in the world Cup. In 1934 they went to Italy, but were knocked out in the first round of the sudden-death tournament by Sweden. There were no survivors from the 1930 side—except the ubiquitous Monti, who was displaying his many-sided talents for the winners, Italy!

Below, left to right, both pages: 1930—Argentina lead . . . but lose. 1966—Rattin (left) is ordered off. 1978—Triumph at last.

Disputes

Disputes with Brazil as well as Uruguay led to Argentina's absence from the World Cup until 1958, by which time Uruguay had recorded their second success and Brazil were embarking on the road to world domination. After colourless performances in both 1958 and 1962, Argentina were again serious contenders in 1966—and again knee-deep in controversy. In their group match with West Germany, Albrecht was sent off for a dangerous tackle, but they qualified for the quarter-finals, where they met England, the host country.

This match was to underline the widening rift between the European and the South American game. Instead of trying to play the fine football they were capable of, Argentina came out looking for trouble, and had the referee regularly reaching for his notebook to record the offenders guilty of a series of deliberate fouls. Their captain and marvellously gifted attacking centre-half Antonio Rattin was constantly at the referee's elbow, provoking him with arguments and complaints. He was finally ordered off when he continued to object to the booking of a colleague—and refused to go. It was more than 10 minutes before he could be persuaded to leave, and he made his way reluctantly and slowly round the pitch, gesturing to the crowd as he went.

Argentina's foolhardiness was emphasized by the fact that their 10

Belo Horizonte

men held out for over 40 minutes before Hurst headed the winner for England 13 minutes from time. England went on to win the World Cup, and Argentina had blown their chance.

Eight years later, in West Germany, Argentine football appeared to have reformed. Without scintillating, they nevertheless reached the last eight after some spirited and popular performances, and they took eventual defeat sportingly. The cynics put it down to the fact that Argentina were due to host the next World Cup—a controversial choice, not only because of their unsavoury record in international football but also because of the terrorism rife in the country at that time.

In the event, the 1978 World Cup went off smoothly, and Argentina emerged finally as winners. They never reached the heights of the Brazilians of previous World Cups, but they played entertaining football, with no hint of the misdemeanours that had characterized them in the past.

They had to beat Peru by four goals in the last of their semi-final group matches to overtake Brazil, and their 6-0 victory was welcomed by all but the Brazilians, whose negative football had lost them many friends and had tarnished memories of their past glories. The final against Holland was a thriller, with captain Daniel Passarella an inspiration in defence and the non-stop Osvaldo Ardiles always at the heart of the action. A Dutch equalizer in the 82nd minute took the match into extra time, but Mario Kempes—the star of the tournament—scored his second and then made one for Daniel Bertoni to clinch the game 3-1. At last Argentina were champions.

England keeper Williams goes up with Gaetjens but cannot stop the goal—1-0 to the USA!

Mention the name Belo Horizonte to an English football fan over the age of 40 and he will cringe with embarrassment. For it is the name of a city in Brazil—it means 'beautiful horizon'—where in 1950, during the finals of the World Cup, England suffered the most humiliating defeat in their history—at the hands of the United States!

A handful of part-timers from a country where 'football' meant the gridiron game and soccer barely merited a mention on the sports pages, the Americans were not given a chance. England had won 23 and drawn 3 of their 30 post-war internationals. Despite the absence of Stanley Matthews, the presence of Finney, Mannion, Mortensen,

and Wright was surely enough to guarantee England—joint favourites with Brazil—a flood of goals.

But they never came—not one. The woodwork was struck four times, a Mullen header was cleared from a position seemingly a yard behind the line, two apparent penalties were not awarded, and the Americans defended valiantly, growing in confidence as the game progressed. And then they scored, with a Gaetjens header from their only real chance—in contrast to the many squandered by England.

True, England were ill-prepared; they were tired from their usual strength-sapping domestic season; and a bumpy pitch with spectators crowded in close was not conducive to the best football. But to lose to the United States! That is a memory that will haunt English sport until the day a team of Englishmen beat the Americans at baseball.

Brazil keep the Cup

Three-time winners

Above: The 17-year-old Pelé, arms aloft, wraps up Brazil's 1958 win with a header. Below right: Pelé celebrates the historic third triumph.

If any team deserved to keep the World Cup, it was the Brazil side of 1970. And by winning the Jules Rimet Trophy for the third time, they did just that.

Brazil made the World Cup what it is—a stage for all that's best in world football. It is not always like that, unfortunately, but Brazil set a standard of excellence for the rest to aim at.

In the fourth World Cup, staged in Brazil in 1950, they had narrowly lost in the final pool to Uruguay, when a draw would have given them the trophy. This was Uruguay's second win, and Italy had won the other two competitions. Who would have thought, then, that Brazil would be the first country to win the trophy three times?

The start of their epic triumph came in 1958, when they got better and better as the tournament progressed—with the dazzling young Pelé, the dashing Vava, the penetrative Didi, and the irresistible Garrincha—culminating with their memorable 5-2 victory in the final over host country Sweden.

In 1962, in what was a substandard World Cup in Chile, Brazil nevertheless emerged again as well-deserved winners, despite losing

BRAZIL'S RECORD

Brazil, the only country to reach the finals of every World Cup, have a remarkable record of success in the tournament. Here is their complete playing record, with their position in each competition on the right.

	P	W	D	L	For	Ag	Pos
1930	2	1	0	1	5	2	–
1934	1	0	0	1	1	3	–
1938	5	3	1	1	14	11	3
1950	6	4	1	1	22	6	2
1954	3	1	1	1	8	5	–
1958	6	5	1	0	16	4	1
1962	6	5	1	0	14	5	1
1966	3	1	0	2	4	6	–
1970	6	6	0	0	19	7	1
1974	7	3	2	2	6	4	4
1978	7	4	3	0	10	3	3
Total	52	33	10	9	119	56	

the injured Pelé after two matches. Amarildo filled the gap admirably, Vava continued to score, and Garrincha excelled himself on the right wing. In addition, keeper Gylmar and full-backs Djalma and Nilton Santos, all winning their second medal, were solid at the back.

The 1966 World Cup was a disaster for the Brazilians. Pelé might have pulled them through had he not been so savagely treated in the two matches he played in that he

swore never to play in the World Cup again.

But, to the glory of the game, he did not keep this promise. He was back on the world's football stage four years later in Mexico to spearhead the finest exhibition of football yet seen in the World Cup and inspire Brazil to a universally popular triumph.

Despite a shaky goalkeeper in Felix, whose errors would have shattered the confidence of lesser sides, Brazil marched on regardless. The weakness in their defence served only to emphasize their superbly inventive attacking football, where the spectacular became commonplace, the impossible always just around the corner.

In winning their six matches, they scored 19 goals and conceded 7. Jairzinho, the powerful and direct right-winger, scored in every match, riding tackles that were only vaguely aimed at the ball. Gerson was master of the midfield, and Rivelino's left-foot dummies and cannonball shots were a revelation. The slight and subtle Tostão was the perfect foil for Pelé up front. And Pelé was Pelé—the goals, the dummies, the telepathic passes, the bubbling enthusiasm. The winning outright of the Jules Rimet Trophy marked the end of an era, and no one could deny Brazil their unique achievement.

World Cup Records

Wins	3	Brazil (1958, 62, 70)
Appearances	11	Brazil (1930-78)
Highest score	9	Hungary (v S. Korea 1954)
	9	Yugoslavia (v Zaïre 1974)
—in final	5	Brazil (v Sweden 1958)
Highest aggregate	12	Austria 7 Switzerland 5 (1954)
Individual		
Appearances	5	Antonio Carbajal (Mexico)
Goals	14	Gerd Müller (W. Germany)
—in one tournament	13	Just Fontaine (France 1958)
—in final	3	Geoff Hurst (England 1966)

Attendance Records

World Cup	199,850	Brazil v Uruguay, Maracana 1950
International	183,341	Brazil v Uruguay, Maracana 1969
Club (Brazil)	177,636	Flamengo v Fluminense, Maracana 1963
Europe		
International	149,547	Scotland v England, Hampden Park 1937
Club (Scottish Cup final)	146,433	Celtic v Aberdeen, Hampden Park 1937
European Cup	135,826	Celtic v Leeds Utd, Hampden Park 1970
—final	127,621	Real Madrid v Eintracht, Hampden 1960
FA Cup (final)	126,047	Bolton v West Ham, Wembley 1923
Scottish League	118,567	Rangers v Celtic, Ibrox 1939
Football League	83,260	Manchester Utd v Arsenal, Maine Rd 1948

Top left: Billy Wright of England, the first player to win a hundred international caps, watched by Duncan Edwards, the youngest man to win a full England cap. **Top right:** The 1923 FA Cup final, the first at Wembley, where a record 126,047 paid to get in and an estimated 40,000 to 70,000 broke in. **Below:** The Brazil side that put a record five goals past Sweden in the 1958 World Cup final. **Right:** A goalmouth incident in the Brazil-Uruguay World Cup decider that drew a world record 199,850 to the Maracana Stadium, Rio de Janeiro, in 1950.

World Cup Finals

1930 Montevideo, Uruguay, 30 July, att. 100,000
Uruguay (1)**4** **Argentina** (2)**2**
Dorado, Cea, Iriarte, Castro   Peucelle, Stabile
Leading scorer: 8 Stabile (Argentina)

1934 Rome, Italy, 10 June, att. 55,000 (Extra time)
Italy (0)(1)**2** **Czechoslovakia** (0)(1)**1**
Orsi, Schiavio   Puc
Leading scorers: 4 Conen (Ger.), Nejedly (Cz), Schiavio (It.)

1938 Paris, France, 19 June, att. 65,000
Italy (3)**4** **Hungary** (1)**2**
Colaussi 2, Piola 2   Titkos, Sarosi
Leading scorer: 8 Leonidas (Brazil)

1950 Rio, Brazil, 16 July, att. 199,850 (Deciding match in final group)
Uruguay (0)**2** **Brazil** (0)**1**
Schiaffino, Ghiggia   Friaça
Leading scorer: 7 Ademir (Brazil)

1954 Berne, Switzerland, 4 July, att. 55,000
West Germany (2)**3** **Hungary** (2)**2**
Morlock, Rahn 2   Puskas, Czibor
Leading scorer: 11 Kocsis (Hungary)

1958 Stockholm, Sweden, 29 June, att. 49,737
Brazil (2)**5** **Sweden** (1)**2**
Vava 2, Pelé 2, Zagalo   Liedholm, Simonsson
Leading scorer: 13 Fontaine (France)

1962 Santiago, Chile, 17 June, att. 69,068
Brazil (1)**3** **Czechoslovakia** (1)**1**
Amarildo, Zito, Vava   Masopust
Leading scorers: 4 Albert (Hung.), Ivanov (USSR), Sanchez (Chile),
Garrincha (Braz.), Jerkovic (Yug.), Vava (Braz.)

1966 Wembley, England, 30 July, att. 93,000 (Extra time)
England (1)(2)**4** **West Germany** (1)(2)**2**
Hurst 3, Peters   Haller, Weber
Leading scorer: 9 Eusebio (Portugal)

1970 Mexico City, Mexico, 21 June, att. 110,000
Brazil (1)**4** **Italy** (1)**1**
Pelé, Gerson, Jairzinho,   Boninsegna
Carlos Alberto
Leading scorer: 10 Müller (West Germany)

1974 Munich, West Germany, 7 July, att. 77,833
West Germany (2)**2** **Holland** (1)**1**
Breitner (pen.), Müller   Neeskens (pen.)
Leading scorer: 7 Lato (Poland)

1978 Buenos Aires, Argentina, 25 June, att. 77,000 (Extra time)
Argentina (1)(1)**3** **Holland** (0)(1)**1**
Kempes 2, Bertoni   Nanninga
Leading scorer: 6 Kempes (Argentina)

From top to bottom: (1) The first World Cup final. The captains, Uruguay's Nasazzi (left) and Argentina's Ferreira shake hands, watched by the curiously attired referee. (2) Ferenc Puskas (right) opens the scoring for Hungary in the 1954 final against Germany. (3) England's Bobby Charlton (far right) slams a thunderbolt shot past the Portuguese keeper in the 1966 semi-final. (4) Star of the 1970 World Cup, Brazil's Pelé stretches to reach the ball in the final against Italy, but this one hit the post.

European Competitions

EUROPEAN FOOTBALL CHAMPIONSHIP

Year	Winners		Runners-up	
1960	USSR	(0)(1)2	Yugoslavia	(1)(1)1
1964	Spain	(1)2	USSR	(1)1
1968	Italy	(0)(1)1	Yugoslavia	(1)(1)1
	Replay	(2)2		(0)0
1972	West Germany	(1)3	USSR	(0)0
1976	Czechoslovakia	(2)(2)2	West Germany	(1)(2)2
	Czechoslovakia won on penalties (5-3)			
1980	West Germany	(1)2	Belgium	(0)1

EUROPEAN CUP

Year	Winners		Runners-up	
1956	Real Madrid	(2)4	Stade de Reims	(2)3
1957	Real Madrid	(0)2	Fiorentina	(0)0
1958	Real Madrid	(0)(2)3	AC Milan	(0)(2)2
1959	Real Madrid	(1)2	Stade de Reims	(0)0
1960	Real Madrid	(3)7	Eintracht Frankfurt	(1)3
1961	Benfica	(2)3	Barcelona	(1)2
1962	Benfica	(2)5	Real Madrid	(3)3
1963	AC Milan	(0)2	Benfica	(1)1
1964	Internazionale	(1)3	Real Madrid	(0)1
1965	Internazionale	(1)1	Benfica	(0)0
1966	Real Madrid	(0)2	Partizan Belgrade	(0)1
1967	Celtic	(0)2	Internazionale	(1)1
1968	Manchester Utd	(0)(1)4	Benfica	(0)(1)1
1969	AC Milan	(2)4	Ajax Amsterdam	(0)1
1970	Feyenoord	(1)(1)2	Celtic	(1)(1)1
1971	Ajax Amsterdam	(1)2	Panathinaikos	(0)0
1972	Ajax Amsterdam	(0)2	Internazionale	(0)0
1973	Ajax Amsterdam	(1)1	Juventus	(0)0
1974	Bayern Munich	(0)(0)1	Atlético Madrid	(0)(0)1
	Replay	(1)4		(0)0
1975	Bayern Munich	(0)2	Leeds United	(0)0
1976	Bayern Munich	(0)1	St Etienne	(0)0
1977	Liverpool	(1)3	B. Mönchengladbach	(0)1
1978	Liverpool	(0)1	FC Bruges	(0)0
1979	Nottingham Forest	(1)1	Malmö	(0)0
1980	Nottingham Forest	(1)1	SV Hamburg	(0)0

FAIRS CUP

1958	Barcelona	2:6	*London	2:0
1960	Barcelona	0:4	*Birmingham City	0:1
1961	AS Roma	2:2	*Birmingham City	2:0
1962	*Valencia	6:1	Barcelona	2:1
1963	Valencia	2:2	*Dynamo Zagreb	1:0
1964	Real Zaragoza	2	Valencia	1
1965	Ferencvaros	1	Juventus	0
1966	*Barcelona	0:4	Real Zaragoza	1:2
1967	*Dynamo Zagreb	2:0	Leeds United	0:0
1968	*Leeds United	1:0	Ferencvaros	0:0
1969	*Newcastle United	3:3	Ujpest Dozsa	0:2
1970	Arsenal	1:3	*Anderlecht	3:0
1971	†Leeds United	2:1	*Juventus	2:1

Match to decide permanent possession (at Barcelona)
	Barcelona	2	Leeds United	1

UEFA CUP

1972	Tottenham Hotspur	2:1	*Wolverhampton W	1:1
1973	*Liverpool	3:0	B. Mönchengladbach	0:2
1974	Feyenoord	2:2	*Tottenham Hotspur	2:0
1975	*B. Mönchengladbach	0:5	Twente Enschede	0:1
1976	*Liverpool	3:1	Bruges	2:1
1977†	*Juventus	1:1	Athletic Bilbao	0:2
1978	PSV Eindhoven	0:3	*Bastia	0:0
1979	B. Mönchengladbach	1:1	*Red Star Belgrade	1:0
1980†	Eintracht Frankfurt	2:1	*B. Mönchengladbach	3:0

*Home team in first leg of two-legged final.
†Final decided on away-goals rule.

CUP-WINNERS CUP

Year	Winners		Runners-up	
1961	Glasgow Rangers	(0)0	Fiorentina	(1)2
	Fiorentina	(1)2	Glasgow Rangers	(1)1
	Fiorentina won 4-1 on aggregate			
1962	Atlético Madrid	(1)1	Fiorentina	(1)1
	Replay	(2)3		(0)0
1963	Tottenham Hotspur	(2)5	Atlético Madrid	(0)1
1964	Sporting Portugal	(1)(3)3	MTK Budapest	(1)(3)3
	Replay	(1)1		(0)0
1965	West Ham United	(0)2	Munich 1860	(0)0
1966	Borussia Dortmund	(0)(1)2	Liverpool	(0)(1)1
1967	Bayern Munich	(0)(0)1	Glasgow Rangers	(0)(0)0
1968	AC Milan	(2)2	SV Hamburg	(0)0
1969	Slovan Bratislava	(3)3	Barcelona	(1)2
1970	Manchester City	(2)2	Gornik Zabrze	(0)1
1971	Chelsea	(0)(1)1	Real Madrid	(0)(1)1
	Replay	(2)2		(0)1
1972	Glasgow Rangers	(2)3	Moscow Dynamo	(0)2
1973	AC Milan	(1)1	Leeds United	(0)0
1974	FC Magdeburg	(1)2	AC Milan	(0)0
1975	Dynamo Kiev	(2)3	Ferencvaros	(0)0
1976	Anderlecht	(1)4	West Ham United	(1)2
1977	SV Hamburg	(0)2	Anderlecht	(0)0
1978	Anderlecht	(3)4	Austria/WAC	(0)0
1979	Barcelona	(2)(2)4	Fortuna Düsseldorf	(2)(2)3
1980	Valencia	(0)(0)0	Arsenal	(0)(0)0
	Valencia won on penalties (5-4)			

Dalglish scores Liverpool's European Cup winner in 1978.

FOOTBALLER OF THE YEAR

1956	Stanley Matthews (Blackpool & England)
1957	Alfredo Di Stefano (Real Madrid & Spain)
1958	Raymond Kopa (Real Madrid & France)
1959	Alfredo Di Stefano (Real Madrid & Spain)
1960	Luis Suarez (Barcelona & Spain)
1961	Omar Sivori (Juventus & Italy)
1962	Josef Masopust (Dukla Prague & Czechoslovakia)
1963	Lev Yachin (Moscow Dynamo & USSR)
1964	Denis Law (Manchester Utd & Scotland)
1965	Eusebio (Benfica & Portugal)
1966	Bobby Charlton (Manchester Utd & England)
1967	Florian Albert (Ferencvaros & Hungary)
1968	George Best (Manchester Utd & N. Ireland)
1969	Gianni Rivera (AC Milan & Italy)
1970	Gerd Müller (Bayern Munich & West Germany)
1971	Johan Cruyff (Ajax & Netherlands)
1972	Franz Beckenbauer (Bayern Munich & West Germany)
1973	Johan Cruyff (Ajax, Barcelona & Netherlands)
1974	Johan Cruyff (Barcelona & Netherlands)
1975	Oleg Blokhin (Dynamo Kiev & USSR)
1976	Franz Beckenbauer (Bayern Munich & West Germany)
1977	Allan Simonsen (B. Mönchengladbach & Denmark)
1978	Kevin Keegan (SV Hamburg & England)
1979	Kevin Keegan (SV Hamburg & England)
1980	Karl-Heinz Rummenigge (Bayern M & W Germany)

English Football

LEAGUE CHAMPIONSHIP

Season	Winners	Pts
1888–89[1]	Preston North End	40
1889–90[1]	Preston North End	33
1890–91[1]	Everton	29
1891–92[2]	Sunderland	42
1892–93[3]	Sunderland	48
1893–94[3]	Aston Villa	44
1894–95[3]	Sunderland	47
1895–96[3]	Aston Villa	45
1896–97[3]	Aston Villa	47
1897–98[3]	Sheffield United	42
1898–99[4]	Aston Villa	45
1899–1900[4]	Aston Villa	50
1900–01[4]	Liverpool	45
1901–02[4]	Sunderland	44
1902–03[4]	The Wednesday	42
1903–04[4]	The Wednesday	47
1904–05[4]	Newcastle United	48
1905–06[5]	Liverpool	51
1906–07[5]	Newcastle United	51
1907–08[5]	Manchester United	52
1908–09[5]	Newcastle United	53
1909–10[5]	Aston Villa	53
1910–11[5]	Manchester United	52
1911–12[5]	Blackburn Rovers	49
1912–13[5]	Sunderland	54
1913–14[5]	Blackburn Rovers	51
1914–15[5]	Everton	46
1915–19	No competition	
1919–20[6]	West Brom. A.	60
1920–21[6]	Burnley	59
1921–22[6]	Liverpool	57
1922–23[6]	Liverpool	60
1923–24[6]	Huddersfield Town	57
1924–25[6]	Huddersfield Town	58
1925–26[6]	Huddersfield Town	57
1926–27[6]	Newcastle United	56
1927–28[6]	Everton	53
1928–29[6]	Sheffield Wednesday	52
1929–30[6]	Sheffield Wednesday	60
1930–31[6]	Arsenal	66
1931–32[6]	Everton	56
1932–33[6]	Arsenal	58
1933–34[6]	Arsenal	59
1934–35[6]	Arsenal	58
1935–36[6]	Sunderland	56
1936–37[6]	Manchester City	57
1937–38[6]	Arsenal	52
1938–39[6]	Everton	59
1939–46	No competition	
1946–47[6]	Liverpool	57
1947–48[6]	Arsenal	59
1948–49[6]	Portsmouth	58
1949–50[6]	Portsmouth	53
1950–51[6]	Tottenham Hotspur	60
1951–52[6]	Manchester United	57
1952–53[6]	Arsenal	54
1953–54[6]	Wolverhampton Wndrs	57
1954–55[6]	Chelsea	52
1955–56[6]	Manchester United	60
1956–57[6]	Manchester United	64
1957–58[6]	Wolverhampton Wndrs	64
1958–59[6]	Wolverhampton Wndrs	61
1959–60[6]	Burnley	55
1960–61[6]	Tottenham Hotspur	66
1961–62[6]	Ipswich Town	56
1962–63[6]	Everton	61
1963–64[6]	Liverpool	57
1964–65[6]	Manchester United	61
1965–66[6]	Liverpool	61
1966–67[6]	Manchester United	60
1967–68[6]	Manchester City	58
1968–69[6]	Leeds United	67
1969–70[6]	Everton	66
1970–71[6]	Arsenal	65
1971–72[6]	Derby County	58
1972–73[6]	Liverpool	60
1973–74[6]	Leeds United	62
1974–75[6]	Derby County	53
1975–76[6]	Liverpool	60
1976–77[6]	Liverpool	57
1977–78[6]	Nottingham Forest	64
1978–79[6]	Liverpool	68
1979–80[6]	Liverpool	60

Maximum points [1]44, [2]52, [3]60, [4]68, [5]76, [6]84

LEADING GOALSCORERS

Season	Winners	
1919-20	Fred Morris (West Brom.)	37
1920-21	Joe Smith (Bolton)	38
1921-22	Andy Wilson (Middlesbro.)	31
1922-23	Charlie Buchan (Sunderland)	30
1923-24	W. Chadwick (Everton)	28
1924-25	F. Roberts (Manchester C.)	31
1925-26	Ted Harper (Blackburn)	43
1926-27	Jimmy Trotter (Sheffield W.)	37
1927-28	'Dixie' Dean (Everton)	60
1928-29	David Halliday (Sunderland)	43
1929-30	Vic Watson (West Ham)	41
1930-31	'Pongo' Waring (Aston Villa)	49
1931-32	'Dixie' Dean (Everton)	44
1932-33	Jack Bowers (Derby)	35
1933-34	Jack Bowers (Derby)	35
1934-35	Ted Drake (Arsenal)	42
1935-36	Raich Carter (Sunderland)	31
	Pat Glover (Grimsby)	31
	Bob Gurney (Sunderland)	31
1936-37	Freddie Steele (Stoke)	33
1937-38	Tommy Lawton (Everton)	28
1938-39	Tommy Lawton (Everton)	35
1939-46	No competition	
1946-47	Dennis Westcott (Wolves)	37
1947-48	Ronnie Rooke (Arsenal)	33
1948-49	Willie Moir (Bolton)	25
1949-50	Dickie Davis (Sunderland)	25
1950-51	Stan Mortensen (Blackpool)	30
1951-52	George Robledo (Newcastle)	33
1952-53	Charlie Wayman (Preston)	24
1953-54	Jimmy Glazzard (Hud'field)	29
1954-55	Ronnie Allen (West Brom.)	27
1955-56	Nat Lofthouse (Bolton)	33
1956-57	John Charles (Leeds)	38
1957-58	Bobby Smith (Tottenham)	36
1958-59	Jimmy Greaves (Chelsea)	32
1959-60	Denis Viollet (Manchester U.)	32
1960-61	Jimmy Greaves (Chelsea)	41
1961-62	Ray Crawford (Ipswich)	33
1962-63	Jimmy Greaves (Spurs)	37
1963-64	Jimmy Greaves (Spurs)	35
1964-65	Andy McEvoy (Blackburn)	29
	Jimmy Greaves (Spurs)	29
1965-66	Roger Hunt (Liverpool)	30
1966-67	Ron Davies (Southampton)	37
1967-68	George Best (Manchester U.)	28
	Ron Davies (Southampton)	28
1968-69	Jimmy Greaves (Spurs)	27
1969-70	Jeff Astle (West Brom.)	25
1970-71	Tony Brown (West Brom.)	28
1971-72	Francis Lee (Manchester C.)	33
1972-73	Bryan Robson (West Ham)	28
1973-74	Mike Channon (Soton)	21
1974-75	Malcolm Macdonald (N'castle)	21
1975-76	Ted MacDougall (Norwich)	23
1976-77	Andy Gray (Aston Villa)	25
	Malcolm Macdonald (Arsenal)	25
1977-78	Bob Latchford (Everton)	30
1978-79	Frank Worthington (Bolton)	24
1979-80	Phil Boyer (Soton)	23

Above: Terry McDermott of Liverpool was voted Footballer of the Year for 1979-80.

Opposite page: Frank Stapleton (centre) heads Arsenal's second goal in the 1979 FA Cup final against Manchester United.

FOOTBALLER OF THE YEAR

1947-48	Stanley Matthews (Blackpool)
1948-49	Johnny Carey (Manchester U.)
1949-50	Joe Mercer (Arsenal)
1950-51	Harry Johnston (Blackpool)
1951-52	Billy Wright (Wolves)
1952-53	Nat Lofthouse (Bolton)
1953-54	Tom Finney (Preston North End)
1954-55	Don Revie (Manchester City)
1955-56	Bert Trautmann (Manchester C.)
1956-57	Tom Finney (Preston North End)
1957-58	Danny Blanchflower (Spurs)
1958-59	Sid Owen (Luton Town)
1959-60	Bill Slater (Wolves)
1960-61	Danny Blanchflower (Spurs)
1961-62	Jimmy Adamson (Burnley)
1962-63	Stanley Matthews (Stoke City)
1963-64	Bobby Moore (West Ham U.)
1964-65	Bobby Collins (Leeds United)
1965-66	Bobby Charlton (Manchester U.)
1966-67	Jackie Charlton (Leeds U.)
1967-68	George Best (Manchester U.)
1968-69	Tony Book (Manchester C.)
	Dave Mackay (Derby County)
1969-70	Billy Bremner (Leeds United)
1970-71	Frank McLintock (Arsenal)
1971-72	Gordon Banks (Stoke City)
1972-73	Pat Jennings (Spurs)
1973-74	Ian Callaghan (Liverpool)
1974-75	Alan Mullery (Fulham)
1975-76	Kevin Keegan (Liverpool)
1976-77	Emlyn Hughes (Liverpool)
1977-78	Kenny Burns (Nottm For.)
1978-79	Kenny Dalglish (Liverpool)
1979-80	Terry McDermott (Liverpool)

FA CUP

Year	Winners		Runners-up	
1872	Wanderers	1	Royal Engineers	0
1873	Wanderers	2	Oxford University	0
1874	Oxford University	2	Royal Engineers	0
1875	Royal Engineers	1	Old Etonians	1
	Replay	2		0
1876	Wanderers	0	Old Etonians	0
	Replay	3		0
1877	*Wanderers	2	Oxford University	0
1878	Wanderers	3	Royal Engineers	1
1879	Old Etonians	1	Clapham Rovers	0
1880	Clapham Rovers	1	Oxford University	0
1881	Old Carthusians	3	Old Etonians	0
1882	Old Etonians	1	Blackburn Rovers	0
1883	*Blackburn Olympic	2	Old Etonians	1
1884	Blackburn Rovers	2	Queen's Park	1
1885	Blackburn Rovers	2	Queen's Park	0
1886	Blackburn Rovers	0	West Bromwich A.	0
	Replay	2		0
1887	Aston Villa	2	West Bromwich A.	0
1888	West Bromwich A.	2	Preston N. End	1
1889	Preston N. End	3	Wolverhampton W.	0
1890	Blackburn Rovers	6	The Wednesday	1
1891	Blackburn Rovers	3	Notts County	1
1892	West Bromwich A.	3	Aston Villa	0
1893	Wolverhampton W.	1	Everton	0
1894	Notts County	4	Bolton Wanderers	1
1895	Aston Villa	1	West Bromwich A.	0
1896	The Wednesday	2	Wolverhampton W.	1
1897	Aston Villa	3	Everton	2
1898	Nottingham Forest	3	Derby County	1
1899	Sheffield United	4	Derby County	1
1900	Bury	4	Southampton	0
1901	Tottenham Hotspur	2	Sheffield United	2
	Replay	3		1
1902	Sheffield United	1	Southampton	1
	Replay	2		1
1903	Bury	6	Derby County	0
1904	Manchester City	1	Bolton Wanderers	0
1905	Aston Villa	2	Newcastle United	0
1906	Everton	1	Newcastle United	0
1907	The Wednesday	2	Everton	1
1908	Wolverhampton W.	3	Newcastle United	1
1909	Manchester United	1	Bristol City	0
1910	Newcastle United	1	Barnsley	1
	Replay	2		0
1911	Bradford City	0	Newcastle United	0
	Replay	1		0
1912	Barnsley	0	West Bromwich A.	0
	Replay	1		0
1913	Aston Villa	1	Sunderland	0
1914	Burnley	1	Liverpool	0
1915	Sheffield United	3	Chelsea	0
1916–19	*No competition*			
1920	*Aston Villa	1	Huddersfield Town	0
1921	Tottenham Hotspur	1	Wolverhampton W.	0
1922	Huddersfield Town	1	Preston N. End	0
1923	Bolton Wanderers	2	West Ham United	0
1924	Newcastle United	2	Aston Villa	0
1925	Sheffield United	1	Cardiff City	0
1926	Bolton Wanderers	1	Manchester City	0
1927	Cardiff City	1	Arsenal	0
1928	Blackburn Rovers	3	Huddersfield Town	1
1929	Bolton Wanderers	2	Portsmouth	0
1930	Arsenal	2	Huddersfield Town	0
1931	West Bromwich A.	2	Birmingham	1
1932	Newcastle United	2	Arsenal	1
1933	Everton	3	Manchester City	0
1934	Manchester City	2	Portsmouth	1
1935	Sheffield W.	4	West Bromwich A.	2
1936	Arsenal	1	Sheffield United	0
1937	Sunderland	3	Preston N. End	1
1938	*Preston N. End	1	Huddersfield Town	0
1939	Portsmouth	4	Wolverhampton W.	1
1940–45	*No competition*			
1946	*Derby County	4	Charlton Athletic	1
1947	*Charlton Athletic	1	Burnley	0
1948	Manchester United	4	Blackpool	2
1949	Wolverhampton W.	3	Leicester City	1
1950	Arsenal	2	Liverpool	0
1951	Newcastle United	2	Blackpool	0
1952	Newcastle United	1	Arsenal	0
1953	Blackpool	4	Bolton Wanderers	3
1954	West Bromwich A.	3	Preston N. End	2
1955	Newcastle United	3	Manchester City	1
1956	Manchester City	3	Birmingham City	1
1957	Aston Villa	2	Manchester United	1
1958	Bolton Wanderers	2	Manchester United	0
1959	Nottingham Forest	2	Luton Town	1
1960	Wolverhampton W.	3	Blackburn Rovers	0
1961	Tottenham Hotspur	2	Leicester City	0
1962	Tottenham Hotspur	3	Burnley	1
1963	Manchester United	3	Leicester City	1
1964	West Ham United	3	Preston N. End	2
1965	*Liverpool	2	Leeds United	1
1966	Everton	3	Sheffield Wed.	2
1967	Tottenham Hotspur	2	Chelsea	1
1968	*West Bromwich A.	1	Everton	0
1969	Manchester City	1	Leicester City	0
1970	*Chelsea	2	Leeds United	2
	Replay	2		1
1971	*Arsenal	2	Liverpool	1
1972	Leeds United	1	Arsenal	0
1973	Sunderland	1	Leeds United	0
1974	Liverpool	3	Newcastle United	0
1975	West Ham United	2	Fulham	0
1976	Southampton	1	Manchster United	0
1977	Manchester United	2	Liverpool	1
1978	Ipswich Town	1	Arsenal	0
1979	Arsenal	3	Manchester United	2
1980	West Ham United	1	Arsenal	0

*After extra time

FOOTBALL LEAGUE CUP

Season	Winners		Runners-up	
Two-legged final				
1960–61	Aston Villa	0:3*	†Rotherham United	2:0
1961–62	Norwich City	3:1	†Rochdale	0:0
1962–63	†Birmingham City	3:0	Aston Villa	1:0
1963–64	Leicester City	1:3	†Stoke City	1:2
1964–65	†Chelsea	3:0	Leicester City	2:0
1965–66	West Bromwich A.	1:4	†West Ham United	2:1
Final at Wembley				
1966–67	Queen's Park R.	3	West Bromwich A.	2
1967–68	Leeds United	1	Arsenal	0
1968–69	Swindon Town	3*	Arsenal	1
1969–70	Manchester City	2*	West Bromwich A.	1
1970–71	Tottenham Hotspur	2	Aston Villa	0
1971–72	Stoke City	2	Chelsea	1
1972–73	Tottenham Hotspur	1	Norwich City	0
1973–74	Wolverhampton W.	2	Manchester City	1
1974–75	Aston Villa	1	Norwich City	0
1975–76	Manchster City	2	Newcastle United	1
1976–77	Aston Villa	0	Everton	0
	Replay	1*		1
	Second Replay	3*		2
1977–78	Nottingham Forest	0	Liverpool	0
	Replay	1		0
1978–79	Nottingham Forest	3	Southampton	2
1979–80	Wolverhampton W.	1	Nottingham Forest	0
1980–81	Liverpool	1*	West Ham United	1
	Replay	2		1

*After extra time. †Home team in 1st leg.

Scottish Football

LEAGUE CHAMPIONS

Season	Winners	Pts
1890-91[1]	Dumbarton	29
	Rangers	29
1891-92[2]	Dumbarton	37
1892-93[1]	Celtic	29
1893-94[1]	Celtic	29
1894-95[1]	Hearts	31
1895-96[1]	Celtic	30
1896-97[1]	Hearts	28
1897-98[1]	Celtic	33
1898-99[1]	Rangers	36
1899-1900[1]	Rangers	32
1900-01[3]	Rangers	35
1901-02[1]	Rangers	28
1902-03[2]	Hibernian	37
1903-04[4]	Third Lanark	43
1904-05[4]	Celtic	41
1905-06[5]	Celtic	49
1906-07[6]	Celtic	55
1907-08[6]	Celtic	55
1908-09[6]	Celtic	51
1909-10[6]	Celtic	54
1910-11[6]	Rangers	52
1911-12[6]	Rangers	51
1912-13[6]	Rangers	53
1913-14[7]	Celtic	65
1914-15[7]	Celtic	65
1915-16[7]	Celtic	67
1916-17[7]	Celtic	64
1917-18[6]	Rangers	56
1918-19[6]	Celtic	58
1919-20[8]	Rangers	71
1920-21[8]	Rangers	76
1921-22[8]	Celtic	67
1922-23[7]	Rangers	55
1923-24[7]	Rangers	59
1924-25[7]	Rangers	60
1925-26[7]	Celtic	58
1926-27[7]	Rangers	56
1927-28[7]	Rangers	60
1928-29[7]	Rangers	67
1929-30[7]	Rangers	60
1930-31[7]	Rangers	60
1931-32[7]	Motherwell	66
1932-33[7]	Rangers	62
1933-34[7]	Rangers	66
1934-35[7]	Rangers	55
1935-36[7]	Celtic	66
1936-37[7]	Rangers	61
1937-38[7]	Celtic	61
1938-39[7]	Rangers	59
1939-46	No competition	
1946-47[5]	Rangers	46
1947-48[5]	Hibernian	48
1948-49[5]	Rangers	46
1949-50[5]	Rangers	50
1950-51[5]	Hibernian	48
1951-52[5]	Hibernian	45
1952-53[5]	Rangers	43
1953-54[5]	Celtic	43
1954-55[5]	Aberdeen	49
1955-56[6]	Rangers	52
1956-57[6]	Rangers	55
1957-58[6]	Hearts	62
1958-59[6]	Rangers	50
1959-60[6]	Hearts	54
1960-61[6]	Rangers	51
1961-62[6]	Dundee	54
1962-63[6]	Rangers	57
1963-64[6]	Rangers	55
1964-65[6]	Kilmarnock	50
1965-66[6]	Celtic	57
1966-67[6]	Celtic	58
1967-68[6]	Celtic	63
1968-69[6]	Celtic	54
1969-70[6]	Celtic	57
1970-71[6]	Celtic	56

Season	Winners	Pts
1971-72[6]	Celtic	60
1972-73[6]	Celtic	57
1973-74[6]	Celtic	53
1974-75[6]	Rangers	56
1975-76[9]	Rangers	54
1976-77[9]	Celtic	55
1977-78[9]	Rangers	55
1978-79[9]	Celtic	48
1979-80[9]	Aberdeen	48

Maximum points: [1]36, [2]44, [3]40, [4]52, [5]60, [6]68, [7]76, [8]84, [9]72.

Celtic v Rangers, the eternal battle: the two giants of Scottish football in a 1968 confrontation.

FOOTBALLER OF THE YEAR

1964-65	Billy McNeil (Celtic)
1965-66	John Greig (Rangers)
1966-67	Ronnie Simpson (Celtic)
1967-68	Gordon Wallace (Raith Rovers)
1968-69	Bobby Murdoch (Celtic)
1969-70	Pat Stanton (Hibernian)
1970-71	Martin Buchan (Aberdeen)
1971-72	David Smith (Rangers)
1972-73	George Connelly (Celtic)
1973-74	Jim Holton (Manchester United)
1974-75	Sandy Jardine (Rangers)
1975-76	John Greig (Rangers)
1976-77	Danny McGrain (Celtic)
1977-78	Derek Johnstone (Rangers)
1978-79	Andy Ritchie (Morton)
1979-80	Gordon Strachan (Aberdeen)

LEADING GOALSCORERS

1919-20	Hugh Ferguson (Motherwell)	33
1920-21	Hugh Ferguson (Motherwell)	43
1921-22	Dunky Walker (St Mirren)	45
1922-23	John White (Hearts)	30
1923-24	David Halliday (Dundee)	38
1924-25	Willie Devlin (Cowdenbeath)	33
1925-26	Willie Devlin (Cowdenbeath)	37
1926-27	Jimmy McGrory (Celtic)	49
1927-28	Jimmy McGrory (Celtic)	47
1928-29	Evelyn Morrison (Falkirk)	43
1929-30	Benny Yorston (Aberdeen)	38
1930-31	Barney Battles (Hearts)	44
1931-32	Bill McFadyen (Motherwell)	52
1932-33	Bill McFadyen (Motherwell)	45
1933-34	Jimmy Smith (Rangers)	41
1934-35	Dave McCulloch (Hearts)	38
1935-36	Jimmy McGrory (Celtic)	50
1936-37	David Wilson (Hamilton)	34
1937-38	Andy Black (Hearts)	40
1938-39	Alex Venters (Rangers)	34
1939-46	No competition	
1946-47	Bobby Mitchell (Third Lanark)	22
1947-48	Archie Aikman (Falkirk)	20
1948-49	Alec Stott (Dundee)	30
1949-50	Willie Bauld (Hearts)	30
1950-51	Lawrie Reilly (Hibernian)	22
1951-52	Lawrie Reilly (Hibernian)	27
1952-53	Lawrie Reilly (Hibernian)	30
	Charlie Fleming (East Fife)	30

1953-54	Jimmy Wardhaugh (Hearts)	27
1954-55	Willie Bauld (Hearts)	21
1955-56	Jimmy Wardhaugh (Hearts)	30
1956-57	Hugh Baird (Airdrieonians)	33
1957-58	Jimmy Wardhaugh (Hearts)	28
1958-59	Joe Baker (Hibernian)	25
1959-60	Joe Baker (Hibernian)	42
1960-61	Alex. Harley (Third Lanark)	42
1961-62	Alan Gilzean (Dundee)	24
1962-63	Jim Millar (Rangers)	25
1963-64	Alan Gilzean (Dundee)	32
1964-65	Jimmy Forrest (Rangers)	30
1965-66	Joe McBride (Celtic)	31
1966-67	Steve Chalmers (Celtic)	23
1967-68	Bobby Lennox (Celtic)	32
1968-69	Kenny Cameron (Dundee Utd)	27
1969-70	Colin Stein (Rangers)	24
1970-71	Harry Hood (Celtic)	22
1971-72	Joe Harper (Aberdeen)	33
1972-73	Alan Gordon (Hibernian)	27
1973-74	Dixie Deans (Celtic)	24
1974-75	Andy Gray (Dundee United)	20
	Willie Pettigrew (Motherwell)	20
1975-76	Kenny Dalglish (Celtic)	24
1976-77	Willie Pettigrew (Motherwell)	21
1977-78	Derek Johnstone (Rangers)	25
1978-79	Andy Ritchie (Morton)	22
1979-80	Doug Somner (St Mirren)	25

SCOTTISH FA CUP

Year	Winners		Runners-up	
1874	Queen's Park	2	Clydesdale	0
1875	Queen's Park	3	Renton	0
1876	Queen's Park	1	Third Lanark	1
	Replay	2		0
1877	Vale of Leven	0	Rangers	0
	Replay	1		1
	Second replay	3		2
1878	Vale of Leven	1	Third Lanark	0
1879	Vale of Leven	1	Rangers	1
	Vale of Leven won replay by default			
1880	Queen's Park	3	Thornlibank	0
1881	†Queen's Park	2	Dumbarton	1
	Replay	3		1
1882	Queen's Park	2	Dumbarton	2
	Replay	4		1
1883	Dumbarton	2	Vale of Leven	2
	Replay	2		1
1884	*Queen's Park won by default from Vale of Leven*			
1885	Renton	0	Vale of Leven	0
	Replay	3		1
1886	Queen's Park	3	Renton	1
1887	Hibernian	2	Dumbarton	1
1888	Renton	6	Cambuslang	1
1889	‡Third Lanark	3	Celtic	0
	Replay	2		1
1890	Queen's Park	1	Vale of Leven	1
	Replay	2		1
1891	Hearts	1	Dumbarton	0
1892	§Celtic	1	Queen's Park	0
	Replay	5		1
1893	Queen's Park	2	Celtic	1
1894	Rangers	3	Celtic	1
1895	St Bernard's	2	Renton	1
1896	Hearts	3	Hibernian	1
1897	Rangers	5	Dumbarton	1
1898	Rangers	2	Kilmarnock	0
1899	Celtic	2	Rangers	0
1900	Celtic	4	Queen's Park	3
1901	Hearts	4	Celtic	3
1902	Hibernian	1	Celtic	0
1903	Rangers	1	Hearts	1
	Replay	0		0
	Second replay	2		0
1904	Celtic	3	Rangers	2
1905	Third Lanark	0	Rangers	0
	Replay	3		1
1906	Hearts	1	Third Lanark	0
1907	Celtic	3	Hearts	0
1908	Celtic	5	St Mirren	1
1909	(Celtic)	2	(Rangers)	2
	Replay	1		1
	Cup withheld following riots			
1910	Dundee	2	Clyde	2
	Replay	0		0
	Second replay	2		1
1911	Celtic	0	Hamilton Acad.	0
	Replay	2		0
1912	Celtic	2	Clyde	0
1913	Falkirk	2	Raith Rovers	0
1914	Celtic	0	Hibernian	0
	Replay	4		1
1915-19	*No competition*			
1920	Kilmarnock	3	Albion Rovers	2
1921	Partick Thistle	1	Rangers	0
1922	Morton	1	Rangers	0
1923	Celtic	1	Hibernian	0
1924	Airdrieonians	2	Hibernian	0
1925	Celtic	2	Dundee	1
1926	St Mirren	2	Celtic	0
1927	Celtic	3	East Fife	1
1928	Rangers	4	Celtic	0
1929	Kilmarnock	2	Rangers	0
1930	Rangers	0	Partick Thistle	0
	Replay	2		1
1931	Celtic	2	Motherwell	2
	Replay	4		2
1932	Rangers	1	Kilmarnock	1
	Replay	3		0
1933	Celtic	1	Motherwell	0
1934	Rangers	5	St Mirren	0
1935	Rangers	2	Hamilton Acad.	1
1936	Rangers	1	Third Lanark	0
1937	Celtic	2	Aberdeen	1
1938	East Fife	1	Kilmarnock	1
		*4		2
1939	Clyde	4	Motherwell	0
1940-46	*No competition*			
1947	Aberdeen	2	Hibernian	1
1948	Rangers	1	Morton	1
	Replay	1		0
1949	Rangers	4	Clyde	1
1950	Rangers	3	East Fife	0
1951	Celtic	1	Motherwell	0
1952	Motherwell	4	Dundee	0

Year	Winners		Runners-up	
1953	Rangers	1	Aberdeen	1
	Replay	1		0
1954	Celtic	2	Aberdeen	1
1955	Clyde	1	Celtic	1
	Replay	1		0
1956	Hearts	3	Celtic	1
1957	Falkirk	1	Kilmarnock	1
	Replay	*2		1
1958	Clyde	1	Hibernian	0
1959	St Mirren	3	Aberdeen	1
1960	Rangers	2	Kilmarnock	0
1961	Dunfermline Ath.	0	Celtic	0
	Replay	2		0
1962	Rangers	2	St Mirren	0
1963	Rangers	1	Celtic	1
	Replay	3		0
1964	Rangers	3	Dundee	1
1965	Celtic	3	Dunfermline Ath.	2
1966	Rangers	0	Celtic	0
	Replay	1		0
1967	Celtic	2	Aberdeen	0
1968	Dunfermline Ath.	3	Hearts	1
1969	Celtic	4	Rangers	0
1970	Aberdeen	3	Celtic	1
1971	Celtic	1	Rangers	1
	Replay	2		1
1972	Celtic	6	Hibernian	1
1973	Rangers	3	Celtic	2
1974	Celtic	3	Dundee United	0
1975	Celtic	3	Airdrieonians	1
1976	Rangers	3	Hearts	1
1977	Celtic	1	Rangers	0
1978	Rangers	2	Aberdeen	1
1979	Rangers	0	Hibernian	0
	Replay	0		0
	Second replay	3		2
1980	Celtic	*1	Rangers	0

* After extra time.
† Dumbarton lodged a protest and were awarded a replay.
‡ Final replayed because of the state of the pitch.
§ Queen's Park lodged a protest and were awarded a replay.

SCOTTISH LEAGUE CUP

Season	Winners		Runners-up	
1945-46	Aberdeen	3	Rangers	2
1946-47	Rangers	4	Aberdeen	0
1947-48	East Fife	0	Falkirk	0
	Replay	4		1
1948-49	Rangers	2	Raith Rovers	0
1949-50	East Fife	3	Dunfermline Ath.	0
1950-51	Motherwell	3	Hibernian	0
1951-52	Dundee	3	Rangers	2
1952-53	Dundee	2	Kilmarnock	0
1953-54	East Fife	3	Partick Thistle	2
1954-55	Hearts	4	Motherwell	2
1955-56	Aberdeen	2	St Mirren	1
1956-57	Celtic	0	Partick Thistle	0
	Replay	3		0
1957-58	Celtic	7	Rangers	1
1958-59	Hearts	5	Partick Thistle	1
1959-60	Hearts	2	Third Lanark	1
1960-61	Rangers	2	Kilmarnock	0
1961-62	Rangers	1	Hearts	1
	Replay	3		1
1962-63	Hearts	1	Kilmarnock	0
1963-64	Rangers	5	Morton	0
1964-65	Rangers	2	Celtic	1
1965-66	Celtic	2	Rangers	1
1966-67	Celtic	1	Rangers	0
1967-68	Celtic	5	Dundee	3
1968-69	Celtic	6	Hibernian	2
1969-70	Celtic	1	St Johnstone	0
1970-71	Rangers	1	Celtic	0
1971-72	Partick Thistle	4	Celtic	1
1972-73	Hibernian	2	Celtic	1
1973-74	Dundee	1	Celtic	0
1974-75	Celtic	6	Hibernian	3
1975-76	Rangers	1	Celtic	0
1976-77	*Aberdeen	2	Celtic	1
1977-78	*Rangers	2	Celtic	1
1978-79	Rangers	2	Aberdeen	1
1979-80	Dundee United	0	Aberdeen	0
	Replay	3		0
1980-81	Dundee United	3	Dundee	0

*After extra time.

INDEX

Heavy type indicates a major entry, italic type an illustration. (All major entries are illustrated.)

ACKNOWLEDGEMENTS

The author wishes to acknowledge the following sources for opinions, views, and other quotations used in this book: *Allison Calling* (George Allison), *Banks of England* (Gordon Banks), *Cliff Bastin Remembers* (Bastin and Brian Glanville), *Soccer at the Top* (Matt Busby), *Forward for England* (Bobby Charlton), *There's Only One United* (Geoffrey Green), *Arsenal—Chapman to Mee* (Ralph Finn), *Football Ambassador* (Eddie Hapgood), *It's All in the Game* (Johnny Haynes), *Denis Law* (Law), *Football is my Business* (Tommy Lawton), *The Stanley Matthews Story* and *Feet First Again* (Matthews), *The Great Ones* (Joe Mercer), *Matt . . . United . . . and Me* (Jimmy Murphy), *Bobby Moore* (Jeff Powell), *Talking Football* (Alf Ramsey), *Clown Prince of Soccer* (Len Shackleton), *Shankly* (Bill Shankly), *40 Years in Football* (Ivan Sharpe), *Great Masters of Scottish Football* (Hugh Taylor), *Arsenal from the Heart* ((Bob Wall), *One Hundred Caps and all That* (Billy Wright), *Manchester United* (Percy M. Young), *Daily Express* (Hugh McIlvanney), *Sunday Express* (Danny Blanchflower).

Photo credits: Mick Alexander/Peter Robinson; Associated Press; BBC Hulton Picture Library; Central Press Photos; Colorsport; Fox Photos; Ray Green; Impact; Liverpool Daily Post & Echo; London Express News & Feature Services; George Outram & Company; Popperfoto; The Press Association; Syndication International; Topix.

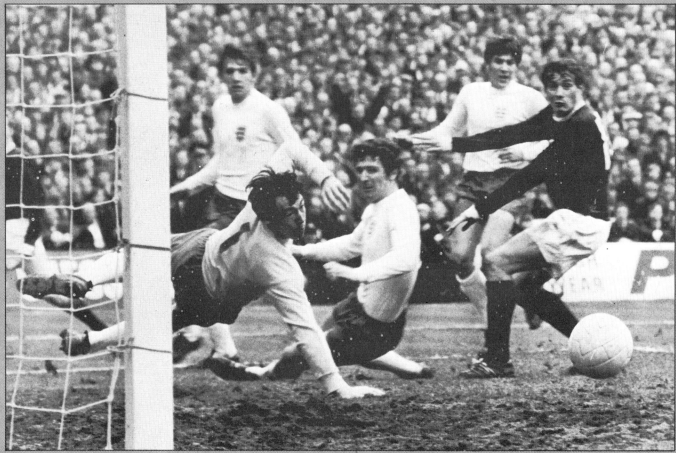